UZBEKISTAN
QUALITY JOB CREATION AS A CORNERSTONE FOR SUSTAINABLE ECONOMIC GROWTH
COUNTRY DIAGNOSTIC STUDY

Kym Anderson, Edimon Ginting, and Kiyoshi Taniguchi

ADB

ASIAN DEVELOPMENT BANK

Notes:
In this publication, "$" refers to United States dollars.

ADB recognizes "Kyrgyzstan" as the Kyrgyz Republic, "China" as the People's Republic of China, "Korea" and "South Korea" as the Republic of Korea, and "Russia" as the Russian Federation.

On the cover: From the top: Daily life, architecture and views of Bukhara, 2016 (Relisa Granovskaya); Daily life, architecture and views of Samarkand, 2016 (Relisa Granovskaya); Construction site on the Talimarjan Power Plant, 2016 (Nikita Makarenko); Daily life, architecture and views of Tashkent, 2016 (Relisa Granovskaya); New turbine installed on Talimarjan Power Plant, 2016. (Relisa Granovskaya); A high-speed train "Afrosiyob" is arriving to Samarkand railway station, 2016 (Relisa Granovskaya).

Contents

Tables, Figures, and Boxes

Tables

Figures

Boxes

Preface

Since its independence, Uzbekistan has achieved sustained growth through its gradual transition to a market-based economy. This involved cautious economic policy reforms such as liberalizing prices of energy and fuel while maintaining a high level of state control. Despite the gradual approach to development challenges following its independence, the country experienced in the 1990s the smallest output decline among former Soviet economies and enjoyed high rates of economic growth from 2004 to 2015, largely driven by the high prices of its major export commodities.

However, the 2014 Russian crisis and the drop in the global prices of many key commodities have severely impacted Uzbekistan's economy in recent years. Consequently, Uzbekistan's economic growth decelerated, manufacturing exports declined, and employment growth was too low to adequately absorb the thousands of labor entrants every year. Given these development challenges, the new government introduced major reforms. The pace of reform is unprecedented, and the government has formulated its long-term economic strategy in its Vision 2030, which aims to double the country's gross domestic product by 2030 through a program of economic diversification.

This book, *Uzbekistan Quality Job Creation as a Cornerstone for Sustainable Economic Growth*, presents an in-depth analysis of ways the country could best consolidate achievements from its recent policy reforms and maintain efforts aimed at accelerating sustainable economic growth to create more and better-paid jobs. The book identifies key elements critical to quality job creation, including fostering macroeconomic stability, reducing underinvestment in physical infrastructure, enhancing human capital, improving firms' access to finance to promote development of the private sector and modernization of the financial sector, and lowering barriers to international trade and foreign investment inflows.

Employment creation can be stimulated by additional government action in three areas. The first priority area is to improve firms' access to finance by focusing on small and medium-sized enterprise development and financial sector modernization. To do this, the government should develop the nonbank finance industry and market-based instruments, establish a high-quality financial structure to modernize the banking sector, and strengthen the use of digital finance solutions to promote financial inclusion. The second priority area of future reforms is to enhance market competition through greater participation in regional and global trade and improve the business climate to attract more foreign direct investment inflows and facilitate job creation. The third priority for government action relates to addressing the longer-term constraints associated with the economy's infrastructure stock and level of human capital. A comprehensive infrastructure program focusing on transport and energy would facilitate the country's access to global markets while concomitantly supporting output and employment growth. Finally, education and skills improvements aimed at fully responding to job market needs are required to meet the challenges of a modern diversified economy.

We at the Asian Development Bank hope that the findings in this book will assist the Government of Uzbekistan in its quest to seek sustainable growth, and highly appreciate the government's support and cooperation throughout the study. We look forward to continuing productive dialogue and engagement with the government and are fully committed to support Uzbekistan in achieving its developmental goals.

Yasuyuki Sawada
Chief Economist and Director General
Economic Research and Regional Cooperation Department
Asian Development Bank

Acknowledgments

The Uzbekistan Country Diagnostic Study was prepared by the Asian Development Bank (ADB) under a regional technical assistance project (TA 8343-REG), Country Diagnostic Studies in Selected Developing Member Countries. The study aims to contribute to the analysis of ongoing economic reforms taken by the Uzbekistan government. The study focuses on how reforms can help to create more good-quality jobs and attempts to look deeper into underlying causes for jobless growth. The study provides concrete and evidence-based policy suggestions that may provide insights to support government planning in the future years.

The study was undertaken by the Economic Research and Regional Cooperation Department (ERCD), under the overall guidance and supervision of Edimon Ginting, deputy director general, ERCD and former director of the Economic Analysis and Operational Support Division (EREA), ERCD. During the CDS' final stretch, the study benefited from the advice of Rana Hasan, director, EREA, ERCD. The study was initially led by Kee-Yung Nam, principal energy economist, Sustainable Development and Climate Change Department, and was completed by Kiyoshi Taniguchi, principal economist, Pakistan Resident Mission, Central and West Asia Department (CWRD).

Each chapter was prepared by a team: Chapter 1 (macroeconomic overview) by Marcel Schroder, Kym Anderson, Edimon Ginting, and Kiyoshi Taniguchi; Chapter 2 (infrastructure) by Kee-Yung Nam, Lotis C. Quiao, Jasmin Sibal, Denise Encarnacion, and Bahtiyor Eshchanov; Chapter 3 (human capital development) by Malika Shagazatova, Kiyoshi Taniguchi, Jasmin Sibal, and Bakhrom Mirkasimov; Chapter 4 (private sector development and access to finance) by Shigehiro Shinozaki; and Chapter 5 (regional cooperation and foreign direct investment) by Jozef Konings and Aigerim Yergabulova.

Overall technical review and economic editing was provided by Kym Anderson, to ensure coherence and quality of the chapter studies, with support from Jill Gale de Villa as copy editor and Tuesday Soriano as proofreader. Overall research and technical support was provided by Maria Rowena Cham and Jasmin Sibal, while Amanda Isabel Mamon supported project administration. Research assistance was provided by Denise Encarnacion, Amador Foronda, Reneli Gloria, and Daryll Naval. Mike Cortes did the graphic design, layout, and typesetting.

The study is a product of extensive consultations with key government ministries in Uzbekistan, its think-tank agencies, and research institutions supporting development and strategy planning. The study team expresses special gratitude to the Institute of Macroeconomic Research and Forecasting, Ministry of Economy, Institute for Fiscal Studies, Ministry of Finance, Central Bank of Uzbekistan, Ministry of Investments and Foreign Trade, Ministry of Labor, and Ministry of Higher and Secondary Specialized Education. Other stakeholders who contributed to the study include Uzbekenergo, the State Committee on Automobile Roads, and O'zbekiston Temir Yo'llari; development partners, cooperatives, state enterprises, and the private sector have also been instrumental in the study.

We thank our university partners from the Tashkent State University of Economics, Westminster International University in Tashkent, and Management Development Institute of Singapore in Tashkent for hosting the study's workshops, seminars, and consultations. We also thank seminar participants from development partners and stakeholders including the American Chamber of Commerce, European Bank for Reconstruction and Development, GIZ Germany, Japan International Cooperation Agency, and the World Bank.

Last, we thank the Asian Development Bank Uzbekistan country team and the Uzbekistan Resident Mission (URM) for generous support and cooperation, including Takeo Konishi, advisor, CWRD; Cynthia Malvicini, country director, URM, CWRD; Safdar Parvez, director, CWRD; Lyaziza G. Sabyrova, principal economist, CWRD; and Mirzo Iskandar Gulamov, CWRD. We also acknowledge the technical support and cooperation provided by the URM economic team: Begzod M. Djalilov, economic officer, URM, and Elyor Mukhamedov, consultant, URM.

Author Profiles

Kym Anderson is a professor of economics at the University of Adelaide in South Australia and at the Crawford School of Public Policy of the Australian National University in Canberra, where he has been affiliated since his doctoral studies at the University of Chicago and Stanford University. During study leave, he worked at the General Agreement on Tariffs and Trade (now the World Trade Organization) Secretariat during 1990–1992 and at the World Bank during 2004–2007. He has published about 400 articles and 40 books. He chairs the Board of Trustees of the International Food Policy Research Institute. He has an honorary doctor of economics degree from the University of Adelaide and a distinguished alumni award from the University of New England. In 2015, he became a Companion of the Order of Australia.

Denise Encarnacion is a consultant at the Sustainable Development and Climate Change Department (SDCC) and previously a research associate at EREA, ERCD, ADB. She has also worked as an evaluation research associate for various evaluation projects in Independent Evaluation Department. Prior to working for ADB, she was an economist for the Philippine government's Department of Environment and Natural Resources for eight years. She has a bachelor's degree in economics from the University of the Philippines in Los Baños, majoring in natural resources economics. She has completed core units in urban and regional planning from the University of the Philippines and obtained a professional license to practice as an urban and regional planner.

Bahtiyor Eshchanov is a senior lecturer in economics at Westminster International University in Tashkent. He holds an MSc in sustainable technologies from the Royal Institute of Technology, Sweden and a PhD in applied economics from the Vrije Universiteit Brussel, Belgium. He has served as a senior economist for the Asian Development Bank (ADB) and department chairman at the Academy of Public Administration under the President of Uzbekistan. He is engaged in national and international research projects in partnership with international financial institutions, including ADB, the Norwegian Institute of International Affairs (NUPI), the Swiss Renewable Energy and Energy Resource Efficiency Program (REPIC), and the United Nations Development Programme. He has publications in peer reviewed journals. In line with teaching industrial economics and energy-environmental economics, he is supervising theses on renewable energy and development economics.

Edimon Ginting is the deputy director general of Economic Research and Regional Cooperation Department (ERCD). He was director of the Economic Analysis and Operational Support Division (EREA), supervising the review of the economic viability of all ADB projects and leading the preparation of country diagnostic studies for ADB's developing member countries (DMCs). He joined ADB in 2007 and has led several large and strategic ADB operations to support economic reforms, including loans to support DMCs' response to the global financial crisis. Before joining ADB, he was an economist at the International Monetary Fund; advisor to the Indonesian Parliament; research economist at the Productivity Commission, Australia; researcher and lecturer at the University of Indonesia; postdoctoral fellow at Monash University; and research economist at Gadjah Mada University. He received his PhD in economics from Monash University.

Jozef Konings is a full professor of economics at the University of Liverpool Management School and at the Katholieke Universiteit Leuven, Belgium. He is a research fellow of the Center for Economic Policy Research in London and director of the Center for Regional Economic Policy (VIVES) at the University of Leuven. He has held visiting positions at the International Monetary Fund, Dartmouth College, the University of Michigan, Ljubljana University, and the Federal Reserve Bank of New York. Between November 2008 and March 2010 he was an economic adviser to President Barroso at the European Commission. He also served as a Dean of the School of Business and Economics at the University of Leuven. His research focuses on emerging markets, global firms, international macroeconomics, and micro drivers affecting macroeconomic fluctuations. He has published in leading academic journals.

Bakhrom Mirkasimov is the dean of research, postgraduate programs, and executive courses and a senior lecturer at Westminster International University in Tashkent. He is the managing editor of the newly launched international peer-reviewed open-access journal *Silk Road: A Journal of Eurasian Development* published by the University of Westminster Press. He is a research affiliate at the International Security and Development Center in Berlin, Germany, and a Global Labor Organization Fellow. Previously, he visited the Center for Economic Research and Graduate Education – Economics Institute (CERGE-EI), Duke University, and Hanover University as a research scholar; worked at the German Institute for Economic Research (DIW Berlin); and served as a consultant to ADB, the International Food Policy Research

Institute, the International Labour Organization, the Stockholm International Peace Research Institute, the United Nations Development Programme, and the World Bank. He studied economics at Humboldt University of Berlin, Vanderbilt University, and Boise State University and has published papers in peer-reviewed scientific journals.

Kee Yung Nam is a principal energy economist at the Energy Sector Group, Sector Advisory Services Cluster, Sustainable Development and Climate Change Department (SDCC), ADB. He has over 30 years of professional experience in the energy sector. Prior to joining SDCC, he was a principal economist, EREA, where he provided significant contributions to ERCD's analytical research and technical advice to operations departments on multiple disciplines including power sector development and reforms; renewable energy; fossil fuel subsidies; transport; impact evaluation; country diagnostic studies; and issues related to economic analysis on investment projects particularly on energy, infrastructure, and environment sectors. Prior to joining ADB, he worked in the International Atomic Energy Agency, International Institute for Applied Systems Analysis, and the United Nations Industrial Development Organization. He received his PhD in economics from the University of Vienna, Austria.

Lotis Quiao is an economics officer at EREA, ERCD, ADB. She has been involved in the division's work on energy for 7 years: reviewing economic analyses of energy projects, preparing power sector assessments in ADB's country diagnostic studies and other publications. Prior to joining ADB, she was a consultant at the World Bank. She has a master's degree in development economics from the University of the Philippines.

Malika Shagazatova is a social development specialist (gender and development) in SDCC, ADB. She has an MBA from the Graduate School of Management of the University of Western Australia and a PhD from Tashkent State Economic University. She has more than 26 years of professional experience, including 17 years across ADB's operations, with direct experience in social development. She has worked as a regional and international consultant with various international organizations, in Central Asia, Mongolia, and the People's Republic of China. Her consultancy experience and research interests include education, training and skills development and labor market needs analysis, gender gaps in education and women's participation in the labor force, and inclusive growth. She has provided consultancy and research services and has led and conducted complex and strategic projects for various international organizations: ADB; the European Training Foundation;

the Japan International Cooperation Agency (JICA); the United Nations Educational, Scientific and Cultural Organization (UNESCO); and the United States Agency for International Development (USAID).

Jasmin Sibal is an economics officer at ADB's EREA, ERCD. She provides operations support particularly in reviewing economic analyses of investment projects and in analytical work related to preparing country diagnostics and impact evaluation studies. As a consultant at ADB she provided research support for the employment diagnostics studies for Cambodia and Fiji, women in the workforce report, and the *Key Indicators* publication. Prior to joining ADB, she was a monitoring and evaluation officer for the Philippine Conditional Cash Transfer program at the Department of Social Welfare and Development and a senior research executive for a large consumer market research agency in the Philippines. She also worked as a research assistant at the University of the Philippines, where she coauthored studies on maternal health, adolescent and risk-taking behaviors, and the decent work country program in the Philippines. She has a master's degree in demography from the University of the Philippines.

Shigehiro Shinozaki is a senior economist at ERCD, ADB. He supports ADB's DMCs in improving small and medium-sized enterprise access to finance through technical assistance projects. His advisory and research expertise includes policy issues in small and medium-sized enterprise development, inclusive finance, and financial sector development especially in developing Asia. Prior to joining ADB, he held expert positions, including as a special officer for development finance at Japan's Ministry of Finance, an advisor to the Indonesian Capital Market and Financial Institution Supervisory Agency (Bapepam-LK) as JICA expert, and an administrator of the Directorate for Financial and Enterprise Affairs at the Organisation for Economic Co-operation and Development (OECD). He holds a PhD in International Studies from Waseda University in Japan and a Master's degree in business administration from École Nationale des Ponts et Chaussées in France.

Marcel Schroder is an assistant professor at the Lebanese American University in Byblos, Lebanon. He previously worked as a lecturer in Economics at the Development Policy Centre, Australian National University, and has been a visiting lecturer at the University of Papua New Guinea. He has a strong interest in policy-oriented research centered around macroeconomic aspects of economic development, especially in resource-rich developing countries. His other interests include issues related to financial globalization and stability in emerging market economies.

Kiyoshi Taniguchi is a principal economist at the Pakistan Resident Mission, Central and West Asia Department, ADB. Previously, he was a principal economist at EREA, ERCD, where he led the preparation of many country diagnostic studies for ADB DMCs. He is also leading impact evaluation study teams. At ADB, he held several economist positions, including at the Private Sector Operations Department, Uzbekistan Resident Mission, and Pacific Department. Prior to ADB, he was an economist for the Poverty Reduction and Economic Management Network of the World Bank. He started his career as an economist at the Food and Agriculture Organization of the United Nations in Rome, Italy. He has held research and teaching positions at the International University of Japan, Westminster International University in Tashkent, and University of the Philippines. He holds a PhD and master's degree in economics from the Ohio State University, bachelor of science in economics with honors from the University of Oregon, and bachelor of law from Chiba University in Japan.

Aigerim Yergabulova is a PhD student at the Center for Regional Economic Policy (VIVES), University of Leuven. Her research interests include firm dynamics, global market power, and the role of firm size distribution in aggregate fluctuations. She holds a Master's degree in economics from Nazarbayev University (Kazakhstan) and a BSc in environmental science from the University of London.

Abbreviations

ADB	—	Asian Development Bank
BRI	—	Belt and Road Initiative
CALISS	—	Central Asia's Labor and Skills Survey
CAREC	—	Central Asia Regional Economic Cooperation
CBU	—	Central Bank of Uzbekistan
CEPII	—	Centre d'Etudes Prospectives et d'Informations Internationales
CIAC	—	Credit Information Analytical Center
CIS	—	Commonwealth of Independent States
CVET	—	continued vocational education and training
DFS	—	digital financial services
DMC	—	developing member country
ECI	—	Economic Complexity Index
ERCD	—	Economic Research and Regional Cooperation Department, ADB
EREA	—	Economic Analysis and Operational Support Division, ADB
EU	—	European Union
FDI	—	foreign direct investment
GDP	—	gross domestic product
GVA	—	gross value added
HEI	—	higher-education institution
ICT	—	information and communication technology
JICA	—	Japan International Cooperation Agency
PPP	—	public–private partnership
PRC	—	People's Republic of China
PV	—	photovoltaic
R&D	—	research and development
RRDC	—	resource-rich developing country
RRF	—	Republican Road Fund
SDCC	—	Sustainable Development and Climate Change Department, ADB
SMEs	—	small and medium-sized enterprises
STEM	—	science, technology, engineering, and mathematics
TVET	—	technical and vocational education and training
URM	—	Uzbekistan Resident Mission, ADB
UTY	—	Uzbekiston Temir Yullari—Uzbekistan Railways
VAT	—	value-added tax
WTO	—	World Trade Organization

Weights and Measures

GWh	—	gigawatt-hour
km	—	kilometer
kV	—	kilovolt
kWh	—	kilowatt-hour
m^3	—	cubic meter
MW	—	megawatt
TWh	—	terawatt-hour

Executive Summary

Key elements of quality job creation include providing macroeconomic stability, reducing underinvestment in physical infrastructure, enhancing human resources, improving access to finance to promote private sector development, and lowering barriers to international trade and foreign investment inflows. This Country Diagnostic Study explores ways Uzbekistan can best (i) consolidate achievements from its recent policy reforms that started in mid-2017, and (ii) maintain reform efforts aimed at accelerating sustainable economic growth to create more and better-paid jobs.

Improving Macroeconomic Performance

The government is currently undertaking a series of major reform measures that have removed various impediments to quality job creation. Most significant was the unification of the exchange rate in September 2017, which led to the disappearance of the black market in foreign currencies. That and other key elements of the reform package have led to a substantial improvement in the economy's investment climate. For example, Uzbekistan's Doing Business ranking improved from 87th in 2016 to 69th in 2020.

Uzbekistan currently has a unique demographic window of opportunity as 500,000 youths are being added annually to the labor supply for the next dozen years. Successfully integrating these job seekers into the labor market could transform Uzbekistan into a rapidly growing and more diversified economy. However, the country is still facing numerous macroeconomic challenges. They include rising inflation and falling fiscal revenue that, with falling prices for some export commodities and a decline in manufacturing exports, is decelerating economic growth and has caused annual employment growth to average only 0.75% during 2015-2017.

Greater employment creation could be stimulated by additional government action in three areas. First, private businesses, especially small and medium-sized enterprises (SMEs), need better access to finance. The most promising action to achieve that is selective privatization of some state-owned banks. Second, competition in the marketplace needs to be further enhanced.

The government could achieve that by disallowing monopolistic practices and phasing out remaining price controls. Third, constraints on building the economy's public infrastructure and human capital need to be eased. A comprehensive infrastructure program would improve the country's access to global markets while concomitantly supporting output and employment growth and thereby reversing the current slowdown. For education, school curricula need to reflect the skills demanded in an increasingly open and modernizing economy, and more efficient use needs to be made of the substantial fiscal expenditure on education.

Boosting Infrastructure's Contribution to Sustainable Growth

The Uzbekistan government recognizes that public infrastructure must be improved if the country is to maintain rapid economic growth over the longer term. The government also sees that good public infrastructure enhances competitiveness, supports industrialization and urbanization, and improves value chains for farmers. Also, living conditions would improve directly because of expanding infrastructure jobs and then indirectly by making other employment more accessible.

As the economy moves toward upper-middle-income status, the demand for transport facilities will grow strongly. Satisfying that demand requires improved road, rail, and air transport infrastructure; logistics centers; and cross-border transport procedures. Greater investment is needed to allow trade to grow and take advantage of the country's geographical position as a center of commerce in Central Asia and as a key transit country.

Roads provide the dominant mode of transport for domestic passengers and short-haul cargo. The road network has improved significantly in recent years, enhancing access throughout the country and facilitating the transport of goods by truck. However, even new roads soon suffer from insufficient funds for periodic routine maintenance. The backlog of rehabilitation and reconstruction work may eventually result in roads being unable to cope with the increased traffic volumes.

As a double-landlocked country, long-distance rail transport has been the main mode of moving freight in and out of the country, exploiting the expanding international railway corridors in the region. Outdated locomotive stock means there have been inefficiencies in both cargo and passenger rail transit, but the gradual replacement of old stock is easing that constraint. By contrast, the country's air network is among the best in Central Asia. Air transport currently carries about 4% of the country's international cargo. It could carry a much greater share, and boost tourism if a more open skies policy brought greater competition to airline services, resulting in improved access and service quality.

The energy sector continues to play a very significant role in the economy of Uzbekistan. It accounted for about one-quarter of total industry output during 1995–2014, and natural gas comprised one-eighth of total exports. Revenue from energy exports has been a key source of government finance. The reliability of energy supplies is vital for sustaining economic growth and development. Heavy dependence on natural gas has posed load management problems: the country continues to struggle with an unreliable power supply that, coupled with rapidly growing demands for electricity, has led to frequent blackouts. Demand-side inefficiencies from outdated production technologies and supply-side inefficiencies due to old infrastructure for power generation, transmission, and distribution, plus an inadequate billing system, have contributed to economic losses, which the World Bank estimated at $1.5 billion in 2016. A low-tariff policy also contributes to inefficiencies by encouraging wasteful electricity consumption and undermining the financial performance of the power utility. This has discouraged investments in maintenance of the electricity infrastructure, which clearly needs to be upgraded and expanded if it is to adequately serve the needs of the rapidly growing economy.

An energy sector plan that provides a framework for the development of the sector should be finalized and implemented. This needs to be supported by an improved regulatory system, by establishing an independent energy regulator and reforming the current inefficient tariff-setting policies. Funding needs to be available to revitalize the energy institutions. Also, a favorable business environment for small-scale renewable energy applications would reduce dependence on natural gas consumption. More active participation in regional energy trade should be encouraged, to meet the growing demands for power at lower cost.

For the transport sector to continue contributing to the country's goal of sustaining its high economic growth rate, continual planning and coordination among the agencies that govern the country's transport modes is required. That is, institutional reforms need to be harmonious and complementary to each other. Investments in improved road and rail infrastructure and in the electrification of railways could reduce transport inefficiencies. Such investments would also help Uzbekistan take advantage of its role as a key transit country between Asia and Europe, and spur cooperation between countries of the region.

Boosting Labor Productivity

Uzbekistan's working age population increased from 11 million in 1990 to almost 19 million in 2017, and an additional 4.3 million are expected to enter the labor force by 2030. Yet the country's high annual economic growth rate (8% during the last 12 years from 2004-2015) has not led to a sufficient rise in the number of jobs being generated. As a result, migration of workers to the Russian Federation and other Commonwealth of Independent States countries has been substantial: over 2 million Uzbeks currently reside abroad. In addition, women's participation in the economy has continued to decline and informal employment has continued to grow.

The structure of domestic employment is moving gradually toward industry and services and away from primary sectors, especially agriculture. The service sector has been accounting for almost 80% of all newly created jobs in the country. Most such jobs require both cognitive and noncognitive skills and hence attract graduates who follow education paths in appropriate fields. However, only 1.5% of the workforce is employed in high-tech industries and science.

Males dominate high-paying jobs. Female workers in the labor market are mostly in professional and service occupations, and slightly fewer women than men are in positions such as legislators, senior officials, and managers. Meanwhile, female participation in the labor force remains low.

Informal workers account for more than half (54%) of the working age population in Uzbekistan, and the majority of them are young people. Reasons for this segment of the workforce being so large include the low level of education of such workers, a complex and uncertain tax system, and a high labor tax burden on large businesses.

Uzbekistan has a strong emphasis on education and so has a relatively high level of human capital. Major education reforms are under way, however. They include moving from 12 to 11 years of compulsory schooling starting in 2018, and strengthening preschool education, higher education, and secondary special and professional education.

While gender parity has been achieved in enrollment rates at primary and secondary levels, disparities begin at the level of specialized secondary and higher education. If this persists, women will continue to have unequal access to better jobs in the future.

Low tertiary enrollment rates suggest access to higher education remains a challenge for many. Centrally determined student admission quotas and high fees make higher education inaccessible for 9 out of 10 school leavers.

Low university enrollments and little interaction between private sector employers and universities have a negative impact on the economy's capacity for technological innovation, adoption, and value creation.

More generally, Uzbekistan's education system is misaligned with the needs of the growing private sector, and is unable to catch up with the economy's rapidly changing structure and labor market demands. The skills supply is not matched with employment opportunities: the academic qualifications of graduates, especially from vocational institutions, do not match the qualifications for available jobs. The incidence of labor discouragement among the young in Uzbekistan is higher than in comparator countries, suggesting weak labor market information.

There is no single accountable agency that ensures proper governance of the education sector. On the contrary, there are many actors with overlapping responsibilities playing partial roles. Nor is there a single national qualification framework in Uzbekistan to simplify the process of developing and modifying the qualifications structure.

The government would benefit from an evidence-based responsive education policy and careful monitoring and evaluation of education reforms of both public investments and public–private partnerships. Overlapping responsibilities between state actors should be reduced through consolidation, and the government should ensure a holistic approach to the development of the education system so as to improve the sector's overall governance and institutional efficiency.

Policies are needed that integrate education, skills, and human capital development with entrepreneurship, SME development, and research and innovation policies. Effective policy formulation and implementation require multilevel governance as well as effective coordination between government agencies and relevant stakeholders.

A national qualification framework should be adopted and integrated into a national occupational classification to reduce the mismatch between labor market demands and learner qualifications. Any investment should aim at increasing the number and enhancing the qualifications of teachers and technical and vocational education and training (TVET) instructors. The government should encourage active participation from the private sector, both large companies and SMEs, in TVET curricula development and implementation. To create more effective learning pathways between TVET and higher education, a system for recognizing prior learning should be introduced that assesses each individual's overall learning experience.

Tertiary enrollment rates should be increased, especially in science, technology, engineering, and mathematics. Special measures need to be introduced to encourage and support girls entering such courses. Investments in information and communication technology (ICT) infrastructure should be increased, including an affordable and functional labor market information system and a higher education management information system. The system should also integrate ICT-based learning opportunities in education and training.

Boosting Development of the Private Sector and Its Access to Finance

Uzbekistan's economic growth has been supported by the expansion of private sector businesses, and accelerated by government efforts to transition to a market-based economy. Such private sector development is critical for a smooth shift from state-driven to private-sector-led economic growth in which SMEs play a key role. The present growth pattern of Uzbekistan has been led by labor-intensive industries such as in agriculture, manufacturing, and construction. Increasingly, the service sector will hold the most potential for high-quality job creation. Services-related SMEs, especially tech-based SMEs, could boost national productivity through innovation and skills development, benefiting from foreign direct investment (FDI) and the Fourth Industrial Revolution.

However, funding constraints limit the innovation capabilities of the private sector. A developed financial sector is an essential facilitator of private sector development. Growth-oriented SMEs are seeking diversified financing options that go beyond traditional bank credit to realize their potential. Financial inclusion, especially SME access to various sources of finance, should be high on the government's policy agenda for encouraging private sector development. The balanced development of banking and the nonbank finance industry, using new digital technologies, is crucial to broaden the financial instruments available for viable SMEs, including start-ups and young entrepreneurships.

The government needs to enhance the business-enabling environment for services-related SMEs in the education, health, transport, tourism, and ICT sectors, as they have the potential to create more high-quality jobs and help boost national productivity. Tech-based SMEs should be a primary target to this end. The government's support measures should include business development services for SMEs and business literacy programs for potential workers.

As Uzbekistan's export structure evolves from a heavy reliance on cotton and natural resources to a more diverse range of processed products and services, new business opportunities for export-oriented SMEs are emerging, including as participants in global value chains. The government's support measures should address promoting the internalization of SMEs and developing agricultural value chains, given the growth potential of agribusiness.

Although the credit market has been expanding in Uzbekistan, SMEs have yet to enjoy all the benefits of that expansion. Credit enhancement schemes supported by a credit bureau, a collateral registry, and credit guarantees should be created and strengthened to modernize the banking sector and enhance access to finance for SMEs. Developing a credit risk database is also worth considering.

The nonbank finance industry and capital market have yet to become a viable substitute for bank lending for private businesses. Meanwhile, the demand for diversified financing options has been increasing among SMEs, especially for long-term finance. The government needs to prepare a road map for developing the nonbank finance industry and market-based instruments, so as to promote their balanced development alongside the banking sector.

The advent of financial technology ("fintech") has been rapidly changing the financial sector's architecture. SMEs are considered a key beneficiary of fintech, given their limited access to traditional lending models. Online supply chain finance could be a pilot case of using digital finance. The government needs to promote financial inclusion and enhance financial and digital literacy for SMEs through establishing a comprehensive national strategy.

Given that the reform of state-owned enterprises can create more space for private businesses, the government needs to consider institutional reforms for SME development as part of ongoing state-owned enterprise reforms. That should include clarifying the role of state-owned banks. To facilitate internal coordination of SME development policies, the creation of a specialized SME agency is worth considering.

Boosting International Trade and Foreign Direct Investment

The roles of international trade and FDI have become increasingly important in a globalized world. Uzbekistan is well behind in exploiting benefits from trade and FDI: since 1995, Uzbekistan's share of total trade in gross domestic product has been the lowest of all Central Asian countries. The country has little engagement with regional and international groups, and is not a member of the Eurasian Economic Union or the World Trade Organization (WTO), but could increase its engagement. Greater integration is also possible through the gas pipelines from Turkmenistan to the People's Republic of China, Kazakhstan, and the Russian Federation, including via the Belt and Road Initiative.

The weighted average import tariff rate is still high in Uzbekistan compared with the average rates for Kazakhstan, the Kyrgyz Republic, and Tajikistan. The highest import tariff protection is for footwear, leather, apparel, and textile manufacturing, even though parts of these industries are among the country's main exports.

In addition, Uzbekistan attracts the least FDI inflows among Central Asian economies, and such flows have declined substantially in recent years. Moreover, the inflows are confined mainly to the extractive sector rather than flowing into a broad range of industries.

Gradual trade liberalization will inevitably be associated with accession to the WTO, when the government completes that process. Further regional trade cooperation also would increase trade flows and result in more and better jobs and improved productivity growth.

Opening up to regional and global trade requires more than just reducing high levels of import tariffs, however. Nontariff trade barriers may be even more of an issue, including cumbersome domestic regulations. Improving the business climate by deregulation would generate a more dynamic business environment, which would allow faster firm growth, attract more FDI, and generate more high-quality jobs. A single public–private or private agency could help promote export opportunities for domestic enterprises and attract investors by providing research on new market opportunities, measuring export capacities, and assisting with all regulatory aspects of establishing a new enterprise in Uzbekistan. Greater investments in transport infrastructure, human capital development, and research and innovation would increase the Uzbek economy's competitiveness and diversity.

UZBEKISTAN

FAST FACTS
as of 2017 or latest available year

PEOPLE AND RESOURCES

Total population: 32.4 million [2018]
Total land area: 42.5 million ha
Total fertility rate: 2.3 births per woman [2017]
Agricultural area: 26.8 million ha [2016]
Forest area: 3.2 million ha [2016]

ECONOMY

Value added by sector (2018):
Agriculture: 32.4%
Industry: 32.0%
Services: 35.6%
GDP (constant 2010 $): 65.8 billion
Per capita GDP (2011 PPP$): 6,240
Remittances (current $): 2.8 billion

SOCIAL INDICATORS

Unemployment rate: 9.3% [2018]
Proportion of population living below
the national poverty line: 11.4% [2018]
Gini index: 0.3% [2018]
Life expectancy rate: 71.4 years
Infant mortality rate: 20 per 1,000 births
Adult literacy rate (15 years and above): 100% [2018]

FOREIGN TRADE

Exports ($): 7.5 billion
Imports ($): 11.9 billion
Top 3 imports: Machinery, metals, transportation equipment [2016]
Top 3 exports: Precious metal, textiles, mineral products [2016]
Top 3 export trading partners: Switzerland,
People's Republic of China, Russian Federation

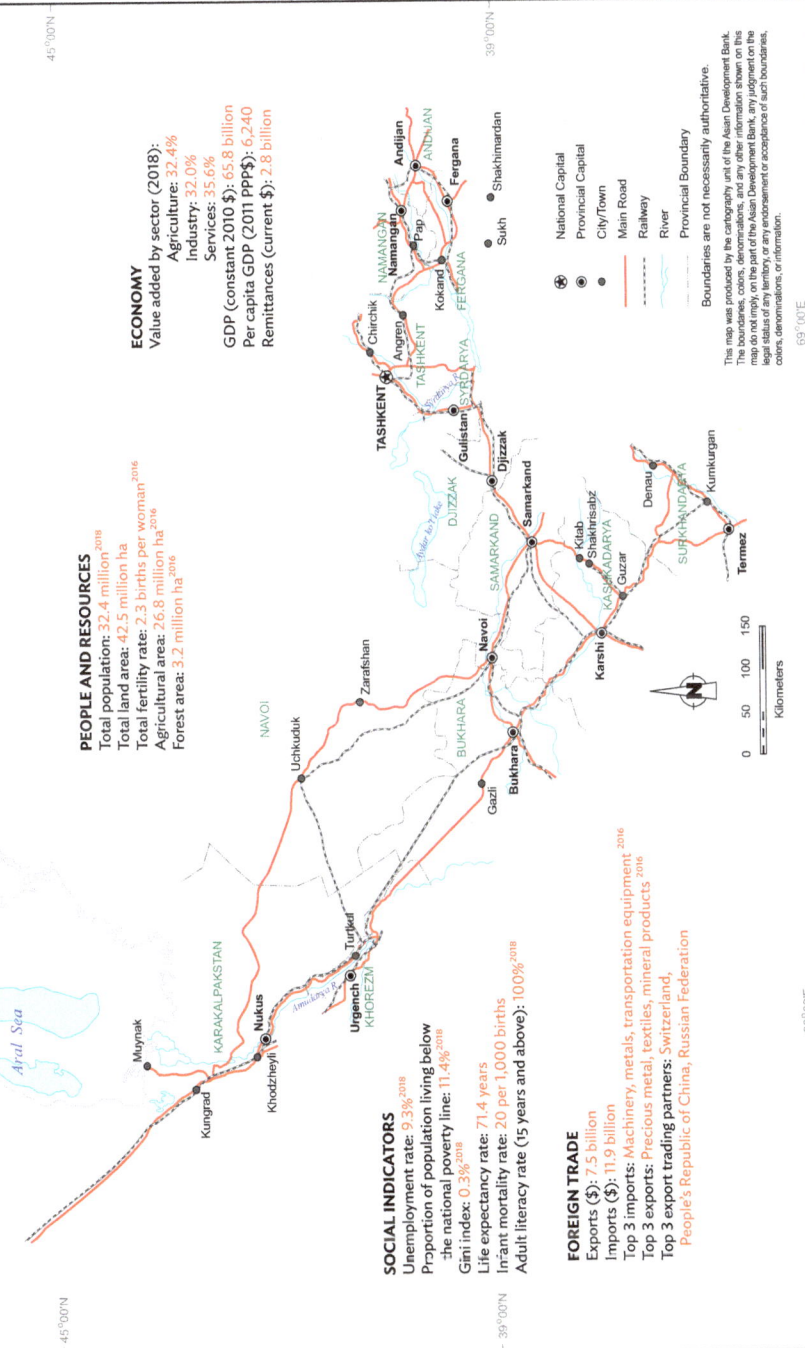

Legend

⊛ National Capital
◉ Provincial Capital
● City/Town
— Main Road
--- Railway
~ River
--- Provincial Boundary

This map was produced by the cartography unit of the Asian Development Bank.
The boundaries, colors, denominations, and any other information shown on this
map do not imply, on the part of the Asian Development Bank, any judgment on the
legal status of any territory, or any endorsement or acceptance of such boundaries,
colors, denominations, or information.

Boundaries are not necessarily authoritative.

Aral Sea

Muynak
Kungrad
Khodzheyli
Nukus
KARAKALPAKSTAN
Turtkel
Urgench
Uchkuduk
NAVOI
Zarafshan
Gazli
Bukhara
BUKHARA
Navoi
Karshi
KASHKADARYA
Guzar
Kitab
Shakhrisabz
Denau
SURKHANDARYA
Kumkurgan
Termez
Samarkand
SAMARKAND
Djizzak
DJIZZAK
Gulistan
SYRDARYA
TASHKENT
Angren
Chirchik
Kokand
FERGANA
Namangan
NAMANGAN
Pap
Andijan
ANDIJAN
Fergana
Shakhimardan
Sukh
KHOREZM

69°00'E
60°00'E
39°00'N
45°00'N

19-2999 19UZB AV

CHAPTER 1

Macroeconomic Performance, Opportunities, and Challenges

Marcel Schroder, Kym Anderson, Edimon Ginting, and Kiyoshi Taniguchi

Uzbekistan is the most populous of the five Central West Asian republics.[1] Its population reached 32.4 million in 2018, which is about 80% of the number of people in the other four Central West Asian republics combined. Uzbekistan is one of only two "double-landlocked" countries in the world.[2] Its economy is dependent on primary exports and belongs to the International Monetary Fund's group of 29 resource-rich developing countries (RRDCs).[3] In the years immediately after gaining independence from the Soviet Union in 1991, Uzbekistan depended heavily on cotton production. In recent years, however, gold and natural gas have become its main exports while wheat, meat, and most manufactured goods are imported.

Following the break-up of the Soviet Union, Uzbekistan transitioned from central planning to an economy based on market principles, albeit to a rather limited extent. President Islam Karimov led the country through the post-independence era until his death in 2016. His approach to economic reform was one of "gradualism." It involved cautiously liberalizing prices, especially those of energy and fuel, and maintaining a high level of state control.

The government up to 2016 promoted an import substitution strategy that was heavily driven by state investments. Credit was directly channeled to state-owned enterprises. The government also imposed high import duties and excise taxes, as well as foreign exchange controls. The latter resulted in a significantly overvalued real exchange rate. Despite these "unorthodox"

---

[1] The four other Central West Asian republics are Kazakhstan, the Kyrgyz Republic, Tajikistan, and Turkmenistan.

[2] The other one is Liechtenstein, which is between landlocked Austria and Switzerland.

[3] According to IMF (2012), RRDCs are classified as such based on two criteria: (i) low-income or lower-middle-income status, based on the World Bank classification; and (ii) at least 20% of total exports are natural resources.

development policies, the country experienced the smallest output decline of the ex-Soviet economies in the 1990s and enjoyed high rates of economic growth during 2004–2015, predominantly due to the recent commodity price boom for its major export goods.

When Shavkat Mirziyoyev was elected President on 14 December 2016, he took over a country facing challenges on multiple fronts. Since mid-2014, the prices for many key commodities (such as natural gas, gold, and copper) have declined, which has hampered Uzbekistan's export earnings. Furthermore, the Russian Federation suffered from a financial crisis in 2014–2015 that reduced both exports and migrant workers' remittances. Consequently, after a decade of formidable economic expansion, Uzbekistan's economic growth decelerated, manufacturing exports declined, and current employment growth was too low to absorb the thousands of young people entering the labor market every year. Uzbekistan risks missing its current demographic window of opportunity, a window that could transform the country into a rapidly growing and diversifying economy.

In light of these challenges, the new government recognizes the need for reform. The President signed in February 2017 the Decree on Strategy of Actions for the Development of Uzbekistan for 2017–2021. The February 2017 Decree outlines a strategy in five priority areas for the country's modernization and liberalization. The government's long-term view is formulated in its Vision 2030, which aims to double gross domestic product (GDP) in the following dozen years by diversifying the economy.

This chapter discusses the various reforms the government enacted in 2017–2019 and analyzes recent macroeconomic developments such as economic growth, fiscal policy settings, external sector performance, the labor market, and inclusion and sustainability. The final section identifies key challenges that might prevent the economy from creating sufficient jobs to reap the demographic dividend, and proposes ways to overcome them for Vision 2030 to become a reality.

1.1. Recent Reforms

The February 2017 Decree encompasses a set of five broad reform areas: (i) improving public administration; (ii) ensuring the rule of law and reforming the judicial system; (iii) developing and liberalizing the economy; (iv) improving education, health care, public infrastructure, and the social safety net; and (v) promoting mutually constructive and beneficial foreign policy.

The government has already implemented a number of reform initiatives. The most significant measure by far was the unification of the exchange rate in September 2017. The sum depreciated by about 50%, from SUM4,210 per dollar to SUM8,067 per dollar (Figure 1.1). This led to the immediate disappearance of the black market premium. The exchange rate regime is now floating, de jure, but is actually de facto a stabilizing arrangement (IMF 2018). Effectively, there are no more restrictions on currency convertibility and the repatriation of profits, which is a boost to Uzbekistan's attractiveness from the viewpoint of foreign investors.

Figure 1.1: Uzbekistan's Exchange Rate, 2013–2019
(SUM/$)

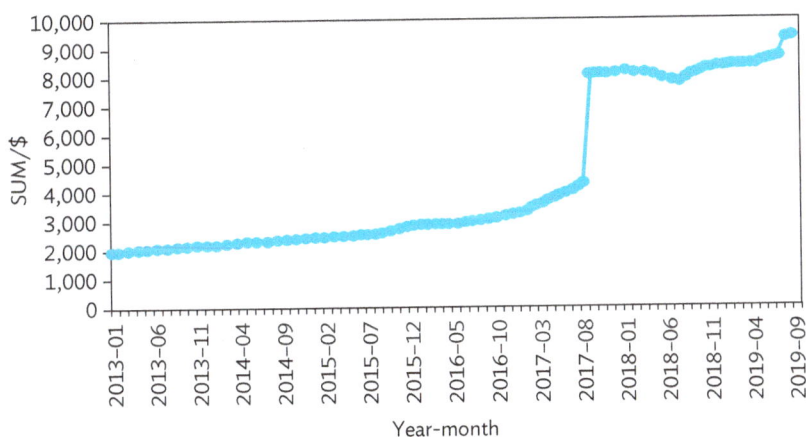

SUM = Uzbekistan sum.
Source: Central Bank of the Republic of Uzbekistan Statistics. http://www.cbu.uz/en/statistics/dks/ (accessed 11 November 2019).

Uzbekistan has also become active in trade policy. The average tariff rate stood at 30% as of July 2017 (International Trade Administration 2017), which is one of the highest in the world. There are signs that the government is committed to push for integrating the Uzbek economy into world markets. Most significant in this regard is the resumption of negotiations for Uzbekistan to accede to the World Trade Organization. Furthermore, effective 1 October 2017, Uzbekistan reduced import duty rates for 1,154 commodity items, of which about half were set at zero. In 2018 the authorities canceled duties on imports of vehicles for transporting agricultural products, electric vehicles, and cars produced no longer than 2 years ago and worth more than $40,000. More gradual tariff reductions for cars and other items are expected in 2019. Uzbekistan also plans to eliminate tariffs on textile imports from the European Union.

The positive impacts of these reforms are already visible and measurable. The reforms are reflected in the country's improved Doing Business ranking, which rose from 87th in 2016 to 69th in 2020. Uzbekistan's ratings improved in almost all categories, especially "getting electricity," "protecting minority investors," and "paying taxes" (Table 1.1). There is thus a marked improvement in the investment climate.

Table 1.1: Ease of Doing Business Rankings, Uzbekistan, 2016 and 2020

Category	Doing Business Rank	
	2016	2020
Ease of doing business rank	87	69
Starting a business	42	8
Dealing with construction permits	151	132
Getting electricity	112	36
Registering property	87	72
Getting credit	42	67
Protecting minority investors	88	37
Paying taxes	115	69
Trading across borders	159	152
Enforcing contracts	32	22
Resolving insolvency	75	100

Note: Rank 1 is the highest, 190 is the lowest.
Source: World Bank (2020).

Trading activity increased significantly. One year after the exchange rate unification, exports expanded by 23%, with food exports rising 45%. Imports rose even faster, by 40%. On the finance front, exchange rate liberalization promoted loan agreements with the European Bank for Reconstruction and Development and several German banks worth more than $1 billion; the loans are aimed at supporting infrastructure and small business projects (Tsereteli 2018). Anecdotally, economic activity also increased substantially in the nontradable sector, with the emergence of numerous restaurants and shops in Tashkent, for example.

Despite the significant recent reform efforts, there is room for more dynamic structural reforms such as privatizing state-owned enterprises, curtailing monopolistic practices, or further liberalizing domestic prices, particularly in the energy sector. Section 1.7 will return to these issues.

1.2. Economic Growth and Inflation

After independence, Uzbekistan's output decline was moderate in comparison to that in other ex-Soviet economies (Figure 1.2). This relatively good output performance was aided by rising international prices for cotton, then Uzbekistan's major export good. Between 1997 and 2003, real GDP growth averaged 4.4%. From 2004 onward, Uzbekistan experienced economic growth rates above 7.0% every year until 2015. This rapid economic expansion was driven by the global commodity price boom (Pomfret 2019). More recently, GDP growth rates decelerated to 4.5% in 2017 and 5.1% in 2018 due to a combination of falling commodity prices and a sharp decline in exports to the People's Republic of China and Kazakhstan. In summary, Uzbekistan's economic performance remains dependent on world commodity prices despite its fairly closed economy.

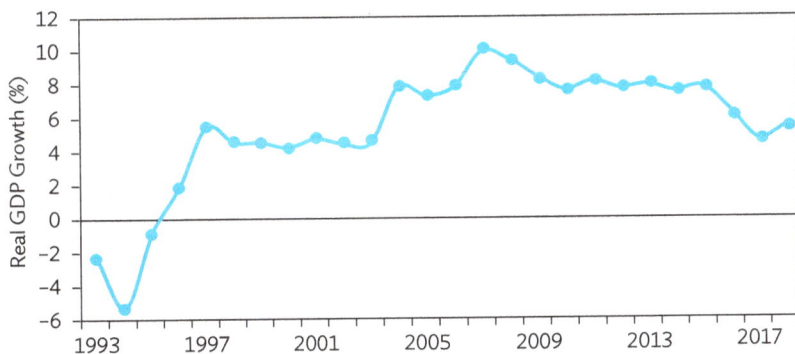

Figure 1.2: Real GDP Growth, Uzbekistan, 1993–2018
(% per year)

GDP = gross domestic product.
Sources: For 1993–2009, World Bank, World Development Indicators. http://www.databank.worldbank.org/, and for 2010–2018 Uzbekistan Statistics. http://stat.uz (both accessed 11 November 2019).

In terms of income levels, Uzbekistan has remained in the lower-middle-income group since 2001 (having briefly been classified as a low-income country during 1998–2000).[4] Average GDP per capita (in 2011 purchasing power parity dollars) more than doubled from $2,913 in 2004, the beginning of the commodity price boom, to $6,240 in 2018 (Figure 1.3). The doubling in income contributed to a halving of poverty. In particular, the poverty

---

[4] World Bank. n.d. Country Classification. https://datahelpdesk.worldbank.org/knowledgebase/articles/378833-how-are-the-income-group-thresholds-determined (accessed December 2018).

headcount at the national poverty line declined from 27.5% in 2001 to about 13.7% in 2015 (CER 2015).

Figure 1.3: GDP per Capita, 1993–2018
(2011 PPP $)

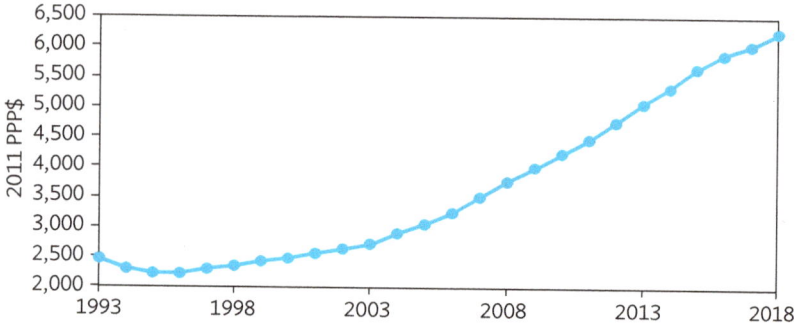

GDP=gross domestic product, PPP = purchasing power parity.
Source: World Bank. World Development Indicators. http://www.databank.worldbank.org/ (accessed 11 November 2019).

There has been a structural shift in production away from agriculture, whose share of GDP was 32.4% in 2018 versus 50.0% in 1993–1995 (Figure 1.4). The share of services increased from 28.1% in 1993 to 35.6% in 2018, while that of manufacturing gew from 17.1% to 26.3% over the same period.

Figure 1.4: GDP by Economic Activity, Uzbekistan, 1993–2018
(%)

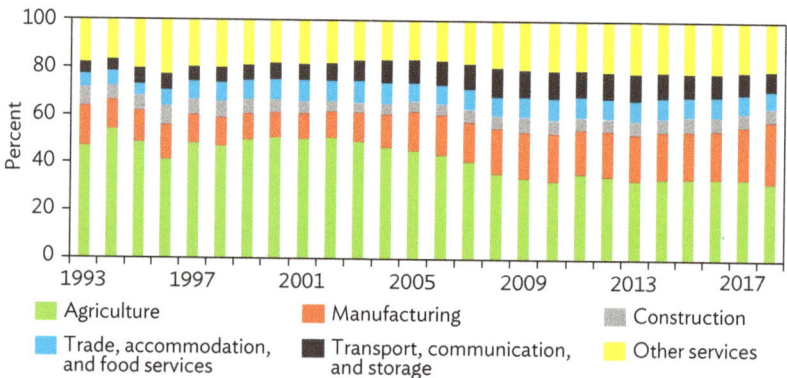

GDP = gross domestic product.
Notes: Percent (%) based on GDP at current basic prices. Manufacturing includes mining and quarrying, and electricity, gas, steam and water.
Sources: ADB. Statistical Data Base System. https://www.adb.org/data/sdbs (accessed 11 November 2019) and Uzbekistan Statistics. http://stat.uz (accessed 11 November 2019).

Uzbekistan has maintained stable, as officially reported, single-digit inflation rates since 2004 (Figure 1.5). Even during the commodity price boom years (2004–2014), annual inflation never exceeded 8%. After the boom, the economic slowdown led to a concomitant decline in the inflation rate, to 5.5% in 2015 and 5.6% in 2016. In early 2018, however, inflation jumped to almost 20%. This was predominantly due to the exchange rate unification in September 2017 as well as the loosening of both fiscal and monetary policies. In response, the Central Bank of Uzbekistan (CBU) tightened monetary policy by selling monetary gold and increasing the refinancing rate from 14% to 16% in September 2018. The inflation rate subsequently declined resulting in an annual average of 17.5% in 2018.

Figure 1.5: CPI and Food Inflation Rates, Uzbekistan, 2000–2018

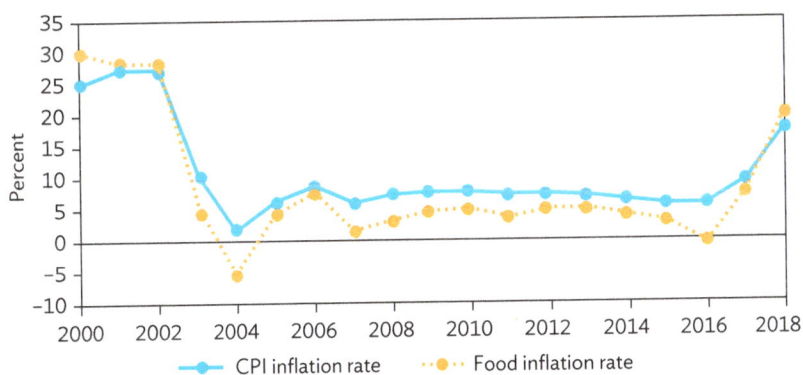

CPI=consumer price index.
Sources: For 2000–2011, ADB (2018) and for 2012–2018, Uzbekistan Statistics. http://stat.uz (accessed 11 November 2019).

Whether these recent measures will be sufficient for inflation to return to single digits is unclear. Pressure on the sum to depreciate is ongoing.[5] Furthermore, monetary transmission via the interest rate channel is weak in Uzbekistan (Hespeler 2013). Inflation is thus likely to persist and may only gradually decline in 2019/20. In the future, the monetary transmission channel will need strengthening to tame inflation more effectively. The CBU's recent effort to develop the government bond market is a first step in the right direction. A strong monetary transmission process will also be a key ingredient to the CBU's planned adoption of inflation targeting over the medium term (IMF 2018). In the meantime, further structural reforms aimed at promoting

---

[5] Interview with Central Bank of Uzbekistan, 4 October 2018.

competitive markets, as discussed in section 1.8, would have the additional side effect of bringing down inflation.

1.3.   Fiscal Policy and Reform

Uzbekistan has a history of prudent fiscal policy. As a result, public external debt is low, at 24.5% of GDP, despite the large currency devaluation in September 2017. Uzbekistan's fiscal policy is moderately pro-cyclical, meaning that when GDP increases by 1%, fiscal spending grows by less than that (Aizenman et al. 2018). During the resource boom years of 2011–2013, the government ran a fiscal surplus. In response to the external shock of lower commodity prices from 2014 onward, the authorities moderately loosened fiscal policy. The augmented fiscal balance recorded a deficit from 2015 to 2018, except in 2017 when government lowered expenditure significantly resulting in a brief surplus. The government has indicated its commitment to fiscal tightening with the aim of not letting fiscal deficits exceed 2% of GDP during 2019–2021. In the future, a move toward an even more counter-cyclical fiscal policy would be beneficial along various dimensions (Box 1.1).

The fiscal deficit is driven by a decline in both total revenue and expenditure. Total revenue in the government's budget decreased from 26.8% of GDP in 2013 to 23.0% in 2018. The drop in revenue is in large part explained by lower value-added tax (VAT), excise taxes, and mining tax (Figure 1.7). Total expenditure decreased slightly less, from 28.2% in 2013 to 24.6% of GDP in 2018.

The government was able to use its fiscal buffers to increase public investment and the wages of public sector employees. Public spending on education and health was maintained at close to 10% of GDP, which is unusually high in international comparison given Uzbekistan's level of income (Figure 1.7). More specifically, in 2014, education accounted for 6.1% of GDP. But due to the overall trend of falling expenditure, it declined to 5.4% in 2018.

The government is in the process of implementing a tax reform, which will significantly overhaul the tax system. As of January 2019, small businesses will no longer receive preferential treatment, except those with yearly revenues not exceeding SUM1 billion. All other businesses will be subject to a compulsory 20% VAT. At the same time, the reform seeks to reduce tax rates on social contributions, the corporate tax rate, turnover tax, property tax, and the administrative burden in order to decrease costs.

Box 1.1: Countercyclical Fiscal Policy

Resource-rich developing countries (RRDCs) such as Uzbekistan are typically subjected to volatile commodity prices, which to a large extent drive the business cycle in such countries. Empirical studies suggest that fiscal policy in developing countries, and particularly RRDCs, typically is pro-cyclical (Kaminsky et al. 2005, Kraay and Serven 2013). This means that spending expands in times of resource booms and contracts during busts. Such a spending pattern both prolongs and amplifies economic expansions and recessions, which can lead to macroeconomic instability. By contrast, counter-cyclical fiscal policy would be beneficial. Indeed, empirical evidence suggests that counter-cyclical fiscal spending dampens business cycles and reduces the probability of a prolonged economic crisis (Ostry et al. 2010).

Moreover, pro-cyclical fiscal policy may indirectly have an adverse impact on long-run economic growth. Countries with high output volatility tend to experience lower economic growth (Ramey and Ramey 1995). Another possible channel is through the so-called Dutch Disease: excessive growth in fiscal spending during booms leads to further erosion of the manufacturing sector's competitiveness. The development literature often argues that manufacturing is special due to the positive externalities that are not present in other areas of economic activity (Rodrik 2008). While whether such externalities exist in practice remains unclear (Eichengreen 2008; Schroder 2017), there is evidence that small states benefit from export diversification through lower output volatility (McIntyre et al. 2018).

Uzbekistan's fiscal policy compares favorably with that of other RRDCs and countries in the region. For example, Kazakhstan and the Kyrgyz Republic, two neighboring countries, have among the most pro-cyclical fiscal policies in the world (Aizenman et al. 2018). In these economies, estimated cyclicality is above 1, i.e., for every 1% increase in gross domestic product, government spending grows by more than 1%. Indonesia and Papua New Guinea, two peer RRDCs, also display an estimated cyclicality of greater than 1. The Uzbek authorities, by contrast, increase fiscal spending by only 0.5% for every 1% increase in the annual gross domestic product growth rate, which, when compared internationally, is moderate.

Nevertheless, moving toward a more counter-cyclical spending would be beneficial. Other Asian countries, some of them also rich in natural resources (such as Brunei Darussalam, Bhutan, Cambodia, and Sri Lanka) on average, decrease fiscal spending when output increases. Uzbekistan should gradually follow suit to reap the benefits.

Sources: Aizenman et al. 2018, Eichengreen 2008, Kaminsky et al. 2005, Kraay and Serven 2013, McIntyre et al. 2018, Ostry et al. 2010, Ramey and Ramey 1995, Rodrik 2008, Schroder 2017.

Figure 1.6: Total Fiscal Revenue and Expenditure (Budget), Uzbekistan, 2013–2018
(% of GDP)

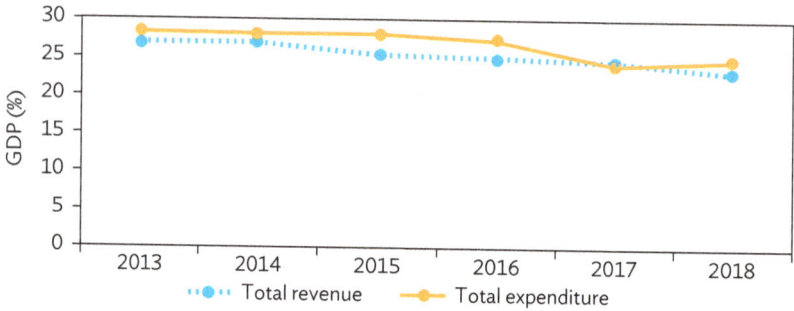

GDP = gross domestic product.
Source: Author's calculations based on data from the Ministry of Finance of the Republic of Uzbekistan (2018).

Figure 1.7: Tax and Expenditure Items (Budget), Uzbekistan, 2013–2018
(% of GDP)

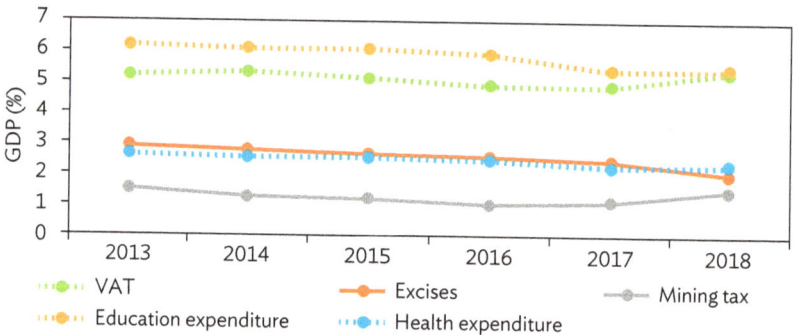

GDP = gross domestic product, VAT = value-added tax.
Source: Author's calculations based on data from the Ministry of Finance of the Republic of Uzbekistan (2018).

The tax reform is commendable and should boost employment creation in Uzbekistan. Before the reform, small and large enterprises were subject to different tax regimes. The standardized system applied to large companies, and a simplified system applied to small firms, where the distinguishing factor was the number of employees. Once a firm exceeded the employee threshold, the tax burden, including a VAT, increased substantially. The old tax system thus generated adverse incentives for enterprises to create formal sector jobs. In 2017, Uzbekistan had about 350,000 firms only 8,000 of which were subject to the standardized tax system. Other side effects were a broken value chain system in that small enterprises that were exempt from paying VAT did not do business with large companies and vice versa. The tax system also hindered benefiting from economies of scale.

The reform will also broaden the tax base, which promises to provide several important benefits. First, will be additional funds for physical, social, and administrative infrastructure. Second, the broadened tax base will cushion the government's revenue against drops in commodity prices in the future. Both factors will contribute to better economic and employment growth outcomes in the long run. Finally, the reform is also likely to lead to more cooperation and competition between small and large enterprises, which will boost their productivity levels.

Despite its expected overall positive impact, the tax reform is not without challenges and shortcomings. While the elimination of preferential treatment for small businesses leads to a more equitable tax system, the proposed flat income tax (12% for both corporate and private) may effectively increase the tax burden of households at or around the poverty level, and thus hurt the poor. The compulsory VAT is also likely to lead to additional price increases amid the already high prevailing inflation rates. At this stage, it is also not clear to what extent small firms will be able to deal with the VAT and other administrative burdens associated with the new tax system. An appropriate grace period would thus be useful, especially for small businesses, so they can adjust their administrative capacities to the new taxation regime.

1.4. External Sector

This section reviews Uzbekistan's recent trends and patterns in export performance, and then assesses the degree of export diversification as well as the current external position.

1.4.1. Export performance

Uzbekistan's post-independence export performance can be broken into two episodes: from the mid-1990s to 2008, and from 2009 onward. During the first period, exports expanded rapidly from $1.6 billion in 1995 to $7.0 billion in 2008 (Figure 1.8), which represents an average annual growth rate of about 12.5%. During that time, there was a major shift away from agricultural to manufactured goods. The latter increased from a mere $127.8 million in 1995 to $2.5 billion in 2008, whereas the former remained virtually unchanged. Consequently, the export share of manufactures increased from 8% to 36%, whereas that of agricultural goods declined from 70% to 14% during that period (Figure 1.9). The boost in manufactured goods exports was mainly driven by increases of passenger vehicle exports.

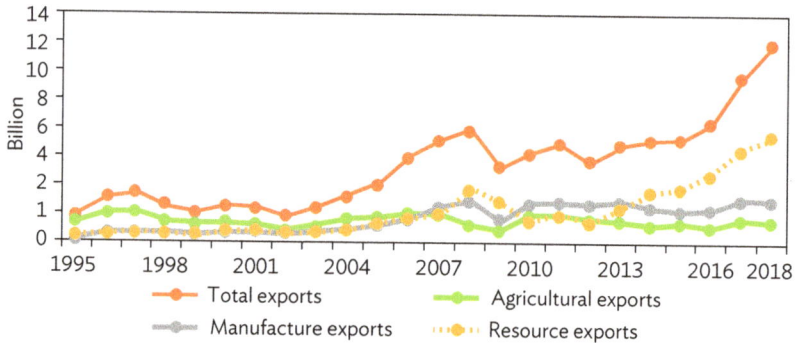

Figure 1.8: Value of Exports, Uzbekistan, 1995–2018
($ billion)

Source: Compiled from UN Comtrade database. http://unctad.org/en/Pages/statistics.aspx (accessed 14 January 2020).

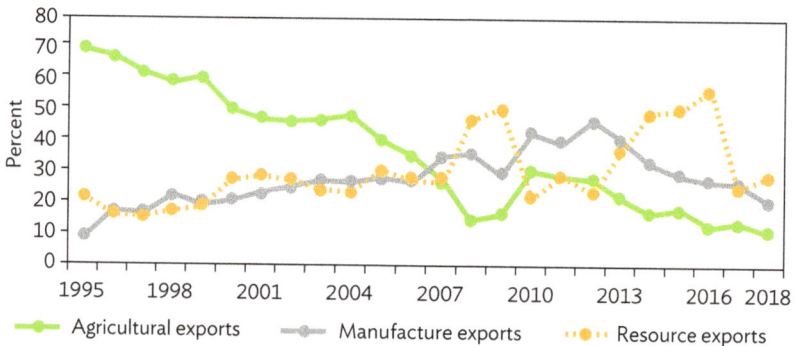

Figure 1.9: Sectoral Export Shares, Uzbekistan, 1995–2018
(%)

Source: Compiled from UN Comtrade. https://comtrade.un.org (accessed 14 January 2020).

However, this favorable trend in export performance reversed in 2009. Since then, total export growth has slowed, with the value of exports declining to $4.9 billion in 2012 before recovering to $7.4 billion in 2016. Importantly, however, the export composition shifted dramatically away from agricultural and manufactured goods, as the share of natural resources exports increased (Figure 1.9). The share of manufactured exports in total exports declined from a record-high of 47.1% in 2012 to 20.6% in 2018. This was driven partly by a lower demand for Uzbek goods in neighboring Kazakhstan and the Russian Federation.[6] On the other hand, the share of resource exports, the bulk of which is gold, has been on an upward trend since 2012. The Uzbek economy's resource dependency has thus increased substantially despite falling commodity prices.

Little progress has been made in export diversification. When classed by the level of technology (Lall classification), the export basket predominantly consists of primary goods, resource-based manufacturers, and gold (Figure 1.10). Medium-technology exports (e.g., cars) declined by 65%, from $1.1 billion in 2011 to $399.8 million in 2015 before recovering to $996.5 million in 2018, while exports of low-technology products increased to almost $1 billion in 2017 before decreasing to $764.1 million in 2018.

Figure 1.10: Exports by Level of Technology, Uzbekistan, 1995–2018

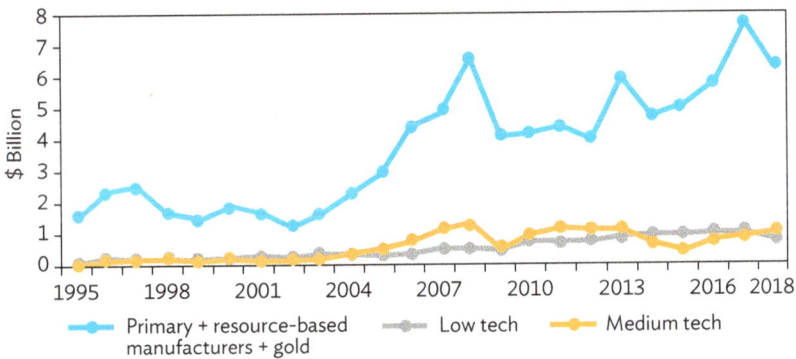

Note: Level of technology is based on the Lall classification.
Source: Compiled from UN Comtrade. https://comtrade.un.org (accessed 11 November 2019).

A product space analysis also suggests limited diversification of the export basket (Figure 1.11). Most products are clustered on the "periphery," implying that the country has not yet developed the capabilities required to produce high-value-added goods such as machinery, metal products, construction materials, ships, or chemicals, all of which are in the middle portion of the product space. Noteworthy in this context is the temporary emergence of a "machinery and transport equipment" cluster, which accounted for 9.3% of the export basket in 2005. However, these products are no longer represented in the export basket, underlining the difficulty for diversifying the economy.

---

[6]   The Russian Federation entered a recession in 2015. As a result, the Russian ruble depreciated significantly, which meant Uzbek car exporters lost out to Russian competitors in the Kazakh car market.

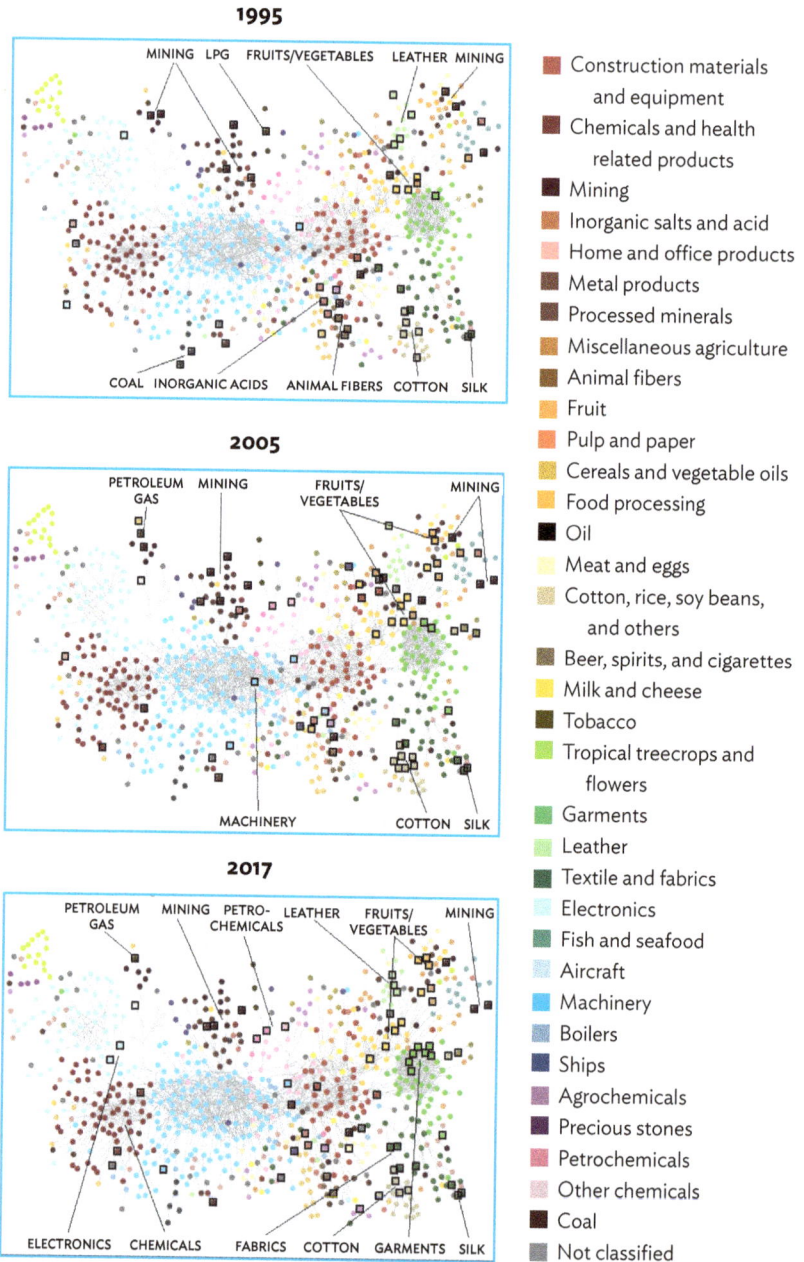

Figure 1.11: Product Space of Exports, Uzbekistan, 1995, 2005, and 2017

1995

2005

2017

Construction materials and equipment
Chemicals and health related products
Mining
Inorganic salts and acid
Home and office products
Metal products
Processed minerals
Miscellaneous agriculture
Animal fibers
Fruit
Pulp and paper
Cereals and vegetable oils
Food processing
Oil
Meat and eggs
Cotton, rice, soy beans, and others
Beer, spirits, and cigarettes
Milk and cheese
Tobacco
Tropical treecrops and flowers
Garments
Leather
Textile and fabrics
Electronics
Fish and seafood
Aircraft
Machinery
Boilers
Ships
Agrochemicals
Precious stones
Petrochemicals
Other chemicals
Coal
Not classified

Source: ADB estimates based on UN Comtrade. https://comtrade.un.org (accessed 11 November 2019).

Figure 1.12 suggests a strong positive association between a country's economic complexity index (ECI) value and its economic performance. Uzbekistan's ECI value (-0.68 in 2016, Figure 1.13) compares favorably with the RRDC average (which was –1.11 in 2016). However, there is a big gap between Uzbekistan's ECI and the average for resource rich countries that have reached at least upper-middle-income status (–0.19).[7] Uzbekistan's ECI did not improve between 1995 and 2016, similar to the RRDC average, although there are exceptions among the RRDC group: the ECI for Angola improved significantly (+0.63), as did that of Indonesia (+0.43), the Lao People's Democratic Republic (+0.22), and Viet Nam (+1.12). The lesson from these countries is that export diversification is possible independent of market conditions and despite vast resource wealth.

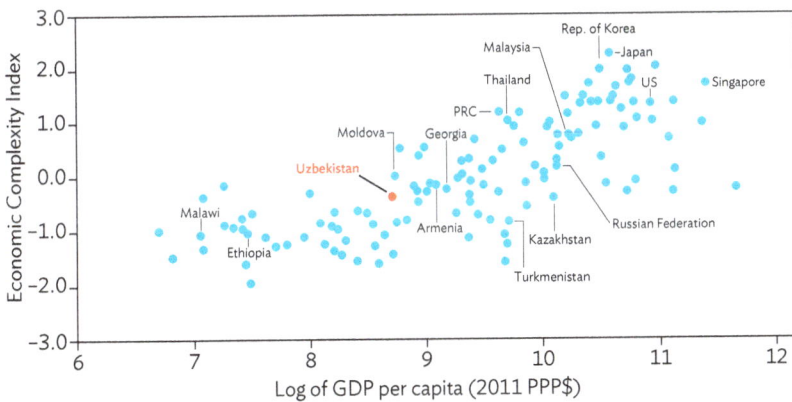

Figure 1.12: Economic Complexity and GDP per Capita, Various Countries, 2017

GDP=gross domestic product, PPP = purchasing power parity, PRC = People's Republic of China, US = United States.
Notes: The Economic Complexity Index is a ranking of countries based on the diversity and complexity of their export baskets. Countries that have a great diversity of productive know-how, particularly complex specialized know-how, are able to produce a great diversity of sophisticated products. The complexity of a country's exports is found to highly predict current income levels, or where complexity exceeds expectations for a country's income level, the country is predicted to experience more rapid growth in the future. The index therefore provides a useful measure of economic development.
Sources: ADB estimates based on UN Comtrade database. https://comtrade.un.org; and World Bank, World Development Indicators. http://www.databank.worldbank.org/ for GDP per capita (both accessed 11 November 2019).

---

[7]   The countries are Brazil, Botswana, Chile, Kuwait, Oman, Qatar, Saudi Arabia, and the United Arab Emirates.

Figure 1.13: Economic Complexity Index Values, Uzbekistan and Other Resource-Rich Countries, 1995–2017

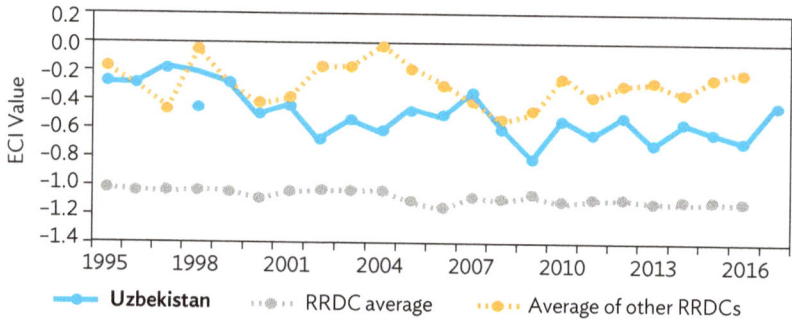

ECI = Economic Complexity Index, RRDC = resource-rich developing country; RRC = resource-rich country.
Source: Compiled from the Atlas of Economic Complexity Data. http://atlas.cid.harvard.edu/about-data (accessed 11 November 2019).

1.4.2. External position

The current account of Uzbekistan's balance of payments has been in surplus since 2002. High GDP growth coupled with fiscal and current account surpluses during this period led to low ratios of external debt to GDP, which were below 20% during 2010–2016. In 2017, this increased to 29.9% of GDP as the currency depreciated and the economy slowed. Foreign direct investment inflows have been significant and were mainly into oil and gas, petrochemicals, and automobile manufacturing. They have declined, however, from a peak in 2010 partly due to the lumpy nature of the investments and partly due to the uncertainty in the global energy market arising from falling commodity prices (Table 1.2).[8]

Table 1.2: External Indicators, Uzbekistan, 2005–2018

	2005	2010	2013	2014	2015	2016	2017	2018
Foreign direct investment ($ million)	191.6	1,636.4	634.7	757.4	66.5	134.1	97.7	412.4
External debt outstanding (% GDP)	27.1	16.6	15.5	17.3	18.1	19.9	29.9	34.9
Remittances ($ million)	...	2,858	6,689	5,653	3,059	2,741	3,901	2,801

... = no data, GDP = gross domestic product.
Sources: For gross official reserves and external debt outstanding, ADB (2018) and IMF (2018); for remittances, World Bank. World Development Indicators. http://www.databank.worldbank.org (accessed 11 November 2019); for foreign direct investment, UNCTAD. http://unctad.org/en/Pages/statistics.aspx (accessed 11 November 2019).

---

[8]   The 2011 peak in foreign direct investment was due to new cooperation arrangements with the People's Republic of China that gained momentum with the launch of a construction project to build a pipeline extension linking Uzbekistan to the Central Asia–China gas pipeline

The unification of the exchange rate is likely to mark a structural break in the external sector's performance. The availability of foreign exchange meant that the demand for imports was no longer compressed. The merchandise trade deficit has widened substantially, from 3.8% of GDP in 2017 to 13.6% in 2018. However, after years of restrictions on imports, this development is not surprising. Once the backlog in imports has cleared, the trade deficit should narrow.

Remittances have declined continuously, from $6.7 billion in 2013 to $2.7 billion in 2016, before recovering slightly to $3.9 billion in 2017 (Table 1.2). In 2018, remittances declined again to $2.8 billion, resulting in a current account deficit of 7.1% of GDP.

The removal of foreign exchange controls and the concomitant current account deficit has put pressure on Uzbekistan's foreign exchange reserves. Between September 2017 and October 2018, they declined by $1 billion, from $27.5 billion to $26.4 billion (Figure 1.14). This level of reserves is still adequate, as it translates to about 18 months of imports, well above the conventional rule of thumb that suggests 3 months of imports.[9] Overall, Uzbekistan's external position can be summarized as healthy despite the recent emergence of a current account deficit. However, should the deficit exceed 5% of GDP for a sustained period, further assessment will be needed, as this might be a cause for concern.

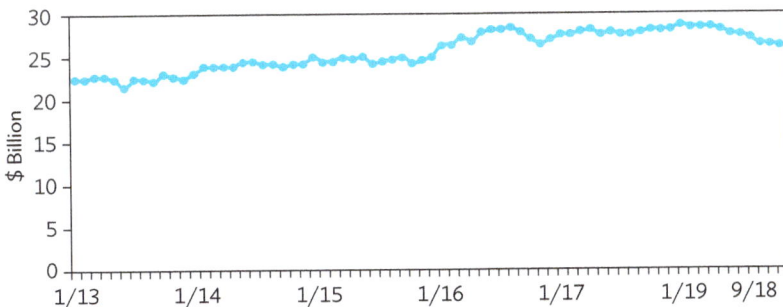

Figure 1.14: Official Reserves, Uzbekistan, January 2013–December 2018

Sources: For 2013-2017: Uzbekistan Statistics. http://stat.uz (accessed December 2018); for 2018: Central Bank of the Republic of Uzbekistan. http://www.cbu.uz/en/statistics/intlreserves/ (accessed 11 November 2019)

---

[9]   A new consensus has emerged that the 3 months of imports rule of thumb is inadequate in an era of financial globalization due to volatile capital flows (e.g., Athukorala and Warr 2002). However, Uzbekistan has low levels of external debt and is not well integrated into world financial markets, so the conventional rule still has merit here.

1.5. Job Creation

The labor market is Uzbekistan's greatest challenge and opportunity at the same time. Estimated 500,000 individuals will enter the labor force every year until 2030. The age dependency ratio has been falling continuously since 2000 and is expected to remain unusually low in the coming decades (Figure 1.15). Also, about 2.6 million migrant workers are employed, often on uncertain terms and with limited rights, in the Russian Federation alone. Successfully integrating job seekers into the labor market will help Uzbekistan achieve upper-middle-income status in the near future. However, the country so far has not seized this unique opportunity as annual employment growth averaged only 0.75% during 2015–2017, while in 2018–2019 employment is expected to expand by only 1% (IMF 2018). Such sluggish employment growth rates are not enough to absorb the yearly increase in the labor supply. There is thus the danger of rising unemployment, labor migration, and dissatisfaction, especially among the youth.

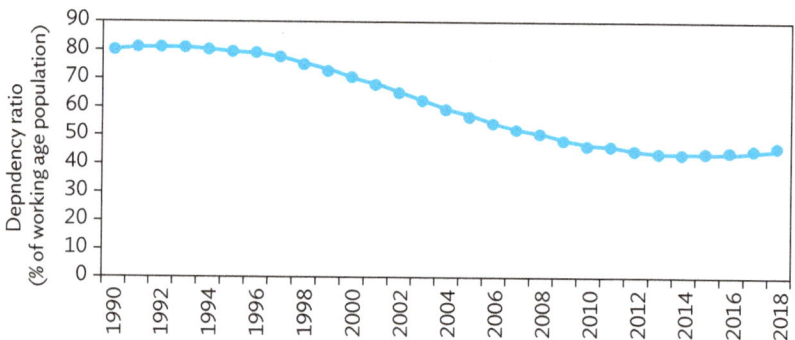

Figure 1.15: Age Dependency Ratio, Uzbekistan, 1990-2018

Source: World Bank. World Development Indicators. http://www.databank.worldbank.org/ (accessed 11 November 2019).

What explains the low employment growth numbers? An important factor is likely to be the steep decline in exports of manufactures in recent years, as discussed in the previous section. This decline hindered the creation of urgently needed high-quality jobs. At the same time, the capital-intensive resources sector, which only offers limited employment opportunities, has expanded substantially. Indeed, in the mid-2000s when manufacturing was expanding more rapidly than the resource sector, employment growth exceeded 3%.

But there are also other reasons. The World Bank (2018) finds that the labor intensity of the manufacturing sector has decreased over time and that this trend continued even though the return to capital has been declining. This is because several past government policies created a bias against labor in favor of capital, even in labor-intensive industries. For example, in 2005–2016, real wage increases consistently outpaced labor productivity gains (World Bank 2018). Other implicit subsidies for capital accumulation occurred through the granting of concessional interest rates and preferential access to foreign exchange at the official rate. Finally, the prereform tax system of granting preferential treatment to small enterprises based on the number of employees also created a bias against job creation.

The government's recent reform measures have removed many of the impediments to employment growth. In a World Bank survey of small and large enterprises, lack of access to foreign exchange, lack of access to raw material, lack of skilled personnel, high taxes, lack of demand for output, and lack of finance were cited as the most important factors that hinder job creation (Table 1.3). The exchange rate liberalization, continuous removal of tariffs, and tax reform addresses several of these key concerns. Eventual accession to the World Trade Organization will give access to new export markets, which will help remedy the issue of limited demand. While substantial progress has been made, more needs to be done to boost employment in the future.

Table 1.3: Ranking of Barriers to Creating Employment, Uzbekistan Enterprise Survey, 2017

	Barrier	Rank by firms	
		Large	Small
1	Lack of access to foreign exchange	1	2
2	Lack of access to raw materials on domestic market	3	1
3	Lack of access to skilled personnel	2	4
4	Too high payroll taxes (social payments) and personal income taxes	5	3
5	Demand limitations	4	6
6	Lack of access to bank credit	6	5
7	Difficult to find good human resource manager	7	9
8	We need more staff, but don't want to exceed the number to remain in "unified taxation" system	10	7
9	Firm offers low wage/no social package: can't attract/retain skilled staff	8	10
10	Lack of workers mobility	12	8
11	We reduce employment or transfer to partial/part time workers	9	13
12	Difficult procedures for hiring personnel	11	11
13	We increase employment when necessary, but do it unofficially	13	12

Note: Large firms were surveyed in the spring of 2017 and small firms were surveyed in July–September 2017.
Source: World Bank's Macroeconomics, Trade and Investment Global Practice surveys conducted for Uzbekistan Growth Diagnostics (World Bank 2018).

1.6. Inclusion and Sustainability

Official data suggest that, since 2001, major reductions have been achieved in absolute poverty, which in turn led to Uzbekistan accomplishing its Millennium Development Goal No. 1 (Improving Living Standards) of halving the poverty rate, which fell from 27.5% in 2001 to 11.4% in 2018 (Table 1.4). At the same time, the Gini measure of inequality also fell, from 0.39 in 2001 to 0.30 in 2018 (Table 1.4).[10]

Table 1.4: Poverty and Inequality Indicators, Uzbekistan, 2001, 2007, 2010, 2013, 2016–2018

Indicator	2001	2007	2010	2013	2016	2017	2018
GDP per capita (constant 2011 PPP $)	2,576	3,525	4,239	5,076	5,880	6,040	6,240
Gini coefficient	0.39	...	0.30	0.29	0.28	0.28	0.3
Poverty in rural areas	30.5	27.1	...	17.3	12.3	...	11.4
Poverty in urban areas	22.5	17.6	...	10.6	...	...	...
Poverty in families with children under 16 years old	...	22.1	...	11.8	...	...	...
Poverty among households headed by women	...	1.3	...	0.3	...	...	...

... = data not available, GDP = gross domestic product, PPP = purchasing power parity.
Sources: For GDP per capita (PPP): World Bank. World Development Indicators. http://www.databank.worldbank.org (accessed 11 November 2019); for national poverty line: ADB Basic Statistics (various years); for the rest: Uzbekistan Statistics. http://stat.uz (accessed 26 March 2018).

Despite these achievements, poverty remains high in rural areas, with four regions recording poverty headcount rates of above 20% in 2012 (Tables 1.5).

Table 1.5: Poverty Incidence by Region, Uzbekistan, 2012
(% of households)

Region	Poverty Incidence (%)	Region	Poverty Incidence (%)
Karakalpakstan[a]	32.5	Navoi	16.6
Kashkadarya	24.9	Samarkand	12.9
Surkhandarya	22.6	Bukhara	12.2
Syrdarya	20.3	Andijan	11.5
Jizzak[a]	18.7	Tashkent Region	10.3
Namangan[a]	17.4	Fergana	9.6
Khorezm[a]	17.2	Tashkent City	2.1

[a] Rural regions.
Source: Uzbekistan Statistics. http://stat.uz (accessed 11 November 2019).

---

[10] The Presidential Address January 2016 suggests a Gini coefficient of 0.28 in 2015. The accuracy of official statistics on poverty is disputed in Bertelsmann Stiftung (2014). According to the Committee of the Republic of Uzbekistan on Statistics, the share of population below the national poverty line is 11.4%.

Despite the decline in inequality, the elasticity of poverty reduction to GDP growth in Uzbekistan is relatively low, with a 1% increase in per capita GDP associated with a 0.5% decrease on average in the national poverty rate.[11] This elasticity of poverty reduction is less than the average for developing countries, consistent with the notion that the recent economic expansion has been by-and-large jobless. But the best way for the poor to participate in the economy is through additional and better employment opportunities. The past policy of implicit subsidies to capital not only encouraged outward labor migration and hindered employment growth, but also put a break on poverty reduction.

According to Ali and Zhuang (2007), three key initiatives are central to inclusive growth: creation of relatively high-productivity jobs, removal of discriminatory barriers to economic and social opportunities, and social protection including social insurance and welfare payments. The government needs to address all three areas, but (as argued in the previous section) employment creation will be critical.

Another important aspect of inclusion and the removal of discriminatory barriers relates to gender equity. In terms of education, health, and social rights, few gender gaps exist. The main issue relates to economic empowerment. As a legacy of the Soviet system, women's participation in the labor market is relatively high, with legal protections available such as maternity leave. Home-based work is recognized formally and attracts pension and unemployment benefits. Nonetheless, the labor market suffers from both horizontal and vertical segregation in gender terms, with women overrepresented in fields such as education and health and underrepresented in the private sector, manufacturing, mining, and transport. Women are also underrepresented in all sectors at managerial and senior levels. This segregation creates an average wage gap of about 35% (ADB 2014). Full inclusion requires progress, particularly through labor market measures, in reducing the economic aspects of gender disparities.

Emerging environmental issues relate to water scarcity, soil degradation, deforestation, and air pollution in urban and industrial centers. Controlled energy and water prices have encouraged overuse: by international standards, Uzbekistan has very low ratios of GDP to both energy and water use. Uzbekistan is a particularly inefficient user of energy, with a ratio of carbon dioxide emissions per unit of GDP more than three times the average for its income level.[12] The district heating system installed in the former Soviet period

---

[11] Ravallion (2001) finds that a 1% rate of growth in average household income or consumption leads to a drop in the poverty rate of between 0.6% and 3.5%.

[12] In 2013, the ratio was 4.9 kilograms of carbon dioxide per unit of GDP in 2005 dollars, compared with the 1.4 kilogram average for lower-middle-income countries.

is a particular source of inefficiency. The Aral Sea, once the fourth-largest inland lake in the world has lost more than half its surface area, largely due to inappropriate irrigation during the Soviet period (World Bank 2014). Climate change will exacerbate these problems, with expected temperature rising sufficiently high to force changes in agricultural practices and measures, such as afforestation and shifts to less water-intensive farming.

1.7.   Key Messages and Policy Recommendations

The key macroeconomic issue for Uzbekistan at this time is to convert jobless growth into more-inclusive economic growth. This means that creating good quality employment opportunities for all Uzbeks must be a top priority. Recent trends are worrying in this regard, as employment growth is historically low and agricultural and manufacturing exports are declining. Relying on the resources sector will not create enough jobs, and will maintain the economy's vulnerability to external shocks. What is needed instead is private business development in the nonresource sector and export diversification.

Recent policy reforms are necessary and are being implemented at a critical time. The lifting of foreign exchange restrictions has led to a substantial improvement in the investment climate. Other measures such as tax reform and removal of many import tariffs promise further improvements. However, the reform efforts may not reach their full positive impact on the economy unless further government action is taken along three additional dimensions.

The first concerns improving firms' access to finance. Even the best investment climate does not help if businesses cannot secure funds to finance their projects. A recent World Bank survey (Table 1.3) indicates that this is a major problem for large and small firms alike. In the Doing Business survey, "getting credit" is one of the few areas where Uzbekistan ranks worse in 2020, at 67th, than in 2016, when it was 42nd (Table 1.1). Fixing this issue should thus be a high priority on the reform agenda. Particular focus should be placed on small and medium-sized enterprises, which contributed 53.3% to GDP and 78.3% to total employment in 2017.

Currently the financial system is dominated by state-owned banks, often with a close relationship with state-owned enterprises in that directed credit and interest rate subsidies have been used to support priority areas. State-owned banks account for more than 75% of banking sector assets (Reuters 2015). The government is aware of the need to develop and modernize the financial sector so that it can play a more effective financial intermediation role, which means reducing reliance on financial controls and moving toward a more market-driven allocation system for funds.

The banking sector is largely resilient to shocks. The bulk of loans in Uzbek banks are made from domestic funding, which helped minimize the impact of the September 2017 exchange rate devaluation on loan repayments. The sector's capitalization has remained broadly stable due to capital injections from the government, which increased after the global financial crisis of 2008–2009. During recent years, all banks have a capital adequacy ratio (capital to total assets) of 11%–15% and, despite the significant acceleration of loans, the ratio of nonperforming loans to total loans has been low at about 3% or less (Figure 1.16).

Figure 1.16: Selected Banking Indicators, Uzbekistan, 2006–2018
(%)

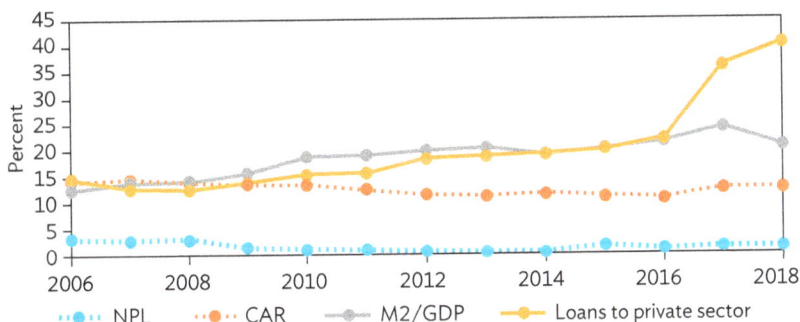

CAR = capital adequacy ratio, GDP = gross domestic product, NPL = nonperforming loan.
Note: The CAR is computed based on total assets (instead of risk-weighted assets).
Sources: Data and computations for M2 to GDP ratio and loans to GDP ratio are based on ADB (2018); other data are from the World Bank. World Development Indicators. http://www.databank.worldbank.org (accessed 11 November 2019).

However, the ratios of deposits, credit, and M2 to GDP are low for the country's income level.[13] While the link between financial development and growth is subject to an ongoing debate (Levine 2005), there is evidence that deep finance alleviates small and medium-sized enterprises' constraints to growth and access to investment funds (Beck and Demirguc-Kunt 2006).

How can be financial development boosted? The key is to avoid negative real interest rates that reduce the demand for liquid assets. Amid the current

---

[13] "M2 is a calculation of the money supply that includes all elements of M1 as well as "near money." M1 includes cash and checking deposits, while near money refers to savings deposits, money market securities, mutual funds and other time deposits." (Investopedia. What is M2? https://www.investopedia.com/terms/m/m2.asp).

inflationary environment, the CBU's recent increase in the refinancing rate is thus a positive action. Concessional interest rates are, however, especially problematic in such an environment and should be avoided. There is also evidence that institutional development, the emergence of a market economy, and secure property rights help financial deepening in transition economies (Hasan et al. 2009). If successful, the government's intended reforms of the administration and judiciary as part of the 2017–2021 National Development Strategy will help financial development. Other important measures would be to (i) lower the current requirement of 125% collateral for loans, which prevents many small and medium-sized enterprises from securing credit; and (ii) introduce international accounting standards in order to attract external finance.[14]

In relation to privatization of state-owned banks, the central economic issue is not whether ownership is public or private, but how efficiently an enterprise operates. Studies suggest that government-owned banks operate less efficiently than private banks (Cole 2009; La Porta et al. 2002; Sapienza 2004). There is also strong evidence that bank privatization in the Russian Federation substantially boosted financial development and lowered unemployment (Berkowitz et al. 2014). Similar success would very likely occur in Uzbekistan. The government should thus consider privatizing at least some of the state-owned banks.

The second priority area of future reforms should be to enhance competition in the marketplace. As also suggested by the International Monetary Fund (2018), the government should take on an active role in reducing monopolistic practices and abandon the use of any remaining price controls. The latter have been used fairly extensively and have affected important goods such as cotton, where growers' prices have been held well below world market levels. Similarly, the prices of energy and water have been held below opportunity cost.

Competition improves firms' productivity levels and thus boosts economic growth. Furthermore, it shifts labor to high-productivity firms, which in turn results in higher wages (Beegle et al., 2012). Thus, contrary to what is often feared, increased competition not only leads to more but also *better* jobs. However, an integral part of this progress is a loss in low-productivity jobs as productivity surges and monopolistic firms lose their market power. The net effect on total employment may thus be negative in the short run. Nonetheless, increased competition will soon pay off. There is empirical evidence that such negative employment impacts are reversed within 1 year (Beegle et al., 2012).

---

[14] Chapter 4 addresses the issues of collateral and international accounting standards.

The third pillar of government action relates to lifting the longer-term constraints associated with the economy's infrastructure stock and the level of human capital.[15] Improved education and training are required to meet the challenges of a modern diversified economy. As mentioned, enterprises surveyed by the World Bank cited the lack of skilled workers as one of their key constraints to creating more jobs (Table 1.3). Current teaching curricula at schools, universities, and other institutions fail to develop the skills needed in the labor market of a rapidly changing economy that is becoming increasingly globalized. There are also concerns over the quality of teachers and access to international teaching material. More efficient use of the government's expenditure on education, which is substantial at 6.5% of GDP in 2017, will be needed to address these issues.[16]

In relation to infrastructure, as a double-landlocked country, Uzbekistan faces an inherent geographical disadvantage in accessing world markets. Indeed, "trading across borders" is the indicator where the country ranks worst in the 2020 Doing Business survey (152nd) (Table 1.1). The cost of cross-border transport is high compared to that in neighboring countries. The Center for Economic Research (2013) estimates transport costs (depending on cargo) to range from 15%–20% to 60%–70% of the value of cargo for exports, which is significantly higher than the 5%–7% in European Union countries. To overcome these obstacles, both rail and road links need major improvement. About 36% of rail lines had been electrified per 2015 data, while local and regional roads need major maintenance (World Bank 2014).

Fixing these issues will take a comprehensive set of measures, which are outlined in section 2.4 of Chapter 2. Enacting such an infrastructure program will support economic growth and boost employment numbers amid the current slowdown. Prudent fiscal policy in the past ensured that there is enough fiscal space to implement these infrastructure projects now. Doing so is also consistent with a counter-cyclical fiscal policy that this chapter argues to be beneficial, provided fiscal spending is restrained during the next boom period.

On a final note, any major and ambitious reform agenda has the dangers of setbacks and potential that economic benefits will take longer to materialize than expected, which may result in reform fatigue. The government has indicated that it is aware of these risks and affirmed in IMF (2018) its commitment to implementing the President's National Development Strategy, which is crucial for Uzbekistan's long-term economic success.

---

[15] Infrastructure and human capital development are analyzed in detail in chapters 2 and 3, respectively.

[16] A detailed set of policy recommendations for human capital development is discussed in section 3.7 of Chapter 3.

References

Aizenman, J., Y. Jinjarak, H. Nguyen, and D. Park. 2018. *Fiscal Space and Government Spending and Tax-Rate Cyclicality Patterns: A Cross-Country Comparison, 1960–2016.* Working Paper 25012. Cambridge, MA: National Bureau of Economic Research. September.

Ali, I. and J. Zhuang 2007. *Inclusive Growth toward a Prosperous Asia: Policy Implications.* ERD Working Paper Series 97. Manila: Asian Development Bank.

Asian Development Bank (ADB). 2014. *Uzbekistan Country Gender Assessment.* Manila.

_____. *Basic Statistics.* Manila. (7 years: 2013-2019).

_____. 2018. *Key Indicators for Asia and the Pacific 2018.* Manila.

_____. Statistical Database System. https://www.adb.org/data/sdbs (accessed 11 November 2019).

Atlas of Economic Complexity. Data. http://atlas.cid.harvard.edu/about-data (accessed 11 November 2019)

Athukorala, P. C. and P. Warr. 2002. Vulnerability to a Currency Crisis: Lessons from the Asian Experience. *World Economy.* 25(1): pp. 33–57.

Beck, T. and A. Demirguc-Kunt. 2006. Small and Medium-Size Enterprises: Access to Finance as a Growth Constraint. *Journal of Banking & Finance.* 30(11): pp. 2931–43.

Beegle, K., G. Hentschel, S. Jesko, and M.G. Rama. 2012. *World Development Report 2013: Jobs.* Washington DC: World Bank.

Berkowitz, D., M. Hoekstra, and K. Schoors. 2014. Bank Privatization, Finance, and Growth. *Journal of Development Economics.* 110: pp. 93–106.

Bertelsmann Stiftung. 2014. *BTI 2014: Uzbekistan Country Report.* Bertelsmann Stiftung.

Center for Economic Research (CER). 2013. *The Transport Sector: Tariff Reductions as a Means to Economic Growth, Development Focus 13.* Tashkent: CER. July.

_____. 2015. *Millennium Development Goals Report: Uzbekistan.* Tashkent: CER.

Central Bank of the Republic of Uzbekistan Statistics. http://www.cbu.uz/en/statistics/dks/ (accessed 11 November 2019).

Cole, S. 2009. Financial Development, Bank Ownership, and Growth: Or, Does Quantity Imply Quality? *The Review of Economics and Statistics.* 91(1): pp. 33–51.

Eichengreen, B. 2008. The Real Exchange Rate and Economic Growth. Commission on Growth and Development. Working Paper No. 4. Washington, DC: World Bank.

Hasan, I., P. Wachtel, and M. Zhou. 2009. Institutional Development, Financial Deepening and Economic Growth: Evidence from China. *Journal of Banking & Finance.* 33(1): pp. 157–70.

Hespeler, F. 2013. A VECM Evaluation of Monetary Transmission in Uzbekistan. *Economic Change and Restructuring.* 46(2): pp. 219–53.

International Monetary Fund (IMF). 2012. *Macroeconomic Policy Frameworks for Resource-Rich Developing Countries.* Washington, DC.

_____. 2018. *Republic of Uzbekistan: Article IV Consultation.* IMF Country Report 18/117. Washington, DC. May.

International Trade Administration (ITA), US Department of Commerce. 2017. Uzbekistan: Import tariffs. https://www.export.gov/article?id=Uzbekistan-Import-Tariffs (accessed 16 November 2018).

Investopedia. What is M2. https://www.investopedia.com/terms/m/m2.asp.

Kaminsky, G., C. Reinhart, and C. Vegh. 2005. *When it Rains, it Pours: Pro-Cyclical Capital Flows and Macroeconomic Policies.* Working Paper 10780. Cambridge, MA: National Bureau of Economic Research. September.

Kray, A. and L. Serven. 2013. Fiscal Policy as a Tool for Stabilization in Developing Countries. Background Note for the 2014 World Development Report: Managing Risk for Development. Washington, DC: World Bank.

La Porta, R., F. Lopez-De-Silanes, and A. Shleifer. 2002. Government Ownership of Banks. *Journal of Finance.* 57(1): pp. 265–301.

Levine, R. 2005. Finance and Growth: Theory and Evidence. In P. Aghion and S. Durlauf (Eds.), *Handbook of Economic Growth*, Volume 1 of *Handbook of Economic Growth.* pp. 865–934. Amsterdam: Elsevier.

McIntyre, A., M. X. Li, and H. Yun. 2018. *Economic Benefits of Export Diversification in Small States.* IMF Working Paper WP/18/86. Washington, DC: IMF

Ministry of Finance of the Republic of Uzbekistan. 2018. Uzbekistan: Review of the Tax System, Technical Assistance Report. April. https://www.mf.uz/media/file_en/state-budget/obzor_nalor_eng.pdf.

Ostry, J., A. Ghosh, J. Kim, and M. Quereshi. 2010. Fiscal Space. IMF Staff Position Note 10/11. Washington, DC: IMF.

Pomfret, R. 2019. *The Central Asian Economies in the Twenty-First Century: Paving a New Silk Road.* Princeton, NJ: Princeton University Press.

Ramey, G. and V. Ramey. 1995. Cross-Country Evidence on the Link between Volatility and Growth. *American Economic Review.* 85(5): pp. 1138–51.

Ravallion, M. 2001. Growth, Inequality and Poverty: Looking Beyond Averages. *World Development.* 29(11): pp. 1803–15.

Reuters. 2015. Fitch: Uzbekistan's Banking Sector Stable, But External Pressures Have Increased. *Reuters*. 27 November 2015. https://www.reuters.com/article/idUSFit94045620151127 (accessed 16 December 2018).

Rodrik, D. 2008. The Real Exchange Rate and Economic Growth. *Brookings Papers on Economic Activity.* Washington, DC: Brookings Institute. pp. 365–412.

Sapienza, P. 2004. The Effects of Government Ownership on Bank Lending. *Journal of Financial Economics.* 72(2): pp. 357–84.

Schroder, M. 2017. The Equilibrium Real Exchange Rate and Macroeconomic Performance in Developing Countries. *Applied Economics Letters.* 24: pp. 506–9.

State Committee of the Republic of Uzbekistan on Statistics (Uzbekistan Statistics). http://stat.uz (accessed 10 March 2018, 16 December 2018, 11 November 2019).

Tsereteli, M. 2018. *The Economic Modernization of Uzbekistan.* Silk-Road Paper. Central Asia-Caucasus Institute & Silk Road Studies Program. Washington, DC and Stockholm. April. https://silkroadstudies.org/resources/pdf/SilkRoadPapers/2018-04-Tsereteli-Uzbekistan.pdf

United Nations Conference on Trade and Development (UNCTAD). n.d. UNCTAD STAT. http://unctad.org/en/Pages/statistics.aspx (accessed 11 November 2019).

UN Comtrade. Database. https://comtrade.un.org (accessed 14 January 2020).

World Bank. 2014. Uzbekistan Vision 2030: Synthesis of background papers on markets and institutions, human development, infrastructure and the environment. May.

————. 2020. *Doing Business 2020: Comparing Business Regulation in 190 Economies.* Washington, DC.

————. 2018. *Growth Diagnostics for Uzbekistan.* Washington DC.

————. n.d. Country Classification. https://datahelpdesk.worldbank.org/knowledgebase/articles/378833-how-are-the-income-group-thresholds-determined (accessed 16 December 2018).

————. World Development Indicators. http://www.databank.worldbank.org/ (accessed 11 November 2019).

CHAPTER 2

Infrastructure as a Foundation for Job Creation

Kee-Yung Nam, Lotis Quiao, Denise Encarnacion, and Bahtiyor Eshchanov

With its aspirations of doubling the country's gross domestic product (GDP), the Government of Uzbekistan recognizes that the economy faces a number of challenges to maintaining its high economic growth over the longer term. They include the dilapidated and often inefficient infrastructure in sectors that can make or break the country's growth objectives. Indeed, in its Development Strategy for 2017–2021, the government has identified infrastructure development as an important factor to enhance competitiveness, support industrialization, and improve living conditions of the population (*Tashkent Times* 2017).

This chapter focuses on the critical issues in the transport and energy sectors by assessing the current status of infrastructure provision and efficiency; reviewing the existing policy, legal, and institutional framework; and identifying challenges confronting the sectors. The chapter also presents a projection of longer-term infrastructure needs to support future growth and identifies strategies to support improved domestic and international connectivity and energy supply security.

The export base has diversified and more than doubled, supporting the country's GDP growth (ADB 2011b). Uzbekistan's location along the ancient trade route between Asia and Europe has positioned it at the center of commerce and trade in Central Asia for many years. Although Uzbekistan is double landlocked, it has been a key transit country and was part of the ancient Silk Road's trade routes. However, the system of transport connection and corridors it inherited from the former Soviet Union has restricted opportunities for accelerating the country's development.

Further development of the transport sector is essential to meet growth targets. Rail has been the main mode of transporting freight in and out of the country, while road transport is the dominant mode for domestic passenger and short-haul cargo. Improvements in both, as well as in logistics centers and cross-border transport procedures, are needed to allow the growth of trade and to take advantage of the country's geographical position as a key transit country.

The energy sector, on the other hand, has played a significant role in the steady economic growth of Uzbekistan after the dissolution of the Soviet Union. The sector accounted for 26% of total industry output during 1995–2014. Energy exports, mainly natural gas, accounted for 13% of total exports during the same period, and have been a key source of government finance. The reliability of energy supply significantly determines the competitiveness of industry. In coming years, the performance of the energy sector will be crucial to sustain GDP growth and double GDP by 2030.

The government acknowledges that an adequate and reliable supply of power is vital to sustained economic growth and development. Demand for power is projected to grow substantially as industrialization proceeds and household incomes increase.

Despite its huge energy endowment, Uzbekistan grapples with energy security issues. Unreliable power supply has limited the activity and profitability of enterprises. In winter, blackouts are common and usually last for at least 2 hours. Inefficiency in the sector is an urgent and pressing issue: in 2016, this resulted in an annual economic loss of about $1.5 billion (World Bank 2016b). In the power sector, inefficiencies have emanated from the use of outdated production technologies, especially in industry and agriculture; from old and inefficient power generation, transmission, and distribution infrastructure; and from inadequate billing and metering systems. The low tariff policy exacerbates the situation by encouraging wasteful electricity consumption. This policy has also undermined the financial performance of the power utility, which has led to limited investments as well as poor operation and maintenance of electricity infrastructure.

2.1   Assessment of the Transport and Logistics Sectors

2.1.1   Transport and logistics overview

Road. Road transport accounts for about 88% of domestic passenger and short haul cargo traffic and about 10% of international carriage of goods (ADB 2016a). The total length of the road network is 185,000 kilometers (km), 42,654 km of which are highways that are further classified as international (3,979 km), national (14,069 km), and regional or local (24,606 km). The rest are urban and rural roads that are managed by cities, municipalities, and local districts (ADB 2016d). About 3,000 km of the road network is also part of the Asian Highway Network.

The quality of Uzbekistan's road network has improved significantly in recent years. In 2004, 66% of the highways were class 3 or below under Asian highway standards. By 2015, all substandard (below class 3) roads and some minimum standard (class 3) roads were upgraded to high-quality roads (class 1 or 2), leaving Uzbekistan with only 22% of the network classified as minimum standard, or class 3 (Table 2.1).

Table 2.1: Road Transport Indicators, Uzbekistan, 2004 to Latest Data

Indicator	2004	Latest
Total Road Network (km)	181,121[f]	185,000 (2015)
Asian Highway Class 1[a] (km)	255	1,195 (2015)
Asian Highway Class 2[b] (km)	765	1,101 (2015)
Asian Highway Class 3[c] (km)	1,618	670 (2015)
Asian Highway Below Class 3[d] (km)	328	none
Paved (% to total roads)	87[e]	87 (2014)
Increase in the volume of trucking transport (%)	10.8[e]	4.6 (2013)
Road density (km of road per km^2 land area)	192	192 (2012)

km = kilometer, km^2 = square kilometer.
Notes:
[a] Class 1 refers to asphalt, cement, or concrete roads with four or more lanes.
[b] Class 2 refers to double bituminous treated roads with two lanes.
[c] Class 3 is also regarded as the minimum desirable standard, usually described as two-lane (narrow) road.
[d] Roads classified below class 3 are road sections below the minimum desirable standard.
[e] Data as of 2005.
[f] Data as of 2002.
Sources: For increases in volume of transport for freight and passenger traffic CER (2013a), for the rest of the data, UNESCAP (2003); UNESCAP (2017); and UNESCAP (2014).

While the road network is able to provide adequate access throughout the country, it suffers from a backlog of rehabilitation work. The design standards of roads throughout the country originated during the former Soviet Union. They are inadequate for the current and future traffic volumes and loads and do not follow road safety engineering principles and international good practice. The economic cost of road crashes is estimated at $63 million, accounting for 2.6% of GDP in 2014 (ADB 2017c). As indicated in Figure 2.1, road safety improved between 2005 and 2015, with road traffic deaths falling from 14.1 per 100,000 people in 2005 to 11.5 per 100,000 people in 2016 (World Bank 2019a).

Figure 2.1: Road Traffic Deaths, Uzbekistan, 2000–2016
(per 100,000 people)

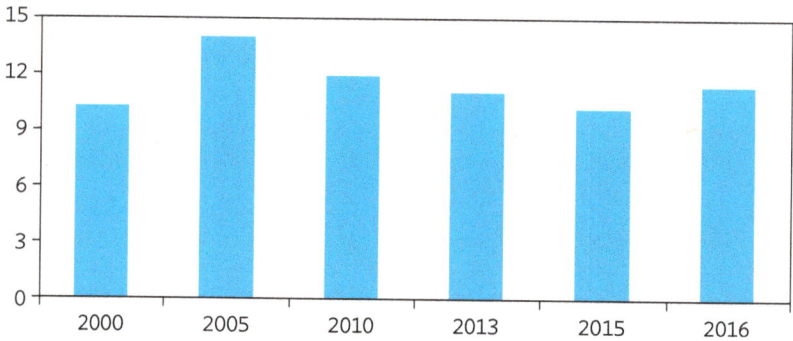

Sources: World Bank (2019a) https://data.worldbank.org/indicator/SH.STA.TRAF.P5?view=chart (accessed 29 July 2019); and WHO (2018).

Road conditions and road upgrading that does not meet requirements have contributed to the road accident incidences (Uzbekistan Statistics 2019). The former state joint-stock company (Uzavtoyul) in charge of road construction and maintenance has faced several issues, such as limited financing, shortage of maintenance machinery and equipment, and limited personnel for road building and maintenance works. Construction, reconstruction, and refurbishment projects prepared and implemented by Uzavtoyul have taken at least twice as long to implement as similar projects in Kazakhstan, for example. This has led to increased costs and the allocation of more resources for unexpected expenses. Projects with long implementation periods are delayed and postponed on frequent occasions, leading to even higher spending and losses.

Total road fund revenues have increased by an average of 22% in the last 6 years, from SUM1,119.8 billion ($138.7 million) in 2011 to SUM4,381.0 billion

($542.9 million) in 2018.[1] Figure 2.2 shows the development and composition of the Republican Road Fund (RRF) income. Proceeds from profit and turnover taxes represent the most substantial source, providing an average of 73% of total income during 2014–2018. The government also collects taxes from road users in the form of fuel taxes; however, the proceeds are not earmarked for roadworks and do not constitute RRF income.

Figure 2.2: Road Fund Revenues, Uzbekistan, 2011–2018 (SUM billion)

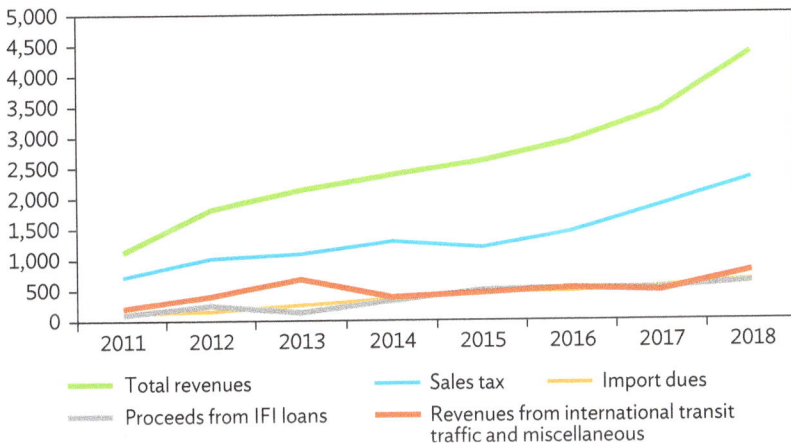

Source: MOF. *Republican Road Fund.* https://www.mf.uz/en/open-data/infografika.html (accessed 14 December 2018).

Road financing data from the RRF and the Asian Development Bank (ADB) show that in 2016 Uzbekistan was spending about 1.3% of its GDP on the road sector, which represented a moderate increase over the previous decade (ADB 2016b). Expenditures on the primary road network for 2012–2017 under the RRF grew by an average of 32% annually. A breakdown by main categories reveals expenditures for construction and reconstruction accounted for an average of 52% during 2011–2017 while road maintenance comprised approximately one-third of the expenditure (Figure 2.3).

Figure 2.3: Development of Republican Road Fund Expenditures, Uzbekistan, 2011–2017
(SUM billion)

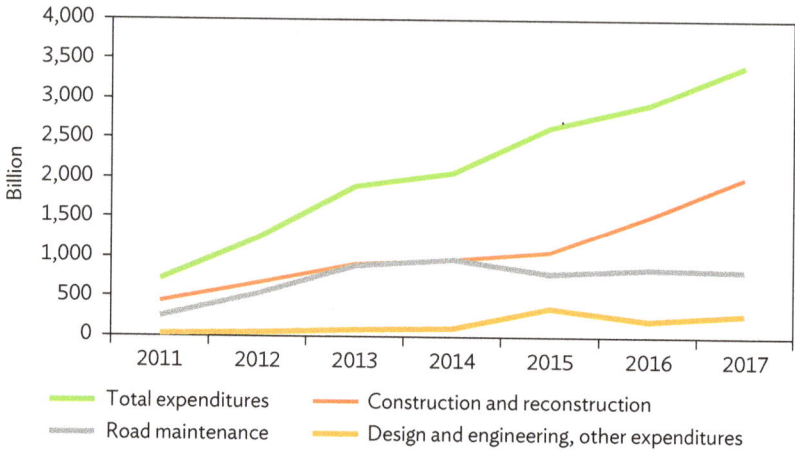

Source: MOF. Republican Road Fund. https://www.mf.uz/en/component/k2/item/56-respublikanskiy-dorozhnyy-fond.html. (accessed 26 March 2018)

The RRF, however, does not differentiate between periodic repairs and routine maintenance. The ongoing efforts at reducing a sizable backlog in deferred maintenance, estimated at $1 billion a year, covers a substantial share of expenditure for reconstruction and rehabilitation (PADECO 2014). Coupled with the relatively low funding for maintenance, this threatens the sustainability of assets and leaves some sections of the road network in poor condition.

An ADB road sector assessment found that about 60% of domestic roads had cracks on more than 10% of the surface area and an average of 10 potholes per kilometer (ADB 2011b). Roads, especially those constructed or refurbished by local companies, are highly prone to climatic anomalies such as highly variable temperature and high precipitation levels. Road surfaces melt due to exposure to direct sunlight and high temperatures, leading to rapid deterioration of the road quality. Lines separating lanes become invisible or disappear in a few weeks, increasing the risk of accidents. Moreover, although Uzbekistan has a dry climate and low precipitation levels, newly opened roads are not able to handle the average rainfall and can flood in lower areas. At certain times, rainwater runs into the metro stations in the capital, Tashkent, and floods the underground pedestrian passages.

Aside from the expected climatic and vehicle use impacts, other factors also affect road conditions. In cities that have central district heating systems, damage to roads can be severe due to refurbishments of heating systems that require digging to access pipes. The result can be a poor road surface where repaving is not to the original standard. This has been a particular issue in Tashkent, where the heating infrastructure is refurbished annually. The city's roads are also affected by the laying of optical wires through the Safe City Project. The Safe City Project was implemented in August 2017 initially in Tashkent, with completion expected in 2019 (Yeniseyev n.d.). The project is expected to be rolled out to all provincial capitals and larger cities by 2021 and the rest of Uzbekistan by 2023. With the project's expansion, the quality of some roads may deteriorate further.

Uzbekistan's road networks facilitate the truck transport of goods.[2] The Uzbek trucking industry is considered underdeveloped, however. Its fleets are old and in serious need of renewal, either through replacement or significant upgrading. In 2010, the trucking fleet was 19 years old on average, compared with 6.7 years in the United States (ADB 2012). Fewer than 2,000 trucks are Uzbek owned, and they are mostly outdated Russian equipment. Foreign-owned trucks from countries such as Iran, the Russian Federation, and Turkey are in much better condition. As a result, the many foreign competitors are taking business away from local trucking companies (WFP Logistics 2019). As of 2013, Uzbek private truckers operated about 34,000 vehicles. To meet projected demands for shipments by 2020, up to 6,500 additional new vehicles may be needed annually in 2019 and 2020 to augment the current supply and to replace at least 50% of the existing trucking fleet (CER 2013b).

Rail. As a double-landlocked country, Uzbekistan relies heavily on rail transport for freight and passenger movements (ADB 2017b). Thus, the railway sector is an instrument for economic development. In line with this, the government, through the Uzbekiston Temir Yullari (UTY—Uzbekistan Railways) is implementing projects to improve the railway system, such as electrifying the railways, constructing new high-speed routes, and renewing the rolling stock. The UTY's current projects include establishing an electrified commuter train network in Tashkent; constructing a new branch of the Tashkent City subway (metro); resuscitating the tramway transport in Samarkand City; and constructing bridges, tunnels, and overpasses for roads.

---

2   The International Road Transport Union identified trucks as the most important way to move goods https://www.iru.org/who-we-are/about-mobility/trucks (accessed 26 March 2018).

As of 2018, the railway network comprised 4,641 route-km of rail track, of which 36% (1,684 km) is electrified (Figure 2.4). These railroad tracks are generally suitable for trains with speeds up to 160 km/hour. High-speed passenger trains that operate between Tashkent, Samarkand, Bukhara, and Karshi can reach speeds up to 250km/hour.

Uzbekistan's electrification rates are among the best in Central and West Asia. Among neighboring countries, electrification rates are 100% in Georgia, 60% in Azerbaijan, and 29% in Kazakhstan. Continued electrification of the railway systems will require more investment for the country to reap energy and environmental benefits and increase transit traffic in the region.

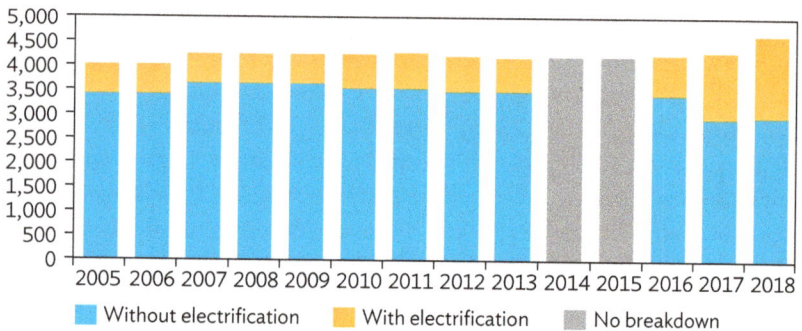

Figure 2.4: Railway Lines, Uzbekistan, 2005–2018
(km)

km= kilometer.
Notes: 2014 and 2015 data are from Uzbekistan statistics data which did not have a breakdown on electrification, 2016–2018 data are as of the first half of these years.
Sources: For 2005–2013 data: Yoshino, N. and U. Abidhadjaev (2015); for 2014–2015 data, Uzbekistan Statistics https://www.stat.uz/en/ (accessed 14 December 2018); for 2016–2018 data: Uzbekistan Railways http://railway.uz/en/gazhk/statisticheskie-dannye (accessed 14 December 2018).

Railways are the main mode of transporting freight in and out of Uzbekistan due to fewer delays at borders than for road traffic. The international railway corridors crossing Uzbekistan span approximately 2,154 km (excluding shared route sections). Railways carry about 75% of international freight. Freight and passenger traffic increased moderately during 2011–2016. Freight traffic grew from 22.5 billion ton-km to 22.9 billion ton-km, while passenger traffic increased from 3.0 billion passenger-km to 3.9 billion passenger-km. The latest available data show that traffic remained the same for freight, at 33 million tons in the first halves of 2017 and 2018; and passenger traffic increased from 10.9 million in the first half of 2017 to 11.7 million in the first half of 2018 (Table 2.2).

Rail cargo is shipped in both goods wagons and intermodal containers, many of which are old and in poor condition. The UTY's rolling stock is outdated and shows a high degree of physical deterioration. About 60% of the rolling stock is unable to provide nominal pulling capacity, often leading to railcars uncoupling from trains, failure to meet delivery deadlines, and reduced volume of rail freight transport (CER 2013a). Nearly 90% of the wagon fleet will need to be replaced in the next decade. The UTY is therefore improving its internal capacity to upgrade its wagon fleet. The UTY's ability to rehabilitate and construct its rolling stock is being improved.

Table 2.2: Rail Transport Indicators, Uzbekistan, 2011–2018

Traffic Volume	2011	2012	2013	2014	2015	2016	1st half 2017	1st half 2018
Freight traffic (million tons)	59.2	61.5	63.7	65.7	67.2	67.6	33.1	33.3
Freight traffic (billion ton-km)	22.5	22.7	22.9	22.9	22.9	22.9	11.6	11.6
Passenger traffic (million passengers)	14.9	15.9	17.4	19.1	20.1	20.5	10.9	11.7
Passenger traffic (billion passenger-km)	3.0	3.4	3.7	3.8	3.8	3.9	3.1	2.1

Sources: Uzbekistan Statistics. https://www.stat.uz/en (accessed 14 December 2018); ADB (2017b); Uzbekistan Railways. http://railway.uz/en/gazhk/statisticheskie-dannye/ (accessed 14 December 2018).

The UTY is embarking on a step-wise program to modernize its locomotive fleet. The current fleet is 75% diesel (28% comprises mainline diesel locomotives and 47% comprises shunting diesel locomotives), with electric locomotives constituting only 25% of the fleet. The latter includes 37 electric locomotives procured within the last 10 years. The locomotive fleet, both diesel and electric, is of advanced age, with the majority having served more than 30 years. Limitations due to the number of electric locomotives and the aging fleet pose a major challenge to the expansion of freight and passenger train services on a reliable basis. The existing fleet is utilized to its maximum potential, making it difficult for the UTY to serve the growing demand. The slow acceleration and top speeds of diesel locomotives and the switching required between diesel and electric locomotives add to transport times and inefficiencies. Locomotive depots remain tailored to servicing diesel locomotives, and require upgrading to suit an increasingly electrified fleet. ADB is currently supporting the Uzbekistan government with the procurement of 24 electric locomotives (ADB 2019).

While the UTY's objective is to maintain its freight market share to ensure long-term financial viability, competition from road haulage has been increasing. Furthermore, while railways have retained a large share of long-distance passenger transport, the UTY is expected to continue to lose passenger and market share to roads.

Air transport. Because Uzbekistan is double-landlocked, aviation plays an important role in cargo transport. Air transport carries about 4% of the international cargo, which includes high-value fruits and vegetables going to the Russian Federation; equipment and parts from Europe; and consumer goods from the People's Republic of China (PRC), the Republic of Korea, and Japan.

Uzbekistan's air network is among the best in Central Asia. The country has 11 international airports.[3] The largest airport is the Tashkent International Airport, which is certified by the International Civil Aviation Organization as an all-weather airport. It is linked with European and Middle Eastern cities through direct flights, and with New York and Los Angeles via connecting flights through Moscow. Uzbekistan Airways, the country's state-owned airline, is the national flag carrier, headquartered in Tashkent. It is reliable and has one of the best safety records in the region.

Navoi International Airport has recently started operating and became the country's largest air cargo center. It offers comprehensive logistic services for air, road, and rail freight. An international multimodal logistics center was established at Navoi International Airport to combine airfreight to the PRC, Europe, India, and Southeast Asia.

2.1.2. Government plans and future demand forecasts

As part of Uzbekistan's rapid development, the demand for transport facilities is expected to grow strongly. The long-term vision for the country has been expressed in several presidential resolutions and speeches. In December 2010, the government issued the *Resolution on Rapid Development of Infrastructure of Transport and Communication Construction for 2011–2015* (Government of Uzbekistan 2010). It targeted the expenditure of $6.9 billion on the sector by 2015. The resolution envisaged large-scale construction and modernization

---

[3]   International airports are Andijan, Bukhara, Fergana, Karshi, Namangan, Navoi, Nukus, Samarkand, Tashkent, Termez, and Urgench (Uzbekistan Airways. About Us. https://www.uzairways.com/en/about-us (accessed 14 December 2018).

of major rail and road links and bridges; renewal of the fleet of the vehicles, railway locomotives, and carriage fleet; and the purchase of new mid- and long-distance passenger airplanes.

In March 2015, Presidential Resolution No 2313, *On the Program of Development and Modernization of Engineering-Communication and Road Transport in the Period 2015–2019* was issued (Government of Uzbekistan 2015b). The document approved the construction of sections of the Uzbek national arterial road and other roads for general use. It also outlined measures to (i) build and reconstruct several sections of motor roads, bridges, overpasses, and road junctions; (ii) purchase in the next 5 years, 993 units of new road repair equipment needed to maintain and carry out routine road repairs; (iii) purchase road construction equipment for more than 150 projects; and (iv) build and reconstruct 1,800 km of the Uzbek National highway and roundabouts for several towns, and modernize roads for local use. The resolution also supports the creation of railway assets, including constructing a new railway line Navoi–Kanimekh–Misken, rehabilitating 240 km of rail track, electrifying several railway sections, purchasing high-speed trains, organizing high-speed traffic on new routes, and purchasing locomotives. The state investment program for the fiscal year 2017/18 aimed to allocate $1.006 billion for financing the railroad projects (Government of Uzbekistan 2016).

Several government programs and policies on transport infrastructure were also put into action in 2017. A comprehensive 5-year program to improve transport infrastructure and diversify foreign trade routes was adopted specifically for three transport corridors: Uzbekistan–Turkmenistan–Iran–Oman, Uzbekistan–Kyrgyz Republic–PRC, and the trans-Afghanistan transport route. The Turkmenabad–Farab railway and road bridges across the Amu Darya, which were opened recently, doubled the volume of cargo transport among the Central Asian countries and increased the possibility of transport and communication linkages with more countries (Kharimova 2018).

Uzbekistan's domestic road freight and passenger traffic are expected to grow at a rate faster than its current GDP. This will be a result of increased per capita income combined with improved roads due to increased resources earmarked for road construction and maintenance, and modernization of facilities. At the assumed high economic growth rate of nearly 8% annually, the volume of freight traffic is forecast to grow at an annual rate of 9.2% until 2030. This would be an overall increase of 4.4 times, from 1,387 million tons in 2013 to 6,041 million tons in 2030. Road transport is expected to have an average annual increase of 9.4%, from 1,259 million tons in 2013 to 5,812 million tons in 2030, and rail transport is expected to grow at 5% annually, from 64 million tons in 2013 to 146 million tons in 2030 (CER 2013a).

A 1% increase in investments in the transport sector will result in a 0.94% greater volume of freight traffic (CER 2013a). To match the projected rise in traffic with an assumed 8% GDP growth rate, investment in the transport sector is projected to increase from 3.5% of GDP (the average annual rate during 2005–2012) to 4.6% in 2030. This amounts to a total investment of nearly $46.7 billion in 2030, with annual investments increasing from $2.1 billion in 2015 to $5.1 billion in 2030.

2.1.3. Cross-border transport

International transport corridors. At present, Uzbekistan's foreign-traded goods are transported along the main transport corridors as shown in Table 2.3.

Table 2.3: Transport Corridors for Foreign-Traded Goods, Uzbekistan

Corridor	Route
Corridor 1	To the Baltic state ports (in transit through Kazakhstan and the Russian Federation)—Klaipeda (Lithuania); Riga, Liepaja, Ventspils (Latvia); and Tallinn (Estonia).
Corridor 2	Through Belarus and the Ukraine (in transit via Kazakhstan and the Russian Federation)—border crossings Chop (Ukraine) and Brest (Belarus), followed by Europe.
Corridor 3	To the Ukrainian port of Ilyichevsk (transiting Kazakhstan and the Russian Federation), exiting to the Black Sea
Corridor 4	Toward the Trans-Caucasian corridor (transiting through Turkmenistan, Kazakhstan, and Azerbaijan), exiting to the Black Sea; also known as the TRACECA corridor.
Corridor 5	To the Iranian port of Bandar Abbas (transiting through Turkmenistan) with access to the Persian Gulf.
Corridor 6	In an easterly direction through the Kazakh-PRC border crossing (Dostyk/Alalshankou) to the eastern ports of the PRC and the Far Eastern port of Nakhodka, Vladivostok, etc.
Corridor 7	To the PRC ports (in transit through the Kyrgyz Republic) with access to the Yellow River and East PRC.
Corridor 8	When the Afghan problem is resolved, alternative south transport corridors could be established to Iranian and Pakistani ports of Bandar Abbas, Chahbahar, Gwadar, and Karachi through Afghanistan.

PRC = People's Republic of China.
Source: Ministry of Investment and Foreign Trade. *International Transport Corridors.* https://mft.uz/en/menu/xalqaro-transport-koridorlari (accessed 7 March 2018).

Uzbekistan is at the center of commerce and trade in Central Asia and at the heart of the Great Silk Road, which allows it to provide the shortest routes connecting Europe to Asia. These routes are the International Transport Corridor Europe–Caucasus–Asia (TRACECA) and three of the six Central Asia Regional Economic Corridors (ADB 2009). Furthermore, Central Asia Regional Economic Cooperation (CAREC) projects are ongoing in Uzbekistan to help address the country's logistical challenges (Box 2.1.).

Box 2.1: Uzbekistan and the CAREC Program

The Central Asia Regional Economic Cooperation (CAREC) program helps address Uzbekistan's logistical challenges by developing regional transport corridors. Uzbekistan joined CAREC in 1997, and, as of 2016, more than $5.33 billion had been invested in energy and transport projects. These projects are based on the principle that better connections among member countries and with global markets will be the key to unlocking the region's vast resources and human potential.

Of the six priority CAREC corridors, Corridor 2-a, 2-b (Mediterranean–East Asia); Corridor 3a-3b (Russian Federation–Middle East and South Asia); and Corridor 6-a, 6-b, 6-c (Europe–Middle East and South Asia) transit Uzbekistan.

Ongoing Transport Projects in Uzbekistan

Project Title	Target Implementation Period
CAREC Corridor 2 (Pap-Namangan-Andijan) Railway Electrification Project	2017–2022
Second CAREC Corridor 2 Road Investment Program—Tranche 3	2015–2018
Pap-Angren Railway	2015–2019
Second CAREC Corridor 2 Road Investment Program—Tranche 2	2012–2020
CAREC Corridor 2 Road Investment Program—Tranche 3	2012–2017
CAREC Corridor 6 (Marakand-Karshi) Railway Electrification Project	2011–2018
Second CAREC Corridor 2 Road Investment Program 2—Tranche 1	2011–2018
Reconstruction and Upgrade of Road in Surkhandarya Region (M39) Project	2009–2015
Locomotive Re-Powering Project	2001–2010

CAREC = Central Asia Regional Economic Cooperation.
Source: CAREC. http://www.carecprogram.org/index.php?page=transport-projects (accessed 14 December 2018)

Trading across borders. Trade facilitation and the cross-border regime in Uzbekistan remain complex and time-consuming. Being a landlocked country, the cost of Uzbekistan's cross-border transport is high compared with that of neighboring countries. From 2005 to 2012, the cost of transport rose by 230% for railway shipments and by 240% for road shipments. Depending on the type of good, the transport costs range from 15%–20% to 60%–70% of the value of cargo for exports, significantly higher than the 5%–7% in European Union countries. The share of the cost of transport in the final price of the bulk of Uzbekistan's consumer goods exports is 2.5–2.6 times higher than the world average (CER 2013b).

A study by the CER (2013a) argued that the increase in the cost of rail transport services is largely because the UTY lacks incentives to reduce costs. From 2008 to 2013, prices for transporting rail freight increased 1.7 times. The relatively high prices for railway freight transport are due to (i) the current cost-plus methodology of setting tariffs for railway transport; (ii) the lack of bidding processes among domestic and foreign freight forwarders to conclude direct freight forwarding contracts with the UTY; and (iii) insufficient development of container freight transport—transporting freight on high-capacity containers is on average 10%–12% less expensive than on railway wagons.

CER (2013a) cited the following reasons for high prices in trucking: (i) rising fuel prices; (ii) an antiquated trucking fleet and the poor condition of road surfaces, resulting in low trucking speeds and higher fuel consumption; (iii) high customs fees for truck imports, generating price increases for trucks in the domestic market, an increase in shipping companies' costs, and an increase in tariffs for truck shipments; and (iv) the trucking companies' small sizes, so they are unable to achieve economies of scale. The rising cost of shipping, despite growing investments in the transport sector, suggests that public and private freight companies do not manage their costs efficiently. Rather, they simply pass on additional costs to customers by increasing their prices.

Uzbekistan also performs poorly in terms of time and cost associated with documentary and border compliance. It takes 128 hours to comply with documentary and border requirements for exports, and 261 hours for imports. The associated costs are $570 for exports and $520 for imports, higher than most countries in the region. Uzbekistan's overall ranking in World Bank's Trading Across Borders indicators in 2020 is 152nd of 190 countries (Table 2.4).

Table 2.4: Indicators of Cost of Trading Across Borders, Selected Countries, 2020

Economy	Rank	Export				Import			
		Border compliance		Documentary compliance		Border compliance		Documentary compliance	
		Time (hours)	Cost ($)	Time (hours)	Cost ($)	Time (hours)	Cost ($)	Time (hours)	Cost ($)
Armenia	43	27	100	2	100	3	0	2	100
Azerbaijan	83	17	214	33	250	14	300	33	200
Georgia	45	6	112	2	0	15	396	2	189
Kazakhstan	105	105	470	128	200	2	0	6	0
Kyrgyz Republic	89	5	10	72	110	69	499	84	200
Russian Federation	99	66	580	25	92	30	520	43	153
Tajikistan	141	27	313	66	330	107	223	126	260
Ukraine	74	6	75	66	192	32	100	48	162
Uzbekistan	**152**	**32**	**278**	**96**	**292**	**111**	**278**	**150**	**242**

Source: World Bank. 2020. *Doing Business 2020: Comparing Business Regulation in 190 Economies*. Washington, DC. (accessed 11 November 2019).

Logistic centers. Uzbekistan has two logistic centers, at Angren (113 km east of Tashkent) and Navoi in southwest Uzbekistan. A diverse group of freight forwarders and logistics companies, including local firms and those from the PRC, Germany, Iran, Kazakhstan, the Republic of Korea, the Russian Federation, Switzerland, and the United Arab Emirates offer logistics services in Uzbekistan. These companies offer mostly traditional forwarding and warehousing services. Logistics systems are characterized by fragmented supply chains as well as inefficient processes for loading and unloading goods from shippers to consignees. Some border crossing points lack sufficient capacity to handle the traffic due to poor equipment and a lack of information and communication technology used in customs operations.

Modern logistics centers include the CJSC Angren Logistics Center (ALC) and the dry port established by Uzbekistan Airways and Korean Air at Navoi airport. The latter involves 15 transcontinental forwarding hub connecting traffic routes between Western, Central, and Eastern Europe; European Commonwealth of Independent States countries; and the PRC, Japan, and Southeast and South Asia. However the system as whole remains poorly developed and needs to be improved for Uzbekistan to take full advantage of its geographical position as a key transit country. Uzbekistan scores poorly in the World Bank's Logistics Performance Index for 2018, ranking 99th (an improvement from the 2016 ranking of 118) of 160 countries (Table 2.5).

Table 2.5: Logistics Performance Index Rank, Selected Countries, 2018

Rank	Country	Overall LPI Score	Customs Rank	Customs Score	Infrastructure Rank	Infrastructure Score	International Shipments Rank	International Shipments Score	Logistics Competence Rank	Logistics Competence Score	Tracking and Tracing Rank	Tracking and Tracing Score	Timeliness Rank	Timeliness Score
5	Japan	4.03	3	3.99	2	4.25	14	3.59	4	4.09	10	4.05	10	4.25
25	Korea, Rep. of	3.61	25	3.40	22	3.73	33	3.33	28	3.59	22	3.75	25	3.92
26	PRC	3.61	31	3.29	20	3.75	18	3.54	27	3.59	27	3.65	27	3.84
71	Kazakhstan	2.81	65	2.66	81	2.55	84	2.73	90	2.58	83	2.78	50	3.53
99	**Uzbekistan**	**2.58**	**140**	**2.10**	**77**	**2.57**	**120**	**2.42**	**88**	**2.59**	**90**	**2.71**	**91**	**3.09**
108	Kyrgyz Republic	2.55	55	2.75	103	2.38	138	2.22	114	2.36	99	2.64	106	2.94
126	Turkmenistan	2.41	111	2.35	117	2.23	136	2.29	120	2.31	107	2.56	130	2.72
130	Mongolia	2.37	127	2.22	135	2.10	117	2.49	140	2.21	152	2.10	93	3.06
134	Tajikistan	2.34	150	1.92	127	2.17	133	2.31	116	2.33	131	2.33	104	2.95
160	Afghanistan	1.95	158	1.73	158	1.81	152	2.10	158	1.92	159	1.70	153	2.38

LPI = Logistics Performance Index, PRC = People's Republic of China.
Source: World Bank. 2018. Logistics Performance Index https://lpi.worldbank.org/international/global (accessed 14 December 2018).

2.1.4. Challenges and opportunities in the transport sector

The transport sector could play a significant role in achieving Uzbekistan's goal of sustaining its very high growth rate. This would require continued planning and coordination among the governing agencies of the transport modes to ensure that development strategies are harmonious and complementary, and to rationalize the functions of each transport subsector. Other serious challenges also need to be confronted.

Continuing electrification of rail networks. For Uzbekistan to continue to be a key transit country between Asia and Europe, its rail network needs to be modernized by increased electrification, to put it on par with neighboring countries' very high electrification rates. Such electrification of the rail network would contribute to energy and environmental benefits and would lower the cost of transporting goods in and out of the country; but it would require increased investment, as acknowledged by the UTY in its development plans.

Regularly replacing and updating dilapidated rolling stock. Because a completely electrified rail system cannot be realized in the short term, a large portion of the country's outdated rolling stock needs to be replaced/updated. Maintenance works also need to be upgraded. Although such activities will divert some funds that may otherwise be used for electrification, neglecting these improvements will mean persistent erratic train schedules and a lower volume of rail freight transport due to mechanical breakdowns and the reduced dependability of rail transport.

Minimizing barriers to trade. A survey of stakeholders in the South Caucasus and Central Asia by the World Economic Forum (WEF) highlighted the need for greater integration into global supply chains (WEF 2014). Improvements in the rail system can spur cooperation among regions and between neighboring countries, and allow easier movement of goods and services. For this to happen, the challenge for Uzbekistan is to reduce the barriers to trade that are within its control.

Identifying financing sources. Developing infrastructure to match the demands created by continued high economic growth requires securing the financing at affordable interest rates.

2.2   Assessment of the Energy Sector

2.2.1. Energy resources

Energy use is a critical issue. Uzbekistan faces the challenge of meeting high future energy demand against a backdrop of inadequate investment in the energy sector that has resulted in slow increases in supply. Energy demand is forecast to increase by 6.9% annually from 2014 to 2030. Demand for natural gas is expected to rise by 1.2% annually from 2015 to 2021 while production is projected to increase by only 0.7% annually. Demand for oil is expected to increase modestly by 0.5% per year while production is projected to decrease by 0.5% during 2015–2026 (BMI 2017). The current process of economic growth is highly resource intensive and unsustainable. In 2013, Uzbekistan consumed about twice as much energy per capita as Armenia and Georgia, and 20% more than the Europe and Central Asia region's average (Figure 2.5).[4]

Figure 2.5: Energy Intensity, Selected Countries, 2014
(toe per 1,000 units of GDP in 2010 PPP)

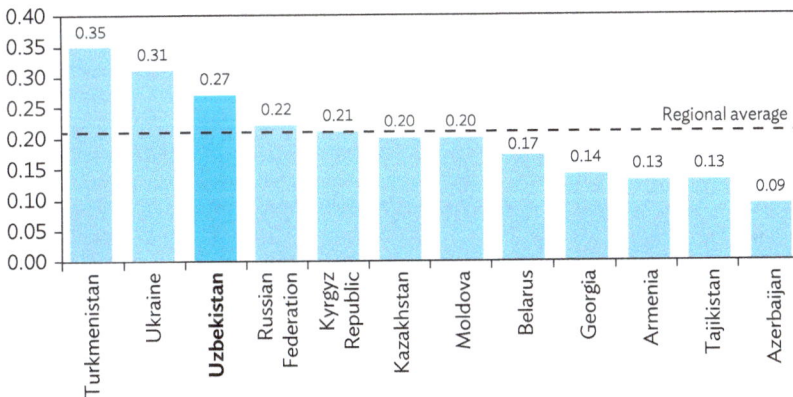

GDP = gross domestic product, OECD = Organisation for Economic Co-operation and Development, PPP = purchasing power parity, toe = tons of oil equivalent.
Note: Dashed line indicates the energy intensity of non-OECD Europe and Eurasia.
Source: IEA (2016).

---

[4]   Assuming a business-as-usual scenario, the country will lose half of its natural resources by 2030 and will experience a deficit in the energy balance of about 65% in 2030, leading to slower GDP growth (CER 2015).

Inefficiency in the energy sector, mainly resulting from the use of outdated technology, is a major contributor to energy resource depletion. Outdated energy processing and delivery systems led to losses of more than 60% of the primary energy mobilized to provide energy services (World Bank 2013). Losses from conversion, transport, and distribution of natural gas amounted to 1.12 kilotons of oil equivalent (ktoe) or about 3.2% of gas supply,[5] while losses from gas flaring have been estimated for 2011 at $500 million or 3% of GDP (World Bank 2013). Use of obsolete district heating technology is another source of energy loss from Uzbekistan's seven large-scale district-heating centers. The heat generation and distribution systems are inefficient and are operating beyond the average 50 years of useful life.

Uzbekistan has rich fossil fuel energy resources composed of natural gas (proven reserves of 1.6 trillion cubic meters), oil (proven reserves of 80.8 million tons), and coal (proven reserves of 1.4 billion tons). Given the 2017 production rate, the reserves-to-production ratios are estimated at 27 years for natural gas, 34 years for oil, and 302 years for coal (ADB 2012). The estimated generation capacity for thermal and hydropower was about 14.3 gigawatts (GW) as of 2017 (Table 2.6). The primary energy supply in 2018 was 41.4 million tons of oil equivalent. The country relied on natural gas for 88% of its primary energy supply, on oil for 7%, and on hydro and biomass for the rest. Uzbekistan is the fourth-largest producer of natural gas in the Europe and Central Asia region[6] in 2016.[7]

Table 2.6: Energy Reserves, Uzbekistan, 2017

Resource	Proven Reserves	Estimated Generation Capacity
Natural gas	1,542 bcm	
Oil	80.8 million tons	
Coal	1,375 million tons	
Thermal		12.4 GW
Hydropower		1.9 GW

bcm = billion cubic meters, GW = gigawatt.
Source: Enerdata. https://www.enerdata.net/ (accessed 9 August 2019).

---

[5] Enerdata. Global Energy & CO_2 Data. https://www.enerdata.net/expertise/energy-co2-data.html (accessed 9 August 2019).

[6] Europe and Central Asia includes Albania, Andorra, Armenia, Austria, Azerbaijan, Belarus, Belgium, Bosnia and Herzegovina, Bulgaria, Channel Islands, Croatia, Cyprus, Czech Republic, Denmark, Estonia, Faroe Islands, Finland, France, Georgia, Germany, Gibraltar, Greece, Greenland, Hungary, Iceland, Ireland, Isle of Man, Italy, Kazakhstan, Kosovo, the Kyrgyz Republic, Latvia, Liechtenstein, Lithuania, Luxembourg, Macedonia, Moldova, Monaco, Montenegro, the Netherlands, Norway, Poland, Portugal, Romania, the Russian Federation, San Marino, Serbia, the Slovak Republic, Slovenia, Spain, Sweden, Switzerland, Tajikistan, Turkey, Turkmenistan, Ukraine, the United Kingdom, and Uzbekistan.

[7] Enerdata. www.enerdata.net (accessed 9 August 2019).

Uzbekistan depended heavily on foreign borrowing to develop its energy sector during the post-Soviet Union years. In the late 1990s, projects in gas exploration and development resulted in increased gas supplies (Figure 2.6). The country has been a net energy exporter since 1995, mainly of natural gas.

Figure 2.6: Total Primary Energy Supply, Uzbekistan, 1990–2018
(mtoe)

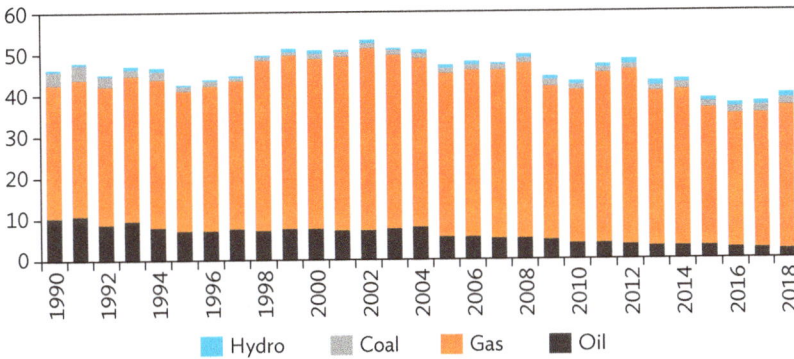

mtoe = million tons of oil equivalent.
Source: Enerdata. https://www.enerdata.net/ (accessed 21 January 2018).

Uzbekistan has four gas processing plants: Mubarek Gas Processing Plant with processing capacity of more than 29 billion cubic meters (m³) per year, Shurtanneftegaz Oil and Gas Processing Plant with a capacity of 12 billion m³/year, Shurtan Gas Chemical Complex with gas processing capacity of 4.5 billion m³/year, and the Joint Venture Uz-Kor Gas Chemical with gas processing capacity of 3.0 billion m³/year.

The government aims to diversify the use of natural gas to include production of polyethylene granules, liquefied natural gas, and polymer products. Uz-Kor Gas, a joint venture with partners from the Republic of Korea, is one of the largest gas chemical factories in Central Asia, with annual production of more than 3.0 billion m³ of natural gas from the Surgil deposit in northern Karakalpakstan. The total length of gas pipelines in Uzbekistan exceeds 13,000 km. The capacity of the gas transport system is 55 billion m³/year. The electricity and residential sectors are the biggest consumers of gas (Table 2.7). About 3% of gas is lost in the system. Gas exports amounted to 15.4 billion m³ in 2018.

Uzbekistan also produces oil, but the quantity has been dwindling due to lack of investment, depletion, and low recovery rates. In renewable energy, only hydropower has been developed on a large scale (World Bank 2013).

Total final energy consumption in 2018 was 27.1 million tons of oil equivalent, mainly in the form of natural gas (65% of total), and the rest as electricity (16%), heat (10%), oil (7%), and coal (2%). Residential and industry groups have been the major consumers of energy; in 2018 they accounted for 40% and 24%, respectively, of the total energy consumption (Figure 2.7). Residential consumers mainly use gas for cooking and heating. About 80% of households are connected to the central gas system. Industrial consumers primarily use electricity to support their operations. The biggest industrial consumers are the smelting and manufacturing companies.

Table 2.7: Supply and Consumption of Gas, by Sector, Uzbekistan, 2018

Sector	Gas Consumption ('000 toe)	Share of Total Primary Supply (%)
Total primary supply	35,150	
Power plants	13,013	37.0
Energy industry Own use	3,550	10.1
Losses	1,116	3.2
Residential	10,000	28.4
Industry	4,418	12.6
Commercial, public services	2,000	5.7
Transport	42.86	0.1
Agriculture	107	0.3
Others	904	2.6

toe = tons of oil equivalent.
Note: "Others" are consumption by unspecified users and for nonenergy uses.
Source: Enerdata. https://www.enerdata.net/ (accessed 9 August 2019).

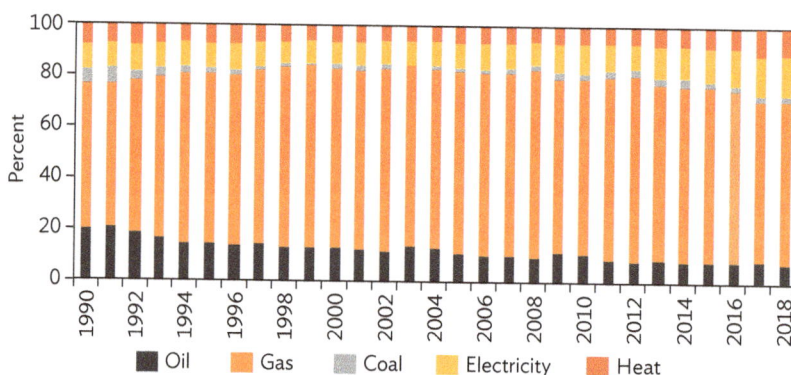

Figure 2.7a: Final Energy Consumption, by Source, 1990–2018

mtoe = million tons of oil equivalent.
Source: Enerdata. https://www.enerdata.net/ (accessed 9 August 2019).

Figure 2.7b: Final Energy Consumption, by Consuming Sector, 1990–2018

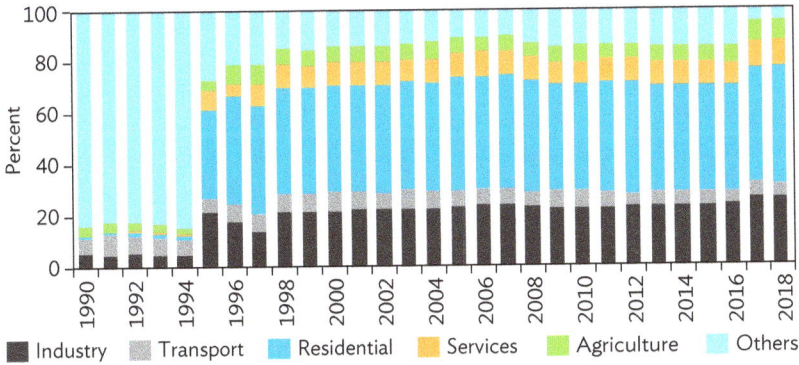

mtoe = million tons of oil equivalent.
Note: "Others" are consumption by unspecified users and for nonenergy uses.
Source: Enerdata. https://www.enerdata.net/ (accessed 9 August 2019).

2.2.2. Current status of the power sector

The state owns and manages Uzbekistan's power sector. Uzbekenergo, a vertically integrated and state-owned company, used to own and operate the majority of power generation, transmission, and distribution assets. Through a presidential resolution signed in March 2019, Uzbekenergo was reorganized into three independent joint-stock companies (JSC) – JSC Thermal Power Plants, JSC National Electric Networks of Uzbekistan and JSC Regional Electric Networks. The JSC Thermal Power Plants will manage thermal generation units. The JSC National Electric Networks of Uzbekistan will operate and develop high voltage transmission lines, while the JSC Regional Electric Networks will be responsible for distribution of power to end-users. This restructuring is part of the government's plan of implementing major state-owned enterprise reforms in 2019–2021, including strengthening corporate governance, unbundling state-owned enterprises' activities, and privatizing or selling minority stakes of selected state-owned enterprises (Government of Uzbekistan 2019).

Uzbekhydroenergo is responsible for all hydropower stations and other hydropower-related units.

The laws and policies affecting the power sector focus on improving the financial viability of the sector to attract new investment, improve the security and sustainability of power supply, and reduce inefficiencies. Box 2.2 lists key legislation related to the sector. The government's strategies include (i) restructuring the power market by demonopolizing energy enterprises and creating a single-buyer generation market, (ii) encouraging private sector participation, (iii) increasing power generation by developing alternative energy sources and hydropower, (iv) addressing the issues related to collection of payments from consumers, and (v) managing demand for electricity through energy efficiency programs. Progress toward these goals has been limited. The reforms that took place during 2001–2008 were toward unbundling the generation, transmission, distribution, and dispatch functions. The objectives were to improve the efficiency of operations and the financial viability of the sector, so as to attract private investors.

Box 2.2: Key Legislation Related to the Power Sector

Fourteen key items of legislation pertain to the power sector.

Decree On Deepening of Economic Reforms in the Energy Sector of Uzbekistan (2001). This presidential decree identified government priorities for reforms in the power sector. The decree called for the demonopolization of energy enterprises, the reduction of state regulation, and the promotion of competition in the power sector. It also called for open access to high-voltage transmission lines.

Resolution On Measures for Organizing the Activities of the Uzbekenergo (2001). This resolution brings reforms based on the priorities of the 2001 decree to deepen economic reforms. The resolution (i) transferred power generation assets from the Ministry of Energy and Electrification to the newly created Uzbekenergo; (ii) created the power sector technical regulator UzGosEnergoNadzor; (iii) allowed Uzbekenergo to offer 49% ownership in thermal power plants and distribution companies, and up to 75% ownership of companies involved in power sector design, construction, and repairs to private investors; and (iv) incorporated UzbekUgol, the national coal company, under Uzbekenergo.

Resolution On Improving the Activities of Economic Management Agencies (2003) and Resolution On Improved Organization of Uzbekenergo Activities (2004). These resolutions separated the high-voltage transmission networks into five zonal branches, united under Uzelectroset, and transferred distribution network assets to separate, regional distribution companies.

Resolution On Measures to Improve the Payment Mechanism for Using Electric Energy (2004) and Resolution On Additional Measures to Strengthen the Accounting and Control System for Selling and Using Electric Energy (2004). The objectives of the two resolutions were to improve the collection rates for electricity.

Continued on next page

Box 2.2 continued

Resolution On Extension of the Process of De-Monopolization and Privatization for 2006–2008. This resolution offered shares in 26 government-owned joint-stock companies. Stakes of 15% each were offered in 12 power distribution companies and nine electricity and heating companies.

Resolution On Measures Aimed at Further Deepening of the Privatization Processes and Active Attraction of Foreign Investments During the Years 2007–2010 (2007). This resolution offered minority shares in Uzbekenergo's power generating assets (the Syrdarya, Novo-Angren, Navoi, Takhiatash, Angren, Tashkent, Fergana, and Mubarek thermal power plants), Uzbekneftegas, and UzbekUgol to private investors.

The Law on Electric Power (2009). The law was intended to create a better-integrated framework for regulating the electricity sector in Uzbekistan, improve energy efficiency in the sector, and attract private investment. The law includes provisions to allow on-site energy generation without licensing and to allow on-site generators to sell electricity back to the grid, and established basic requirements for independent operators of electricity distribution systems. The law made it possible for Uzbekenergo to suspend electricity supply to consumers for violating their supply agreements or damaging electricity meters.

Decree On Measure for Further Development of Alternative Energy Sources (2013). The decree promotes research and development of alternative sources of energy, mainly solar and biogas. Such energy sources are considered important contributors to sustainable development and competitiveness of the economy.

Resolution On Creating the International Institute for Solar Energy (2013). This resolution created the International Institute for Solar Energy. It defines the tasks of the institute as developing solar energy for industrial consumers, promoting the use of solar energy in other sectors, and assisting the development of large solar projects.

Law On the Rational Use of Energy (2015). This law directs the implementation of national, regional, and sectoral programs and projects to promote efficient use of energy, management of production and consumption of energy, introduction of renewable energy sources to replace hydrocarbons, promotion of energy efficient technology and appliances, and creation of an energy efficiency demonstration zone.

Resolution of the President No. PP-2947 On Program of Measures for Further Development of Hydropower Generation for the Period 2017–2021 (2017). The resolution spells out the measures for developing hydropower energy during

Continued on next page

Box 2.2 continued

2017–2021. The decree aims to increase electricity generation from hydropower plants, improve the efficiency of existing plants and water resources management, and meet the increasing domestic demand for electricity.

Decree of the President No. UP-5044 On Setting up Joint-Stock Company "Uzbekhydroenergo" (2017). The decree established Uzbek Hydro Energy by merging the hydro assets of Uzbekenergo and UzSuvenengro. The decree also set the preferential tariff for hydropower resources at 85% of the retail tariff.

Sources: World Bank (2013); Sustainable Development Knowledge Platform (2013) https://sustainabledevelopment.un.org/content/documents/869energyuzbek.pdf as updated by authors; Government of Uzbekistan, various laws and decrees.

Uzbekistan's total installed capacity is 14,263 megawatts (MW), comprising 62% gas, 19% coal, 14% oil, and 134% hydropower plants.[8] The 12 thermal power plants have a total installed capacity of 10,700 MW. The 31 hydropower plants have a total installed capacity of about 1,700 MW (*Azernews* 2017). Generation from renewable energy remains insignificant. Uzbekistan is heavily dependent on natural gas for electricity generation, which accounted for 76% of total electricity generated in 2016; hydropower accounted for 21%, and oil and coal accounted for the rest.

The government aims to develop hydro and coal for electricity generation, to diversify the generation mix. Initial measures have resulted in a very modest increase in generation from hydropower, of about 3.0% between 2013 and 2018 (Figure 2.8). The share of hydropower in total generation has declined from 21.3% in 2013 to 19.8% in 2018. This is despite the President's resolution for developing hydropower energy signed on 2 May 2017. Electricity generation from coal increased by 16% from 2013 to 2018. In 2014, five 300 MW oil- and gas-fired units were converted to coal-based units that use locally sourced coal. Generation from oil has declined continuously since 2004, following the government's effort to reduce dependence on imported oil (Figure 2.8).

Uzbekistan's power system was the backbone of the Central Asia Unified Power System—an integrated transmission infrastructure that used to connect Kazakhstan, the Kyrgyz Republic, Tajikistan, Turkmenistan, and Uzbekistan. After the dissolution of the Soviet Union, this interconnection became a source of conflict. Trade among countries has declined since then. Uzbekistan

---

[8]   Enerdata. https://www.enerdata.net/ (accessed 9 August 2019).

exports power to Afghanistan while it imports power from the Kyrgyz Republic. Trade with Tajikistan has been halted for political reasons. Uzbekistan was a net power importer from 2003 to 2014 (World Bank 2013). From 2015 to 2017, Uzbekistan was able to curtail its import of electricity and became a net power exporter. However in 2018, it again became a net power importer (Figure 2.9).

Figure 2.8: Electricity Generation, by Source, Uzbekistan, 1990–2018 (GWh)

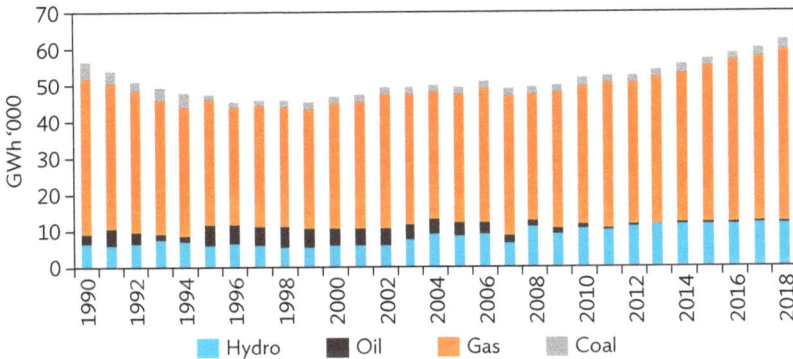

GWh = gigawatt-hour.
Source: Enerdata. https://www.enerdata.net/ (accessed 14 August 2019).

Figure 2.9: Electricity Balance Trade, Uzbekistan, 1990 to 2018 (TWh)

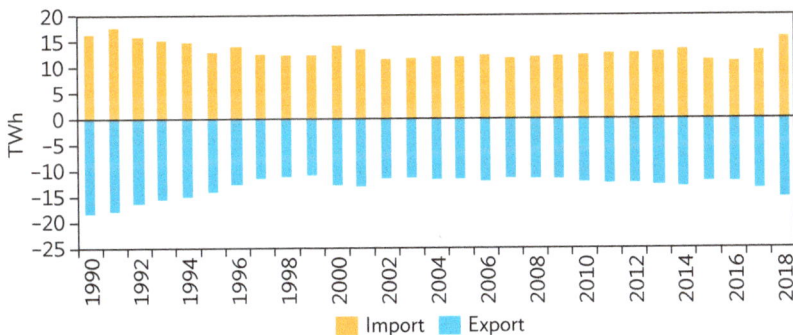

TWh = terawatt-hour.
Source: Enerdata. https://www.enerdata.net/ (accessed 14 August 2019).

Electricity consumption in Uzbekistan increased gradually, at a compound average annual growth rate of 1.4% during 1995–2018. A relatively high upsurge began in 2010 driven by the industry and residential sectors. In 2018, the country's electricity consumption was 48,041 gigawatt-hours, with industry (39% of the total) and agriculture (33%, mainly for irrigation) accounting for bulk of the consumption (Figure 2.10). Household electricity consumption has also increased with the increased ownership of appliances. Electricity consumption per capita gradually decreased from 1990–2016, but it slowly increased from 2017–2018 (Figure 2.11).

Figure 2.10: Electricity Consumption, by Sector, Uzbekistan, 1990–2018
(GWh)

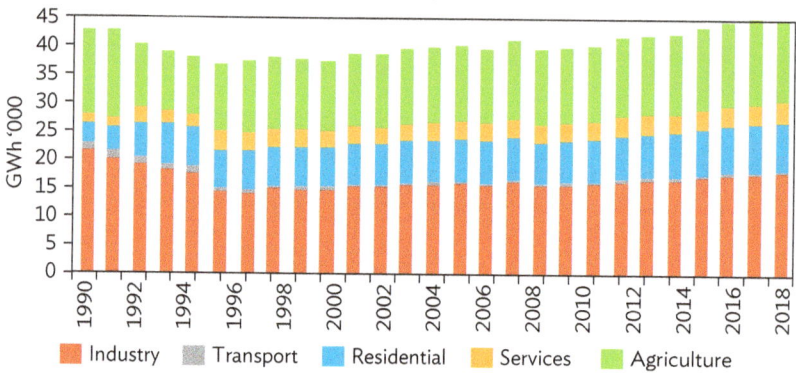

GWh = gigawatt-hour.
Source: Enerdata. https://www.enerdata.net/ (accessed 14 August 2019).

Figure 2.11: Electricity Consumption per Capita, Uzbekistan, 1990–2016
(kWh)

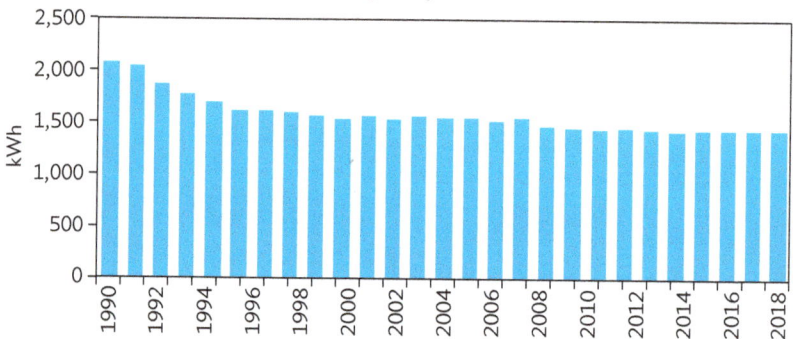

kWh = kilowatt-hour.
Source: Enerdata. https://www.enerdata.net/ (accessed 14 August 2019).

2.2.3. Challenges confronting the power sector

Legal, institutional, and regulatory issues. The energy sector lacks a comprehensive development plan, but the government has been working on a draft. The sector is guided by the Development Strategy for 2017–2021 and by operational plans contained in presidential resolutions that prioritized the following areas: (i) improving electricity efficiency and reducing energy intensity; (ii) developing renewable sources of energy to supply 21% of the country's energy needs; (iii) shifting from consumption of natural gas to coal; (iv) harnessing hydropower potential; (v) increasing electricity generation to support the growth of industries and to increase electricity exports; (vi) reducing losses from gas flaring; and (vii) increasing production of oil and gas by improving the rate of oil recovery, oil conversion, and gas processing efficiency (ADB 2012 and Global Legal Insights 2017).

With finalization of the energy plan still pending, energy projects in Uzbekistan have been identified and implemented in an ad hoc manner. The lack of a coordinated and integrated energy sector plan often leads to inefficient use of energy resources and underinvestment in critical energy infrastructure. There is no systematic approach to identifying and prioritizing the most-efficient energy projects. Feasibility studies and cost–benefit analyses of future projects are not conducted regularly. Institutions involved in the energy sector have limited capacity to plan and manage energy projects, leading to delayed implementation and escalated costs of projects. One case of concern is the 100 MW Samarkand Solar-Photovoltaic (PV) station, whose construction has been delayed due to a series of retenders with various contractors.

Until 2019, Uzbekistan did not have a dedicated and independent regulatory unit to ensure fair competition, employ effective tariff-setting methodology, and set and monitor service standards. The regulatory responsibility was shared between the Ministry of Finance and the State Committee, and the role of each was not clearly identified. In February 2019, the President ordered the establishment of the new Ministry of Energy as part of the effort to restructure the power sector. The Ministry of Energy was formed in March; one of its functions is to develop and implement regulations in the oil, gas, and power subsectors. This initial reform initiative is intended to help improve the performance of the energy sector.

There is very limited private participation in the power sector. This risks inefficient provision of services to consumers and insufficient investment in infrastructure development. The government has restructured Uzbekenergo to attract private capital to its generation and distribution segments. A deficient legal and institutional framework for private participation has limited the entry of private investments in large-scale thermal and small-scale renewable power generation projects. With respect to public–private participation (PPP) arrangements, the laws do not cover government support, lenders' rights, and compensation of the private investor for losses in the event of contract termination on the grounds of public interest. The laws are also silent on the right to create any security interests over the project assets (ADB 2016e). The Law on Electricity prohibits independent power producers from feeding electricity to the grid. While the Law on Rational Energy Utilization introduces project-specific feed-in tariffs that allow recovery of capital investment and operation and maintenance cost of renewable energy facilities, this has not yet been applied to private investors. In terms of institutional arrangements, there is no dedicated public authority to serve as a central unit for PPPs (ADB 2016e).

Poor supply reliability. According to the World Bank Enterprise Survey 2013, electrical outages happen almost six times a month in Uzbekistan, each lasting for about 5 hours. These numbers are worse than the average of the Eastern Europe and Central Asia region. Poor supply reliability has negatively affected profitability of businesses. Losses due to electrical outages amount to 6.6% of annual sales of enterprises. About 5% of manufacturing enterprises use generators that mostly run on diesel to support their operations. Those that own generators on average rely on them for 24% of their electricity needs (Table 2.8). Electricity from diesel-fired generation units is expensive. The generation cost is roughly SUM261 per kilowatt-hour (kWh), about 27% higher than the tariff to residential consumers in Uzbekistan in 2017.[9] Even getting electricity connection is a challenge for new enterprises. Among all respondents surveyed in all sectors (representing 390 enterprises), 32% identified that getting electricity was the most limiting factor for their firms' operations (Figure 2.12).

---

[9] Data on the generation cost of diesel-fired generators are from World Bank (2013), adjusted to approximate the generation cost in 2017 and converted to sum using the average exchange rate in 2013 (SUM2,097.2/$1.00).

Table 2.8: Enterprise Survey Results, Uzbekistan, 2013

Indicator	Uzbekistan	Eastern Europe & Central Asia
Number of electrical outages in a typical month	5.7	1.5
If there were outages, average duration of a typical electrical outage (hours)	4.8	3.3
If there were outages, average losses due to electrical outages (% of annual sales)	6.6	2.2
Percent of firms owning or sharing a generator	5.1	17.8
If a generator is used, average proportion of electricity from a generator (%)	23.9	9.6

Source: World Bank. *Enterprise Survey.* Uzbekistan (2013). http://www.enterprisesurveys.org/data/exploreeconomies/2013/uzbekistan#infrastructure (accessed 29 August 2019)

Electricity supply and demand mismatches arise during winter when electricity demand surges, as electricity is mainly used for heating. Supply is unreliable due to transmission bottlenecks, aging electricity generation plants, and insufficient investment. The issue is more pronounced in the southern and western regions, where blackouts are common and last 2–6 hours a day in winter months. The country experienced a severe power shortage in 2012, when rolling blackouts occurred almost throughout Uzbekistan. In cities, blackouts lasted for several hours daily; in rural villages electricity was not available for weeks. During the winter crisis in 2010, unserved energy amounted to about 860 gigawatt-hours or about 1.7% of total consumption. Economic losses due to the shortage are estimated at $52 million (World Bank 2013). The possibility of supplementing electricity supply with imported electricity has been limited because of the unreliable operations of the Central Asia Unified Power System.

Figure 2.12: Business Environment Obstacle for Firms, Uzbekistan, 2013

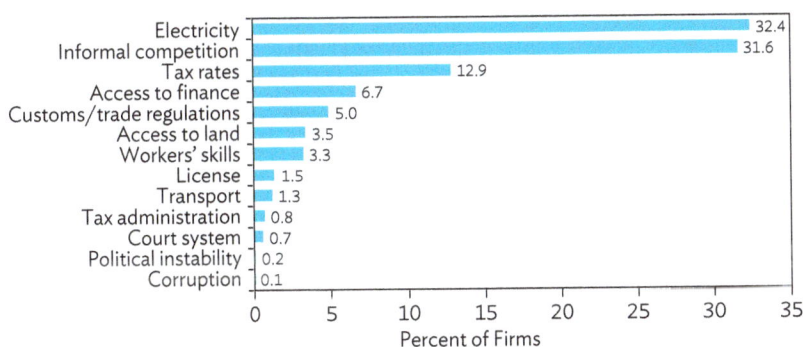

Source: World Bank. Enterprise Survey. Uzbekistan (2013). http://www.enterprisesurveys.org/data/exploreeconomies/2013/uzbekistan#infrastructure (accessed 29 August 2019)

High demand for electricity. The government's target of increasing manufacturing's share of GDP from 12% in 2012 to 22% in 2030 would involve a large increase in demand. In addition, expected higher household incomes will drive purchases of electric appliances and machines such as air conditioners, refrigerators, and computers, and thus add to electricity consumption. CAREC has forecast electricity demand in 2020 and 2030 under various scenarios (Figure 2.13). Comparing the demand forecasts with CAREC's own supply forecast from 2012 implies shortages by 2020 in a high-growth scenario. According to CAREC's analysis, the thermal power plants capacity will diminish to 5.7 GW by 2020. New thermal power plants will add 6 GW of available capacity. Together with hydropower plants, the total available capacity is estimated at about 13 GW, which could generate 65.2 terawatt-hours (TWh) of electricity per year (Table 2.9).

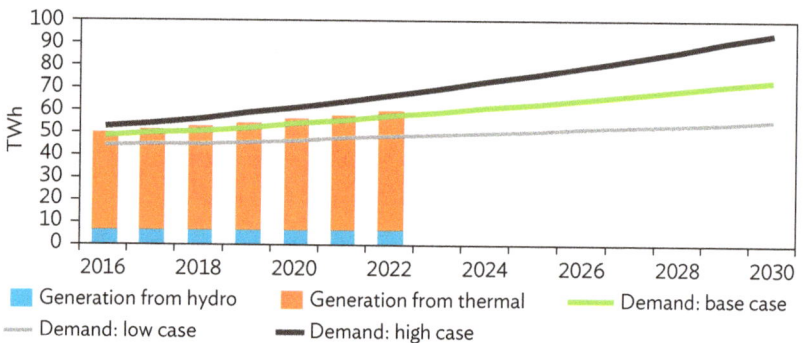

Figure 2.13: Electricity Demand Projection, Uzbekistan, 2016–2030 (TWh)

TWh= terawatt-hour.
Source: Grunwald (2012).

Uzbekenergo provides more optimistic forecasts of power generation—from 61.7 TWh in 2017, it suggests an increase of 77% by 2020 and four-fold by 2050. Per capita generation is forecast to increase from about 1,900 kWh in 2017 to 2,110 kWh in 2020 and to 5,900 kWh in 2050 (Table 2.10). A resolution sets an ambitious goal (Table 2.11) of increasing the hydropower generating capacity to 2,176 MW in 2020 and 3,038 MW in 2025 by constructing 11 new and modernizing 11 existing hydropower plants (Government of Uzbekistan 2017). Additional capacity of 5,406 MW from thermal and 804 MW from renewable energy up to 2030 are in Uzbekenergo's most recent plan (Table 2.12). The additional capacity will come from modernizing, rehabilitating, and expanding existing power plants, and constructing new ones in Uzbekistan during 2017–2030.

Table 2.9: Electricity Supply Projection, Uzbekistan, 2015–2020

Item	2015	2016	2017	2018	2019	2020
Thermal Power Plants						
Installed capacity, existing TPPs (MW)	9,000	8,000	7,500	7,000	6,700	5,700
Installed capacity, new TPPs (MW)	727	1,997	2,897	3,797	4,697	6,067
Total installed capacity, all TPPs (MW)	9,727	9,997	10,397	10,797	11,397	11,767
Available capacity, all TPPs (MW)	9,216	9,710	9,516	10,248	10,967	10,998
Hydropower Plants (HPPs)						
Installed capacity, all HPPs (MW)	2,005	2,005	2,005	2,005	2,005	2,005
Available capacity, all HPPs (MW)	1,990	1,990	1,990	1,990	1,990	1,999
Available capacity, all HPPs during winter (MW)	866	866	866	866	866	866
Total installed capacity (MW)	11,732	12,002	12,402	12,802	13,402	13,772
Total available capacity (MW)	11,206	11,700	11,506	12,238	12,957	12,997
Total available capacity in winter (MW)	10,082	10,576	10,382	11,114	11,833	11,864
Total generation (GWh)	58,806	59,847	60,904	61,979	63,567	65,222
Hydro (%)	12.7	12.5	12.2	12.0	11.7	11.4
Thermal (%)	87.3	87.5	87.8	88	88.3	88.6
Trade						
Export (MW)	1,200	1,200	1,200	1,200	1,200	1,200
Import (MW)	0	0	0	0	0	0
Balance (MW)	1,200	1,200	1,200	1,200	1,200	1,200

GWh = gigawatt-hour, MW = megawatt, TPP = Thermal Power Plants.
Source: Grunwald (2012).

Table 2.10: Uzbekistan's Power Generation, 1991, 2016, 2017, and Projections 2017–2050

	1991	2016	2017	2020ᶠ	2025ᶠ	2030ᶠ	2040ᶠ	2050ᶠ
Population (million people)	21.1	32.1	32.6	33.4	35.4	37.1	40.6	42.7
Annual growth rate (%)		1.8	1.6	1.4	1.2	1.0	1.0	0.5
Power generation (TWh)	54.1	59.0	61.7	70.4	88.6	108.6	165.4	250.1
Power generation per capita (kWh/capita)	2,564.0	1,838.0	1,891.8	2,107.8	2,502.8	2,927.2	4077.0	5,863.2

ᶠ = forecast, kWh = kilowatt-hour, TWh = terawatt-hour.
Source: Uzbekenergo (2018).

Table 2.11: Generating Capacity of Hydropower Plants, Actual and Targeted, Uzbekistan, 2017–2025
(MW)

Item	Generating capacity in 2016 (actual)	Future Generating Capacity					
		2017	2018	2019	2020	2021	2025
Construction of new HPPs	...	0	0	72.0	123.3	342.7	984.7
Modernization of existing HPPs	...	1,838.9	1,854.6	1,879.6	2,053.1	2,053.1	2,053.1
Total	**1,793.9**	**1,838.9**	**1,854.6**	**1,951.6**	**2,176.4**	**2,395.8**	**3,037.8**

... = not available, HPP = hydropower plant, MW = megawatt.
Source: Government of Uzbekistan (2017).

Table 2.12: Generation Expansion Plan, by Source, Uzbekistan, 2018–2030
(MW)

Type	Projects (units)	Capacity (MW)
Thermal power plants	29	5,406
Of which:		
1.1. CCGT or gas turbines	19	4,956
1.2. Coal block stations	2	300
1.3. Modernization of Syrdarya TPP blocks	6	150
1.4. Transition of 6th and 7th units of New-Angren to coal	2	0
2. Hydraulic power plants	18	343
3. Solar and wind power plants:	4	402
3.1. Solar power plants	3	300
3.2. Wind power plants	1	102
Total	**51**	**6,553**

CCGT = combined cycle gas turbine, MW = megawatt, TPP = thermal power plant.
Source: Uzbekenergo. http://www.uzbekenergo.uz/en/ (accessed 17 July 2018).

Ten thermal power stations will be rehabilitated and refurbished under Uzbekenergo's development plan. The developments will add four new 900 MW blocks in the Navoi, New Syrdarya, Talimarjan, and Turakurgan power stations.

Demand- and supply-side inefficiencies. As discussed above, demand- and supply-side inefficiencies have made Uzbekistan one of the most energy- and electricity-intensive countries in the region. Electricity intensity in 2016 was

0.77 kWh per unit of GDP, well above all neighboring countries except the Ukraine, and despite its continuous decline since the mid-1990s (Figure 2.14). Agriculture has been the most electricity intensive sector (except in 1994). Industry followed, but with notable improvements in electricity intensity in recent years, which may be due to the government's effort to modernize the sector.

Figure 2.14a: Electricity Intensity, Uzbekistan, 1990–2016
(kWh per unit of GVA in constant 2010 $)

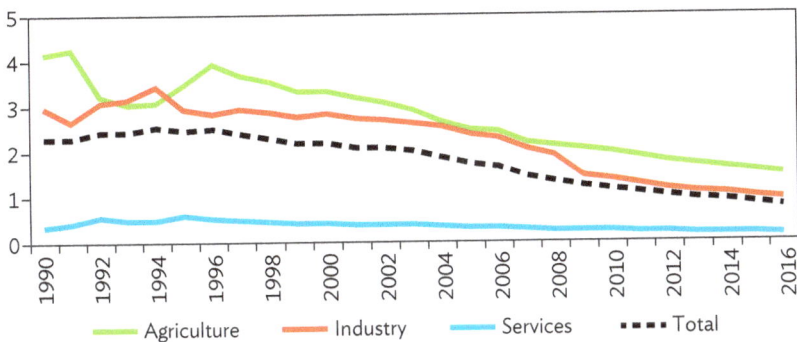

GVA = gross value added, kWh = kilowatt-hour.
Sources: Calculated using final electricity consumption data from Enerdata. https://www.enerdata.net/ (accessed 10 May 2017) and GDP data from World Bank. World Development Indicators. http://databank. worldbank.org/wdi (accessed 10 May 2017).

Figure 2.14b: Electricity Intensity, Selected Countries, 2016
(kWh per unit of GDP in constant 2010,$)

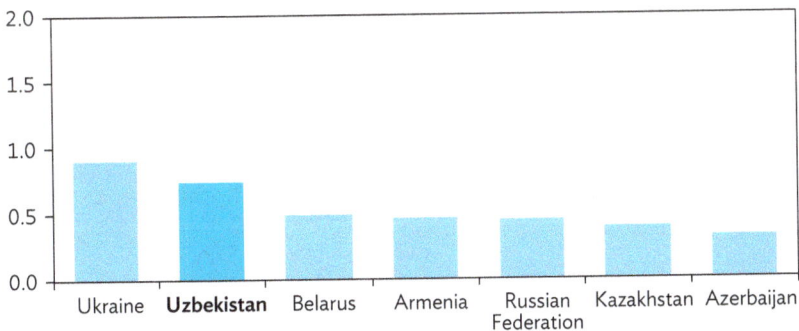

GDP = gross domestic product, kWh = kilowatt-hour.
Sources: Calculated using final electricity consumption data from Enerdata. https://www.enerdata.net/ (accessed 10 May 2017) and GDP data from World Bank. World Development Indicators. http://databank. worldbank.org/wdi (accessed 10 May 2017).

Demand-side inefficiencies in the use of electricity emanate from the use of outdated equipment and technology across sectors, most especially in agriculture. Inefficiencies in the agriculture sector stem from the heavy reliance on old pumping infrastructure used for irrigation, with more than 65% of it past its useful life (World Bank 2013). In industry, activities such as metallurgy and the manufacture of bricks, cement, and chemicals still operate the most electricity-intensive technologies. Households are electricity-intensive: ADB (2004) found that Uzbek households consumed up to three times more than the average of households in Eastern Europe. With electricity mainly used for space heating, household electricity consumption doubles during the winter.

Supply-side inefficiencies in the power sector stem from the aging thermal power plants and transmission and distribution systems. Uzbekistan has the oldest generation assets among the neighboring countries of Kazakhstan, the Kyrgyz Republic, and Tajikistan. About 40% of the installed capacity is past or close to the end of its operating life, with most assets 40–50 years old and in poor condition. In 2013, the average efficiency of thermal power plants was only 33%, well below the efficiency of modern combined cycle gas turbines, at 53%–56% (Table 2.13).

Table 2.13: Efficiencies of Thermal Power Plants, Uzbekistan, 2013

Plant	Available Capacity (MW)	Reported Efficiency (%)
Talimardjan TPP	900	55
Sirdaya TPP	2,840	34
Novo-Angren TPP	1,960	32
Tashkent TPP	1,758	33
Navoi TPP	1,181	30
Takhiatash TPP	690	30
Angren TPP	445	31
Fergana CHPP	289	25
Mubarek CHPP	56	30
Tashkent CHPP	28	23
Other TPPs	39	...
Weighted average efficiency		33
Efficiency of modern combined cycle gas turbines		53–56

... = not available, CHPP= combined heat and power plant, MW = megawatt, TPP= thermal power plant.
All data are as of 2013, except for Talimardjan which is as of 2016.
Sources: World Bank (2013) and ADB (2016d=c).

Uzbekistan's transmission system is composed of 1,850 km of 500 kilovolt (kV) lines, 6,200 km of 220 kV lines, and 15,300 km of 110 kV lines (as of February 2017). The country's transmission system is connected to the Kyrgyz

Republic and Tajikistan by 200 kV and 500 kV transmission lines (Enerdata 2015). The distribution system is composed of 13,593 km of 35 kV lines, 93,983 km of 6 kV to 10 kV lines, and 105,834 km of 0.4 kV lines. The system is old, with an average age of 35 years (Table 2.14).

Table 2.14: Length of Transmission and Distribution Infrastructure, Uzbekistan, 2017

Voltage Level	Length (km)	Average Age (years)
Transmission lines		
500 kV	2,257	33
220 kV	6,200	35
110 kV	15,300	33
Distribution lines		
35 kV	13,592	35
6 kV to 10 kV	93,983	38
0.4 kV	105,834	no data available

km = kilometer, kV = kilovolt.
Source: Data from World Bank (2013) updated based on information from Uzbekenergo.

Aging power systems cause high transmission and distribution losses. Based on Uzbekenergo data, system losses were over 18% in 2014, with transmission losses at 4% and distribution losses at 14%.[10] Technical losses were mostly from the low-voltage transmission and distribution lines (0.4 kV to 35 kV) due to poor operation and maintenance of the system. Commercial losses are as high as 30%. Total losses of the electricity sector are estimated at 33%–35% of overall production.

Outdated distribution assets and manual operations have led to inaccurate and inefficient revenue collection. The current metering and billing system is inadequate, outdated, and susceptible to tampering and potential manipulation of charges by customers and tariff collection officers. Uzbekenergo's revenues are mostly generated domestically, with regional sales from electricity export to Afghanistan amounting to only 5% of total revenues. Uzbekenergo's revenue collection was only about 80% or less of the potential in 2014. Despite continued efforts to improve the metering and accounting system, Uzbekenergo had accumulated $1.5 billion of receivables in 2016, an increase from $1.0 billion in 2010. The government has created a special bureau for all communal services (electricity, gas, and other communal services) under the Prosecutor General's office to improve collections from customers.

---

[10]   Data are from ADB. n.d. Projects. Uzbekistan: Advanced Electricity Metering Phase 4 Project. https://www.adb.org/projects/41340-015/main#project-pds (accessed July 2018).

Energy efficiency and conservation has been at the forefront of Uzbekistan's energy policy. Uzbekistan has the second-highest efficiency potential in the region (second to Kazakhstan), estimated at 32.4 million tons of carbon equivalent. Efficiency savings from the power and heat sector alone is estimated at 9.6 million tons of carbon equivalent (CCEE 2015).

Based on the law on Rational Use of Energy, Uzbekistan's road map for improving energy efficiency for 2015–2019 provides for the mainstreaming of energy efficiency measures in town planning, expanding coverage of energy audits, conducting energy certification of apartments and buildings, energy labelling household appliances, and developing hydropower (Box 2.3). Uzbekistan's energy efficiency and conservation thrust sees industry as one of its priority sectors. In 2010, the government and the World Bank created a $25-million funding facility for industrial enterprises undertaking energy-saving investments. The facility was expanded to $100 million in 2013. It identified industrial enterprises such as manufacturing of building materials, food processing, and textile manufacturing as target candidates for the facility. The project aims to save more than 200 GWh of electricity and lessen carbon dioxide emission by 400,000 tons. Across all sectors, the Center for Economic Research (2015) suggests complete replacement of incandescent bulbs with more energy efficient bulbs (e.g., LED) and upgrading of outdated heating boilers and pumps.

Rehabilitation and updating of electricity generation, transmission, and distribution infrastructure is critical to improving the efficiency of the power sector. CER (2015) recommends complete modernization of power distribution networks and transformers by 2020. New technology such as advanced electricity metering can help address commercial losses. Installation of smart metering systems is being rolled out nationwide to allow two-way communication between the utility and customer meters, and enable the utility to remotely disconnect and reconnect supply, thus minimizing manipulations by utility officers at the site.[11]

Large future investments. The government expansion plans for the sector summarized in Tables 2.10–2.13 will require substantial investment (Table 2.15). For hydropower alone, the 22 projects laid out in Presidential Resolution No. PP-2947 will require $2.2 billion. The government will fund 61% of that, while external funding will provide the rest. Sources of external funding include the Asian Development Bank, Asian Infrastructure Investment Bank, and Eximbank China.

---

[11]   ADB. n.d. Projects. Uzbekistan: Advanced Electricity Metering Phase 4 Project. https://www.adb.org/projects/41340-015/main#project-pds (accessed 16 July 2018).

Table 2.15: Required Investment for Hydropower Plants, Uzbekistan
($ million)

Project	Cost	Source of Financing	
		Government	FDI and Lending
New Construction (11 projects)	1,730.5	1,195.6	534.9
Modernization	507.1	168.3	338.9
Total	**2,237.6**	**1,363.9**	**873.8**

FDI = foreign direct investment.
Source: Government of Uzbekistan (2017).

Huge investments are required to rehabilitate and extend the transmission and distribution networks. Additional high-voltage transmission lines are needed to supply electricity in the densely populated Fergana Valley. Where no large power generation facilities exist, a circular transmission network should be created to allow transmission within the country, and to further integrate regional grids. In the short term, the government aims to construct six high-voltage transmission lines that will cost about $570 million. The government has estimated that a total of $1.3 billion will be needed for investments in transmission and distribution systems by 2020. This will include modernizing switchyards and constructing new distribution-level infrastructure, such as advanced electrical meters for individual customers.

Uzbekenergo had also increased its long-term investment from SUM1.3 billion to SUM1.5 billion to replace aging and inefficient generation assets. In the past, the government has provided the investments. With the huge investment requirement, funding from the public coffers will not suffice and should be supplemented by private investments. However, private sector participation in the power sector is currently negligible due to the sector's poor economic performance, and insufficient financing of the sector has stifled the modernization and reconstruction of power infrastructure. Investment directed to the electricity generation sector has been growing but at a slow pace, accounting for just 3.5% of the total annual investments of the company during 2007–2017.

Increasing investments through private funds requires adjusting electricity tariffs to cover long-run supply costs. The tariff hikes since 2012 had enabled the Uzbekenergo to slowly recover operating and maintenance costs and other administrative expenses. The current electricity tariffs for all of Uzbekenergo's subsidiaries were on a cost basis to cover these costs. The 2018 tariff rates are SUM178.40/kWh for industry and SUM228.60/kWh for residential users

Box 2.3: Uzbekistan's Energy Efficiency Policy

Uzbekistan's Energy Efficiency Policy is anchored on the Law On the Rational Use of Energy. The main directions of the state policy are

- implementation of national, regional, and sectorial targeted programs and projects;
- stabilization of production and consumption of energy, which is necessary for intensive development of the national economy;
- introduction of renewable energy sources to replace hydrocarbons;
- optimization of energy production and consumption;
- stimulation of the production of energy-saving equipment and products with minimal power consumption;
- enacting of energy efficiency regulations on energy producing/using equipment and products;
- organization of statistical observations of energy production and consumption;
- organization of energy efficiency management;
- organization of energy audits of enterprises, institutions, and organizations;
- energy examination of products, existing and reconstructed facilities, technology, and equipment;
- creation of energy efficiency demonstration zones to implement energy efficiency projects; and
- encouragement of the development of energy efficient and environmentally friendly technologies and products.

In May 2015, the government implemented the Program Roadmap for Improving Energy Efficiency, the Introduction of Energy Efficient Technologies and Systems in the fields of Economy and Social Sphere in 2015–2019. The program provides for

- drafting the Law On Renewable Energy Sources,
- reviewing all town-planning norms and rules to provide for the requirements of energy efficiency,
- expanding the range of consumers for energy audits,
- conducting energy certification of apartment houses and public buildings in major cities,
- transferring domestic cement plants to the "dry" method of production,
- introducing energy labeling of household electronic appliances, and
- developing and approving the program of development of hydroenergetics in 2016–2020.

Source: Akhmedov (2015).

(Table 2.16).[12] The cost of hydropower to Uzbekenergo had risen significantly with the takeover of Uzbekhydroenergo. Uzbekenergo used to pay SUM5/kWh for its own hydropower plants and SUM167/kWh from Uzsuvenergo. Uzbekenergo signed a power purchasing agreement with Uzbekhydroenergo for SUM192/kWh.

Table 2.16: Tariff Rates, Uzbekistan, 2001–2018
(sum per kWh)

Year	Industry	Residential	Year	Industry	Residential
2001	4.8	4.7	2014	131.8	65.9
2002	8.7	8.7	2015	153.6	76.8
2003	13.1	13.1	2016	178.4	89.2
2012	104.4	52.2	2017		191.0
2013	116.1	58.1	2018		228.6

kWh= kilowatt-hour.
Sources: Enerdata. https://www.enerdata.net/ (accessed 21 January 2018); Uzbekenergo . http://www.uzbekenergo.uz/en/ (accessed 17 April 2018).

Uzbekistan's power sector has struggled to fund new investments because of its poor financial performance. Uzbekenergo recorded losses of SUM741 billion in 2014 and SUM408 billion in 2015, and a profit of SUM314 billion in 2016. The improvement in 2016 was driven by adjustments of electricity tariffs to high annual inflation rates and a subsidized fuel price, despite low-moderate electricity sales growth averaging 2.5% during 2014–2016. However, the significant adjustment of the exchange rate in 2017 was considered the single largest risk to Uzbekenergo's financial standing, given that the majority of its borrowing is denominated in foreign currency. Based on ADB's financial statement projections, without substantial tariff adjustments, the sector's performance will deteriorate during 2017–2026 and accumulated losses will reach SUM12,662 billion in 2026 (Table 2.17). The sector's sustainability remains highly sensitive to the timely implementation of the financial recovery action plan supported by the government, and the prioritization of key internal financial management reforms.

Heavy dependence on natural gas. Excessive use of natural gas poses a problem for load management. Most of the gas-fired plants are designed as baseload generation and their efficiency is compromised when used for meeting the peak load. Uzbekistan may diversify power sources by promoting renewable energy (such as wind) and trading with other countries, but this has not progressed very far (World Bank 2013).

---

[12] The exchange rate of $1/SUM3,065 was used for conversion.

Table 2.17: Uzbekenergo's Projected Financial Performance, 2017–2026

	2017	2018	2019	2020	2021	2022	2023	2024	2025	2026
Total revenue	5,909	7,489	8,002	8,550	9,536	11,950	12,747	13,598	14,506	15,477
Cost of goods sold	-5,918	-6,848	-7,718	-7,718	-8,518	-9,603	-10,277	-10,965	-11,652	-12,310
Other OPEX	-1,031	-1,273	-1,454	-1,454	-1,621	-2,031	-2,167	-2,312	-2,466	-2,631
EBIT	-1,041	-632	-614	-621	-603	316	302	321	388	535
Finance expense	-300	-228	-310	-300	-287	-369	-867	-905	-991	-986
Exchange rate										
Loss	-8,272	-1,089	-1,139	-1,368	-1,699	-1,948	-2,462	-2,773	-3,005	-2,981
Profit for the year	-9,613	-1,949	-2,063	-2,289	-2,588	-2,001	-3,028	-3,357	-3,608	-3,431

EBIT = earnings before interest and taxes, OPEX = operating expense.
Note: Projections adopted conservative assumptions of real increase of end–user tariff at 4.4% and fuel price at 4.3% that are estimated based on historical trends in tariff adjustments from 2010 to 2017.
Source: ADB (2017a).

So far, the government's approach to the challenge has been to convert natural-gas-fired power plants to coal and develop renewable energy. The government intends to convert seven units (five units have been converted) of the Novo–Angren power plant to run on coal. While this is less costly than building a new plant, conversion lowers the power plants' efficiency.

The government is considering increasing the share of hydropower in the power mix to 15.8% in 2025. The government's push for developing renewable energy also targets solar energy to account for 2.3% and wind energy to account for 1.6% of the country's power by 2025 (Yeniseyev 2017). Uzbekistan's hydroelectric potential is about 21.09 TWh, of which only 6.27 TWh are being harnessed. About 90% of the canals and rivers are used for irrigation purposes, which makes the introduction of hydropower generation challenging.

The tender of the first 100 MW solar PV station in Samarkand is completed, and construction started in 2017. Presently, there is only one solar PV station, in Namangan Province, which can produce 500 kWh to 600 KWh of electricity a year (*UzDaily* 2015). Technical assessment of the second 100 MW Sherobod solar PV station is under way, with plans to construct five 100 MW solar plants in the country by 2021. Total investments for the plan are expected to reach $1.1 billion (Bellini 2017).

2.3 Policy Recommendations

Power, road, and rail infrastructure share common challenges. The following recommendations flow from the foregoing analysis:

(i) **Continue collaboration and coordination among institutions to come up with a coherent master plan for infrastructure**. Ensure coordination among all levels in planning and implementing infrastructure projects. The current institutional setup encourages coordination at the top level, with either the Deputy Prime Minister's Office or the responsible department at the Cabinet of Ministers in charge of cross-sectoral coordination. Coordination at the bottom levels also needs to be strengthened to promote efficient and effective decision-making.

(ii) **Implement institutional reforms to ensure projects are prioritized, improve the financial performance of the sector, and attract private sector investment**. Given the large financing gap, it is crucial to allocate limited resources efficiently by institutionalizing economic analyses of projects. Economic analysis is an analytical framework for estimating the costs and benefits of a project as a basis for comparing projects systematically. This allows sound project appraisal, evidence-based decision-making, and minimal political maneuvering. The private sector is a potential source of investment. A good starting point for determining how to attract private capital is a thorough assessment of the enabling environment for private participation. The results should be the basis for legal, regulatory, and institutional reforms to create a more favorable environment for private companies to participate in infrastructure projects.

(iii) **Augment investments in infrastructure.** This is necessary to finance road maintenance, further electrify railways, upgrade the rolling stock of railways and truck fleets, develop logistics infrastructure, expand the generation capacity, and upgrade power networks.

(iv) **Make the infrastructure sector more climate-resilient.** While planning infrastructure projects, take the increasing incidence of climate anomalies and natural disasters into account, as well as the diminishing water resources, which will challenge all infrastructure subsectors.

(v) **Explore new sources of funds to construct new and update and maintain existing infrastructure.** The PPP is a promising financial mechanism for infrastructure projects. The introduction of efficient PPPs would enable more rapid financing of infrastructure projects; strengthen national financial institutions; increase the country's capacity to diversify sources of the state budget; expand the export potential of the country by reducing inefficient domestic resource use; and, where foreign investors are involved, enhance efforts to promote cooperation on regional trade and sustainable development. PPPs may be pilot-tested by contracting out services such as billing and collections.

(vi) **Create dedicated and independent public–private electricity, natural gas, oil, road, railway, and water utility funds**. The proposed funds, plus well-designed economic and legal frameworks, could establish transparent and favorable public–private financing mechanisms that will directly and indirectly increase the government's capacity to leverage private and other public resources; create a pool of long-term capital; promote the long-term viability of infrastructure financing mechanisms and growth of utility (infrastructure) companies; offer access to knowledgeable and professional teams of investors who can provide managerial support to the companies in question; and contribute to awareness-raising and capital-building efforts.

(vii) **Build the institutions capacities for planning, accounting, and research.** Invest in training staff, with the help of external experts. Establish a database of information and a system of analyzing data to support evidence–based decision-making. Partner with schools to hire competent professionals in transport- and energy-related government agencies.

In addition to the foregoing recommendations that apply to all infrastructure, the transport, logistics, and energy sectors in Uzbekistan need some specific changes in order to become drivers of economic development. The following are recommendations to improve the performance of transport and logistics.

(i) **Improve the operations of transport institutions by strengthening project preparation and implementation and streamlining procurement.** This is necessary to improve reviews of cost estimates to avoid cost escalation during project implementation, to make the procurement system more transparent, and to improve project completion rates by establishing a system for monitoring the progress of projects and establishing incentives for efficient implementation.

(ii) **Review design standards of roads and railroads and ensure that they are aligned with international standards.** Avoid lanes narrower than 3.0 meters, which, according to safety norms, do not allow speeds over 50 km per hour and cannot serve trucks.

(iii) **Address the problem of an aging truck fleet.** Consider enhancing systems for long-term soft bank lending to purchase modern trucks, reducing customs fees for truck models that are not produced domestically, enhancing the current legal framework and creating incentives for renewing truck fleets, and establishing stringent standards for efficient fuel consumption and making exhaust gas emissions limits more stringent (CER 2013a).

(iv) **Implement tariff reforms in the railway subsector.** This will incentivize the railway company to increase its freight turnover while reducing prices. The reforms may include improving the system for tariff setting, whereby the number of adjustment factors are minimized and all types of cross-subsidization in railway transport are reduced.

(v) **Improve customs and border procedures for imports and exports.** To enhance the flow of traffic across borders, simplify customs laws and regulations, harmonize border crossing procedures, establish joint border crossing facilities with neighbors, and automate procedures of border control agencies to improve control and facilitate data exchange.

(vi) **Develop the infrastructure for multimodal logistics centers, labor and management training, and market access to private entrepreneurs.** Border infrastructure needs to be modernized and made more efficient to support the growth of the logistics industry.

The following recommendations are specific to improving the performance of the energy sector, to enable it to play a more significant role in Uzbekistan's economic growth.

(i) **Implement an energy sector plan that outlines the framework for developing the sector**. Base the plan on a comprehensive assessment of the sector's hard and soft infrastructure. The plan should spell out the sector's vision, priority areas, and targets for the short, medium, and long terms. The plan should also consider actions necessary for completing the unbundling process in the power sector with an overarching goal of attracting private sector investment. Set up a monitoring and evaluation system to ensure the effective implementation of the plan.

(ii) **Fund energy development initiatives.** Such initiatives would include exploring and developing oil and gas fields for thermal power plants and developing renewable sources of power. This will help diversify the country's power mix, lessen dependence on natural gas consumption for local electricity generation, and increase otherwise foregone export revenues.

(iii) **Continue active participation in regional energy trade.** This will help meet demand for power during peak periods more efficiently and will open opportunity for earning foreign revenue from the transit and sale of electricity. Uzbekistan has been an active participant in the CAREC process, and the country's abundant energy resources offer an opportunity to earn substantial foreign exchange from power exports. Uzbekistan will also benefit from the exchange of knowledge among participating countries and from access to international experts to enhance institutional capacity in the power sector.

(iv) **Create a favorable business environment for small-scale renewable energy application, especially in the residential and commercial sectors.** Attract transnational companies to offer small-scale residential renewable energy solutions, such as solar PV systems. Establish compensation mechanisms (such as feed-in tariffs, net metering, and green certificate trades) for renewable energy sources. Direct a large part of international financial institution loans to sustainable and green energy solutions. Create credit lines with international financial institutions to support small businesses engaged in the application and servicing of renewable energy technologies.

(v) **Rehabilitate and modernize power sector technologies, infrastructure, and equipment.** This will address inefficient generation, transmission, and distribution, and will minimize energy resource depletion. Rehabilitation and modernization strategies should have finite, measurable, and accountable targets.

(vi) **Improve electricity metering at all levels, with special emphasis on metering the end-use consumers.** Disseminate the ongoing smart metering pilot project countrywide so as to allow prepaid electricity supply and thereby virtually eliminating commercial losses by decreasing them to as low as 1%–2%.

(vii) **Further improve the regulatory system through the established Ministry of Energy as the independent energy regulator**. A good regulatory system should be built on the principles of independence, transparency, and consumer and investor protection. Independence of the regulator means autonomy from the government in terms of function and financing. Transparency means predictability of decision-making. This requires the regulator to promulgate rules, regulations, and policies, and to enforce them objectively. Key policy documents and guidelines should be publicly available. Investor and consumer protection requires carefully balancing the interests of the government, service suppliers, and consumers (UNIDO 2009). This is particularly crucial in deciding on a tariff determination methodology, which should be anchored on the goals of protecting consumers and facilitating investment while supporting the development goals of the government.

(viii) **Review the tariff setting policy.** Aim at creating cost-recovering tariffs for electricity consumers. Revise the current subsidized tariff policy, which stimulates excessive consumption. Energy efficiency and conservation require a shift in consumer behavior, which in turn requires the right energy price-setting mechanism, regulations, and sufficient infrastructure (IGES 2013).

(ix) **Improve load management by introducing multiple tariffs.** This will reduce demand more efficiently and effectively during the peak demand hours. As Uzbekistan is in a single time zone and daylight hours do not shift significantly from East to West, peak and nonpeak tariffs should be introduced.

(x) **Support financial reforms within the power sector**. Ensure timely implementation of a financial recovery action plan and financial management reforms. Monitor results of the initial implementation of the action plan and reform measures. Consider tapping external experts to enhance strategies for improving revenue collection, pursuing corporate reforms, and rationalizing investment plans.

References

Akhmedov, S. 2015. Energy Efficiency Policy in Uzbekistan. PowerPoint presentation, Asian Energy Forum 2015, Manila, 16 June.

Alfen, H., S. Kalidindi, S. Ogunlana, and Shou Qing Wang. 2009. *Public–Private Partnership in Infrastructure Development: Case Studies from Asia and Europe.* V7. Weimar: Bauhaus–Universität Weimar.

Asian Development Bank (ADB). 2004. Final Report: Technical Assistance to the Republic of Uzbekistan for Energy Needs Assessment. Volume 1: Review and Assessment of Technical Needs. TAR: UZB–36382. Manila

_____. 2009. *Uzbekistan: Trade Facilitation and Logistics Development Strategy Report.* Manila.

_____. 2011a. *Uzbekistan Country Partnership Strategy 2012–2016.* Central and West Asia Department: Diversifying Uzbekistan. Manila.

_____. 2011b. *Uzbekistan Country Partnership Strategy 2012–2016. Central and West Asia Department: Diversifying Uzbekistan.* Sector Assessment (Summary): Transport and Information and Communication Technology. Manila.

_____. 2012. *An Infrastructure Road Map for Uzbekistan.* Mandaluyong City.

_____. 2016a. ADB to Upgrade Highways, Improve Road Safety in Kashkadarya. News release. 6 December. https://www.adb.org/news/adb-upgrade-highways-improve-road-safety-kashkadarya

_____. 2016b. Kashkadarya Regional Road Project: Sector Assessment (Summary): Transport (Nonurban). https://www.adb.org/sites/default/files/linked-documents/50063-001-ssa.pdf

_____. 2016c. News and Events. Project Results and Case Studies. State-of-the-art Technology Boosts Energy Efficiency, Saves Money at One of Uzbekistan's Largest Plants. 20 October. https://www.adb.org/results/state-art-technology-boosts-energy-efficiency-saves-money-one-uzbekistan-s-largest-plants (accessed 16 July 2018.)

_____. 2016d. *Report and* Recommendation *of the President to the Board of Directors: Proposed Loan to the Republic of Uzbekistan: Kashkadarya Regional Road Project.* Sector Assessment (Summary): Transport (Nonurban). https://www.adb.org/sites/default/files/linked-documents/50063-001-ssa.pdf.

_____. 2016e. *Study for a Power Sector Financing Road Map within Central Asia Regional Economic Cooperation.* Manila.

_____. 2017a. *Report and Recommendation of the President to the Board of Directors: Proposed Loan and Administration of Technical Assistance Grant to the Republic of Uzbekistan: Power Generation Efficiency Improvement Project. Financial Analysis (accessible from the list of linked documents in Appendix 2).* Manila

_____. 2017b. *Report and Recommendation of the President to the Board of Directors: Proposed Loan to the Republic of Uzbekistan for the Central Asia Regional Economic Corridor 2 (Pap–Namangan–Andijan) Railway Electrification Project.* Sector Assessment (Summary): Railway Transport. Manila

_____. 2017c. *Safely Connected: A Regional Road Safety Strategy for CAREC Countries, 2017–2030.* Manila.

_____. 2019. ADB to Help Modernize Uzbekistan's Railway Fleet, Improve Services. News release. 21 May. https://www.adb.org/news/adb-help-modernize-uzbekistans-railway-fleet-improve-services (accessed 29 July 2019).

_____. n.d. Projects. Uzbekistan: Advanced Electricity Metering Phase 4 Project. https://www.adb.org/projects/41340-015/main#project-pds (accessed 16 July 2018).

Azernews. 2017. New Largest HPP to Appear in Uzbekistan. 15 November.

Bellini, E. 2017. Uzbekistan Set to Launch 500 MW Solar Plan. *PV Magazine.* 24 March. https://www.pv-magazine.com/2017/03/24/uzbekistan-set-to-launch-500-mw-solar-plan/ (accessed 16 April 2018).

Business Monitoring International (BMI). 2017. Uzbekistan Oil and Gas Report 2017 Q3 2917. BMI's Industry Report and Forecast Series. May 2017. London.

Center for Economic Research (CER). 2013a. *Mid-Term and Long-Term Perspectives of Transport and Transit in Uzbekistan in the Context of Economic Transformation: Problems and Solutions.* Tashkent.

_____. 2013b. The Transport Sector: Tariff Reductions as a Means to Economic Growth. *Development Focus.* 13. July 2013.

_____. 2015. *Uzbekistan Toward 2030: Transition to the Resource-efficient Growth Model.* UNDP Country Office in Uzbekistan. Tashkent.

Central Asia Regional Economic Cooperation. http://www.carecprogram.org/index.php?page=transport-projects (accessed 19 July 2017 and 14 December 2018).

Copenhagen Centre on Energy Efficiency (CCEE). 2015. *Accelerating Energy Efficiency: Initiatives and Opportunities—Eastern Europe, the Caucasus and Central Asia.* Copenhagen.

Enerdata. 2015. Uzbekistan: Country Energy Report. https://www.enerdata.net/

_____. https://www.enerdata.net/ (accessed 21 July 2018, 6 March 2018, 9 and 14 August 2019).

_____. Global Energy & CO$_2$ Data. https://www.enerdata.net/expertise/energy-co2-data.html (accessed 9 August 2019).

Global Legal Insights. 2017. Uzbekistan Energy 2017. 5th Edition. https://www.globallegalinsights.com/practice-areas/energy/global-legal-insights---energy-5th-ed./uzbekistan

Government of Uzbekistan. 2010. President of Uzbekistan's *Resolution on Rapid Development of Infrastructure of Transport and Communication Construction for 2011–2015*. Tashkent.

_____. 2015a. Law on Rational Use of Energy. Tashkent.

_____. 2015b. Presidential Resolution No 2313, *On the Program of Development and Modernization of Engineering-Communication and Road Transport in the Period 2015–2019*. Tashkent.

_____. 2016. Decree of the President of Uzbekistan No. 2697 from December 23, 2016 on *Investment Program of the Republic of Uzbekistan for 2017*. Tashkent.

_____. 2017. Resolution of the President No. PP–2947 On Program of Measures for Further Development of Hydropower Generation for the Period 2017–2021 dated 2 May 2017. Tashkent.

_____. 2019. Presidential Decree No. PP–4249, On the Strategy for Further Development and Reform of the Power Sector of Uzbekistan. Tashkent.

Grunwald, S. 2012. Central Asia Regional Economic Cooperation Power Sector Master Plan. Final Report. October. Manila: Asian Development Bank. https://www.adb.org/projects/documents/central-asia-regional-economic-cooperation-power-sector-regional-master-plan-tacr

Institute for Global Environmental Strategies (IGES). 2013. PAT Scheme. Energy Outlook for Asia and the Pacific. Presented at the Asian Development Bank, Manila.

International Energy Agency (IEA). 2016. *Key World Energy Statistics 2016*. Paris.

International Road Union. https://www.iru.org/who-we-are/about-mobility/trucks

Karimova, Z. 2018. *The Diplomat. Connecting Asia: Uzbekistan Looks to Capitalize on Central Asia's Transport Potential*. 12 April. https://thediplomat.com/2018/04/connecting-asia-uzbekistan-looks-to-capitalize-on-central-asias-transport-potential/ (accessed 22 May 2018).

Ministry of Finance (MOF) of the Republic of Uzbekistan. Republican Road Fund. https://www.mf.uz/en/component/k2/item/56-respublikanskiy-dorozhnyy-fond.html (accessed 26 March 2018).

_____. Republican Road Fund. https://www.mf.uz/en/open-data/infografika.html (accessed 14 December 2018).

Ministry of Investment and Foreign Trade of the Republic of Uzbekistan. *International Transport Corridors*. https://mft.uz/en/menu/xalqaro-transport-koridorlari (accessed 7 March 2018).

PADECO Co. Ltd. 2014. Road Asset Management System. Final Report. Asian Development Bank Loan No. 2635-UZB as quoted in Asian Development Bank. 2016. Kashkadarya Regional Road Project: Sector Assessment (Summary): Transport (Nonurban). (accessed from https://www.adb.org/sites/default/files/linked-documents/50063-001-ssa.pdf)

State Committee of the Republic of Uzbekistan on Statistics (Uzbekistan Statistics). 2019. News of Uzbekistan. https://www.stat.uz/en/press-center/news-of-uzbekistan/4538-the-main-problem-is-the-lack-of-knowledge-and-skills-of-drivers-and-pedestrians (accessed 29 July 2019)

————. http://stat.uz (accessed 14 December 2018).

Sustainable Development Knowledge Platform. 2013. *Renewable Energy Initiatives in Uzbekistan 2013.* https://sustainabledevelopment.un.org/content/documents/869energyuzbek.pdf

Tashkent Times. 2017. Uzbekistan's Development Strategy for 2017–2021 Has Been Adopted Following Public Consultation. 02 February. http://tashkenttimes.uz/national/541-uzbekistan-s-development-strategy-for-2017-2021-has-been-adopted-following-

United Nations Economic and Social Commission for Asia and the Pacific (UNESCAP). 2003. Asian Highway Handbook. https://www.unescap.org/sites/default/files/Full%20version.pdf (accessed 26 July 2019).

————. 2014. Uzbekistan—Country Profiles. 9 December. https://www.unescap.org/sites/default/files/Uzbekistan_Country-profiles_SYB2014.pdf (accessed 26 July 2019)

————. 2017. Status of the Asian Highway in Member Countries. 26 September. https://www.unescap.org/sites/default/files/Asian%20Highway%20Database-%2025%20September%202017.xls (accessed 26 July 2019)

United Nations Industrial Development Organization (UNIDO). 2009. *Sustainable Energy Regulation and Policymaking for Africa. Module 5: Structure, Composition and Role of an Energy Regulator.* https://www.unido.org/sites/default/files/2009-02/Module5_0.pdf

Uzbekenergo. 2018. Presentation of Uzbekenergo's Strategic Development Plans for 2018–2050. Tashkent.

————. http://www.uzbekenergo.uz/en/ (accessed 17 April 2018, 17 July 2018).

Uzbekistan Airways. About Us. https://www.uzairways.com/en/about-us (accessed 14 December 2018).

Uzbekistan Railways (Uzbekiston Temir Yullari—UTY). http://railway.uz/en/gazhk/statisticheskie–dannye/ (accessed 14 and 15 December 2017).

UzDaily. 2015. Pilot Photovoltaic Power Plant Officially Launched in Namangan Region. 8 April. https://www.uzdaily.com/articles–id–31791.htm (accessed 16 April 2018).

World Bank. 2013. *Uzbekistan Energy/Power Sector Issues Note*. Washington DC.

_____. 2015. *Project Appraisal Document on a Proposed Loan to the Republic of Uzbekistan for a Pap–Angren Railway Project.* Washington D.C.

_____. 2016. *Systematic Country Diagnostic for Uzbekistan*. Washington, DC.

_____. 2019a. Uzbekistan Data on Mortality Caused by Road Traffic Injury (per 100,000 people) as of 10 July 2019. World Development Indicators. https://data.worldbank.org/indicator/SH.STA.TRAF.P5?view=chart (accessed 29 July 2019)

_____. 2019b. Uzbekistan Data on Official Exchange Rate (LCU per US$, period average). World Development Indicators. https://data.worldbank.org/indicator/PA.NUS.FCRF?view=chart (accessed on 29 July 2019).

_____. 2020. *Doing Business 2020: Comparing Business Regulation in 190 Economies*. Washington, DC. https://www.doingbusiness.org/en/data/exploretopics/trading-across-borders (accessed November 2019).

_____. Enterprise Survey. Uzbekistan (2013). http://www.enterprisesurveys.org/data/exploreeconomies/2013/uzbekistan

_____. Logistics Performance Index. https://lpi.worldbank.org/international/global (accessed 14 December 2018).

_____. PPI Project Database. https://ppi.worldbank.org/en/ppi (accessed July 2018).

_____. World Development Indicators. http://databank.worldbank.org/data/reports.aspx?source=world–development–indicators (accessed 21 January 2018, 29 July 2019).

World Economic Forum (WEF). 2014. *World Scenario Series: Scenarios for the South Caucasus and Central Asia*. Geneva.

World Food Programme (WFP) Logistics. 2019. Logistics Capacity Assessments (LCA) tool of the World Food Programme Logistics. https://dlca.logcluster.org/display/public/DLCA/LCA+Homepage (accessed 29 July 2019)

World Health Organization. 2018. Global Status Report on Road Safety 2018. Geneva. https://www.who.int/violence_injury_prevention/road_safety_status/2018/en/ (accessed 29 July 2019).

Yeniseyev, M. 2017. Energy: Uzbekistan Moves toward Developing Renewable Energy Sources. Caravanserai. 13 June. http://central.asia–news.com/en_GB/articles/cnmi_ca/features/2017/06/13/feature–01 (accessed 16 April 2018).

_____. n.d. Caravanserai (website). Tashkent 'Safe City' Project to Unify
Security Information Systems. http://central.asia-news.com/en_GB/
articles/cnmi_ca/features/2017/09/20/feature-01 (accessed 2 March
2018).

Yoshino, N. and U. Abidhadjaev. 2015. *An Impact Evaluation of Investment
in Infrastructure: The Case of the Railway Connection in Uzbekistan.*
ADBI Working Paper Series No. 548. Tokyo: Asian Development
Bank Institute. http://www.adb.org/publications/impact-evaluation-
investment-infrastructure-case-railway-connection-uzbekistan

CHAPTER 3

Unlocking the Potential for Labor Productivity Growth

Malika Shagazatova, Kiyoshi Taniguchi, Jasmin Sibal,
and Bakhrom Mirkasimov

Two and a half decades since its independence, Uzbekistan's human capital development is at a crossroads. Rapid economic restructuring and the lack of a complementary skills development plan has led to large imbalances between the supply and demand for skills, which is especially the case among transition economies (Kupets 2016), and Uzbekistan is no exception to this trend. The Soviet-style education system is grossly misaligned with a growing private sector and is unable to catch up with the economy's rapidly changing structure and labor market needs, technological change, and globalization.

Individual economic performance levels have been linked to the level of human capital, as human capital theory predicts (Kwon 2009; Wu 2013). Hence, improving the various dimensions of human capital can stimulate economic growth in developing countries. This chapter analyzes four distinguishing elements linked to human capital development in Uzbekistan (WEF 2017):

- capacity—the level of formal education as a result of past investments in education;

- development—formal education of the next generation's workforce and continued upgrading and changing of the current workforce's skills;

- deployment—skills application and accumulation among the adult population; and

- know-how—breadth and depth of specialized skills use at work.

The chapter highlights the issues related to human capital development and skills mismatches in Uzbekistan and provides some policy suggestions to address them. Section 3.1 depicts the country's demographic dynamics. Section 3.2 describes the country's social and economic development since its independence; section 3.3 tackles Uzbekistan's state of education, including the gap between the supply of and demand for skills; section 3.4 presents labor market outcomes; section 3.5 discusses labor migration; and section 3.6 concludes by summarizing policy options for closing these gaps.

3.1.   Demographic Dynamics

Uzbekistan's working age population has increased from 11 million in 1990 to almost 19 million in 2017. As the working age population increases and birth rates decline, the total dependency ratio—the ratio of the young (aged 0–14) plus old (over age 65) population to that of working age—has declined substantially, from 82% in 1990 to less than 50% in 2017. At present, Uzbekistan is on the threshold of what can be described as a golden age of economic growth, where labor participation will be at historically high levels and lead to record economic growth, placing Uzbekistan on the road to rapid economic development. A key to this will be the pace at which Uzbekistan engages skilled youth in place of its unskilled older workers. Taking advantage of the demographic dividend can lead not only to growth but also can push Uzbekistan's economy toward upper-middle-income status.

Between 2010 and 2040, an additional 8.9 million labor entrants are expected, increasing Uzbekistan's labor supply to 27.8 million (Figure 3.1). Therefore more jobs are needed to absorb the expected new labor entrants. The additional working age population will reduce the country's dependency ratio to 46.0% by 2040, possibly leading to additional economic growth or a demographic dividend. However, after 2040, the working age population is expected to start shrinking as the share of the older population increases more quickly, leading to a path similar to that experienced by the aging economies in Europe, with a shortage of young workers and a high dependency ratio (World Bank 2016a).

Enabling the expected demographic shift to rapidly expand the consumer base and raise productivity can help fuel faster economic growth by taking full advantage of this window of opportunity. In doing so, it is important to boost the creation of more jobs that match the current supply of skills, and likewise support the development of skills to match future demand. This will help prepare the country as it contends with an aging population and a higher dependency ratio starting in 2040 (World Bank 2016a).

Figure 3.1: Population by Major Age Group and Dependency Ratio, Uzbekistan, 1990–2060

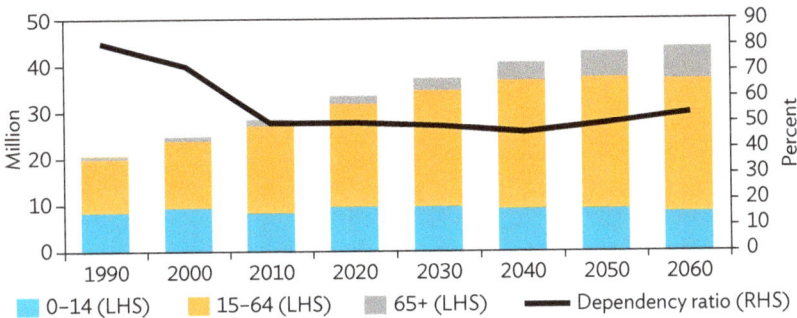

LHS = left-hand scale, RHS = right-hand scale.
Notes: (i) 1990–2010 population based on estimates, 2020–2050 based on medium variant projections; as of 1 July of the year; (ii) dependency ratio is the ratio of dependents—people younger than 15 or older than 64—to the working age population—aged 15–64.
Source: UNDESA, Population Division (2019).

3.2. Economic Structure and Drivers of Economic Growth

Since Uzbekistan's independence, its economy has undergone industrial modernization and structural diversification. After plummeting to record lows subsequent to independence, since 2001 the country's gross domestic product (GDP) per capita has recovered and it grew at an average rate of about 5% per year until 2017 (Figure 3.2). During this period, GDP per capita more than doubled. Growth was mainly driven by natural resource exports, strong global commodity prices, and substantial international remittances (IMF 2015).

As a result, many Uzbek citizens have experienced improved living conditions, albeit unevenly across the country (Uzbekistan Statistics 2017). The share of the population living below the national poverty line was nearly halved, from 27.5% in 2001 (UNDESA 2011) to 11.4% in 2018 (ADB 2019). Uzbekistan's more industrialized areas, including the Fergana Valley, Tashkent city, and Tashkent Region, saw the largest reductions in poverty rates. Improvements in health and education were closely linked to improvements in living conditions.[1]

---

[1] For example, the mortality rate among children under 5 years old declined by 49.2% between 1991 and 2017, although it is still relatively high at 22.5 per 1,000 live births (World Bank. World Development Indicators. http://datatopics.worldbank.org/world development-indicators/ accessed 7 August 2019).

Likewise, income inequality, as measured by the Gini coefficient, narrowed from 0.39 in 2001 to 0.29 in 2013 (World Bank 2016c).[2]

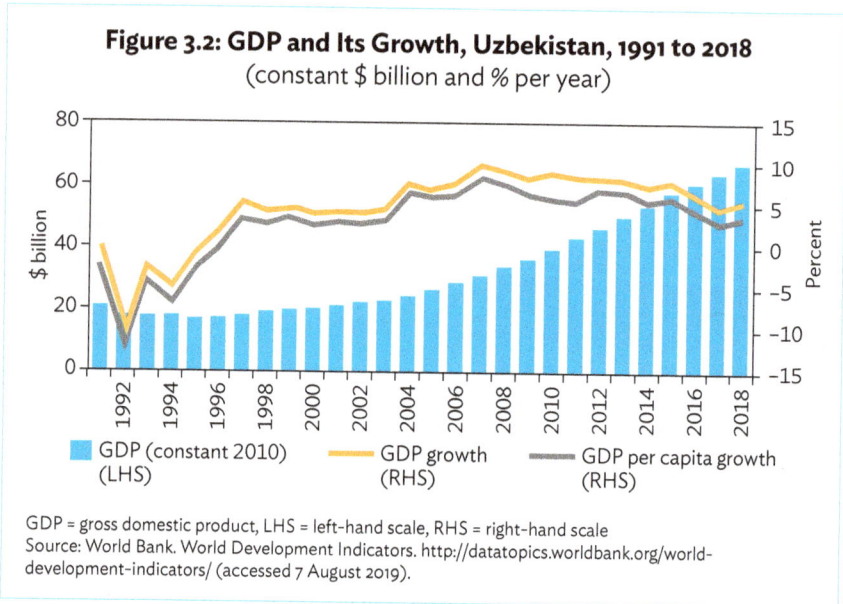

Figure 3.2: GDP and Its Growth, Uzbekistan, 1991 to 2018
(constant $ billion and % per year)

GDP = gross domestic product, LHS = left-hand scale, RHS = right-hand scale
Source: World Bank. World Development Indicators. http://datatopics.worldbank.org/world-development-indicators/ (accessed 7 August 2019).

Historically, natural resource exports have been the country's major source of foreign exchange. However, since 2012, the share of Uzbekistan's natural resource exports has been declining and hence so have rents from those activities as a share of GDP (Figure 3.3). This might suggest the government's policies to diversify the economy have been effective, although declines in commodity prices also contributed in recent years.

The high economic growth reported in the first decade of the 21st century was mostly due to high commodity prices. While growth indicators were strong in 2016–2017, GDP growth decreased from 7.8% in 1960 to 5.3% in 2017, and to 5.2% year-on-year in the first three quarters of 2018. These figures are comparable to estimates by the Asian Development Bank and International Monetary Fund (Holzhacker 2018) and have been accompanied by growth in services, particularly tourism, as well as industrial production and construction.

The reported annual economic growth was approximately 8% on average in the last 10–15 years, but this growth did not lead to an equivalent rise in

---

[2]   However, Sabyrova (2017) argues that Gini indicators should be assessed with "a grain of salt" in Central Asia. One of the arguments is that Gini coefficients are computed based on household surveys and many better-off households refuse to participate in such surveys and/or the data on their real incomes is not publicly available.

Figure 3.3: Share of Natural Resource Rents in GDP, Uzbekistan, 1991–2017
(% of GDP)

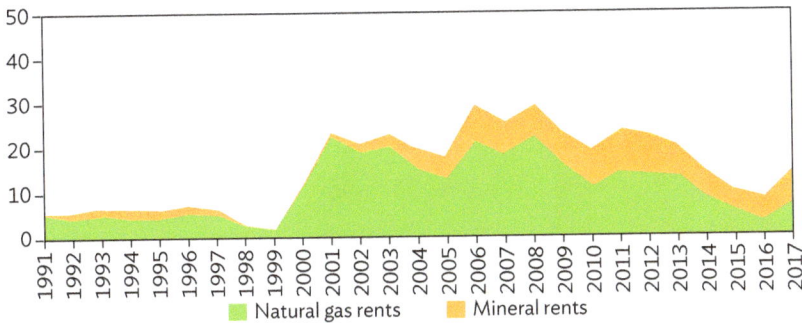

GDP = gross domestic product.
Source: World Bank. World Development Indicators. http://datatopics.worldbank.org/world-development-indicators/ (accessed 7 August 2019).

employment and creation of sustainable jobs, as it was mostly in capital-intensive sectors. Throughout that period the level of migration of workers to the Russian Federation and other regions was substantial, and women's participation in the economy continued to decline while informal employment continued to grow.

In February 2017, the Government of Uzbekistan began to implement a large-scale program of political and economic reforms for 2017–2021. The government identified five priority areas for the country's development:

- public administration reform;
- judiciary system reform, including reforms to strengthen the rule of law and parliamentary reform;
- economic development and liberalization, modernizing agriculture and industry to make their goods and services more competitive;
- social reforms to achieve income growth and better jobs and improved health care, education, and housing; and
- security reforms centered on national stability as well as a balanced foreign policy.

Implementation of the reform program is focusing on achieving Uzbekistan's 2030 goals, namely more than doubling the 2012 per capita gross national income, from $1,700 to over $4,000, thus achieving upper-middle-income status.

The new development strategy commits the government to double Uzbekistan's GDP by 2030 while increasing the share of industry in the economy to 40%. The strategy outlines the key sectors with the greatest potential to drive economic growth until 2021: the textile industry (moving away from cotton production to cotton processing), industrial and building materials production, agricultural and food processing, pharmaceuticals, and tourism (Aliyeva 2017, UZAFI 2017). Eight special programs designed to develop these sectors and 657 investment projects worth approximately $40 billion in total, including projects in the new free economic zones, are envisioned to be implemented. The government is also committed to increasing the share of the service sector and the role of small and medium-sized enterprises (SMEs) in the national economy, as outlined in the strategy.

By 2021, the government plans to achieve full processing of cotton and has already taken steps to increase the volume of cotton fiber processing. For example, 112 contemporary high-tech factories are planned to be opened, rehabilitated, or upgraded, which will enhance the country's potential for exporting processed cotton (aimed at $2.5 billion per year) and generating over 25,000 jobs.

Uzbekistan's public sector alone cannot sustain the demand for jobs, so a well-functioning private sector and relevant investments are necessary to create well-paying, skilled jobs and social security, and to sustain economic growth and improve the welfare of the poorest 40% of households. In the last 18 years, the role of SMEs and entrepreneurs in sustaining Uzbekistan's economic growth has been increasing, from 30% of GDP in 2000 to 53% in 2017, and the SME share of total employment has risen from 10% to 27%.

3.3. Education and Skill Development

Uzbekistan has a high level of human development, ranking 105th of 189 countries. This is partly due to education: the average years of schooling have increased by 2.4 years since 2000 and the expected years of schooling has risen by 0.7 years. The increase is reflected in the country's Human Development Index value growing from 0.595 in 2000 to 0.710 in 2017 (UNDP 2018).

The overall state budget spending on education is one of the highest in the world (approximately 8% of GDP), but the share of this spending on tertiary education is one of the lowest, at 0.4% of GDP.[3] There is also a misalignment

---

[3] In comparator countries, about 20% of the state education budget is spent on tertiary education, and in some, for example Malaysia, as much as 30% is spent on tertiary education (World Bank 2014).

in the spending on tertiary education, salaries for teachers remain low by international standards, while student stipends are generous and almost universal (World Bank 2014).

Major education reforms, including decreasing compulsory schooling from 12 to 11 years, have been initiated in 2018, by presidential decree.[4] Other reforms include strengthening preschool and higher education and improving secondary special and professional education (Table 3.1).

3.3.1. Preschool education

Due to various factors, but mainly financial constraints, coverage of preschool education has been declining in the country, particularly in rural areas. From 2000 to 2017 the number of kindergartens in cities decreased, from 6,704 to 5,128, and (even more profoundly) in the rural areas, where the number of preschool education institutions dropped by almost 50%, from 3,888 to 2,049.

Table 3.1: Education System, Uzbekistan, 2018

	Preschools	Secondary and Specialized Schools and Academic Lyceums	VET and Professional Colleges	Bachelor's Degree	Master's Degree	Doctorate Studies
Duration		11 years	6 months to 2 years	4 years	2 years	
Type	Preschool education	Compulsory basic and secondary education	Vocational education and training	Higher education		Postgraduate education
Student Age	From 3 to 6–7	From 6–7 to 17–18	From 17–18	From 17–18		

VET = vocational education and training.
Source: Authors.

Ensuring accessibility and increasing the preschool coverage to 50% of children by 2021 by expanding the network of preschool educational institutions is a key objective of the Government Development Strategy. In

---

4   Presidential Decree No. PP-2829, On Measures to Further Improve the Activities of Educational Institutions of Secondary Special and Vocational Education, issued on 14 March 2017, was aimed at a systematic solution of problems in lyceum activities. In accordance with the resolution, 4 lyceums will be abolished and 54 lyceums, located far from universities and having low rates of graduates' admission to universities, will be gradually transformed into professional colleges. In total, of the 144 lyceums, 67 will be closed. At the same time, students starting grade 10 will study general education subjects 5 days a week and 1 day will be devoted to professional education (Government of Uzbekistan 2017b).

2017, the Ministry of Preschool Education was established and a road map was approved for developing preschool education in the country.[5]

In 2018, access to preschool education started to improve, with the number of preschool educational institutions increasing, both public and private, and an increased average coverage of children aged 3–7.[6] About 859,000 children were covered by preschool education, which is about 34% of all children aged 3–7. New initiatives to develop public–private partnerships in preschool education are showing positive results.[7]

Preschool education and attendance is positively correlated with employment opportunities. Ajwad et al. (2014) found that in Uzbekistan, attending preschool is often the precursor to attaining higher education, and that it increases the probability of employment and of having better work in the future. While increasing access to preschool education, attention must be paid to teacher training, including development of professional skills and improved teaching standards to ensure that children develop key competencies through the means appropriate for their age.

3.3.2.   Secondary education

With the introduction of the 11-year education system in 2017, textbooks and a curriculum were rapidly created for year 10 students. Schools are obliged to teach using uniform textbooks and curriculum prepared by the Ministry of Public Education, yet the last time these obligations were implemented was a decade ago. Hence the secondary school curricula are outdated and not very relevant, while textbooks for colleges and lyceums have replaced secondary school textbooks. Developing new curricula and textbooks in the languages of instruction is thus urgently required, although it is a time-consuming and costly process. Since the 2017/18 school year, 8.5 million textbooks and teaching aids have been published for grade 10 students, but more are needed. At the same time, 116,000 year-10 teachers have been required to take short teacher training courses to refresh their professional knowledge and enhance their teaching skills.

---

[5]   Government of Uzbekistan (2018a) Presidential Decree No. UP-3651. On Measures for Promoting and Developing Preschool Education System. 5 April 2018.

[6]   In 2018, according to the Ministry of Preschool Education, there were 6,154 preschool educational institutions in the country, of which 5,586 were state and 568 were private preschools (*The Korea Times* 2018).

[7]   The Ministry of Preschool Education engaged a private consulting company for a preschool education institutions inventory exercise. This identified missing entities (branches of the state preschool education institutions) that were not initially counted in reporting. Another public–private partnership initiative is outsourcing of catering services, which is being pilot tested in several regions.

Through its reforms, the government is also attempting to address other urgent issues in secondary education. They include a lack of computer classes and modern laboratory equipment, and of access to high-speed internet in over 90% of schools (Government of Uzbekistan 2018c). The government pays special attention to investments in construction and modernization of secondary schools and has allocated SUM11,662 billion from the 2018 state budget for refurbishing infrastructure and supplying schools with modern equipment.

3.3.3. Vocational education

Uzbekistan adopted the National Program of Personnel Training in 1997, a principal objective of which was to provide skills needed to succeed in a market-based economy. This made 9 years of secondary schooling and 3 years of vocational technical education mandatory and free for all. Under this system, after completing the secondary level, young people aged 15–18 were required to choose between attending academic lyceums or professional colleges. Academic lyceums target young people aiming to enter higher education and therefore focus on academic subjects needed to enter universities. Professional colleges target young people who want to join the labor market with specific technical/professional skills and therefore specialize in technical and vocational training. College graduates are also able to later join the higher education track as the curriculum in professional colleges covers many of the subjects covered in academic lyceums.

The Government of Uzbekistan invested heavily in building new colleges and lyceums, as well as providing them with new textbooks and equipment, including equipment for workshops. From only 47 academic lyceums and 301 professional colleges operating in 2001, about 144 academic lyceums and 1,423 professional colleges were operating as of the 2015/16 academic year. The number of students at the tertiary level has increased as the number of professional colleges and lyceums has more than quadrupled between 2000 and 2015. The compulsory nature of secondary general education and professional college enrollment has also resulted in greater gender parity since 2009.

The National Program of Personnel Training in Uzbekistan has been quite successful in serving its intended objectives (Maclean, Jagannathan, and Sarvi 2013). Guided by coordination councils from professional colleges at regional and national levels, the system benefited from participation of employers' associations and trade unions in its policymaking to ensure it addresses issues of graduates' labor-market entry. At the same time, although the progress of developing the vocational and technical education system in Uzbekistan has been impressive, specifically in infrastructure development and coverage, its quality and governance need improving. An in-depth survey of over 200 enterprises in Uzbekistan indicates that while 80% of firms are satisfied with the skills of university graduates, less than 60% of firms express satisfaction with the skills of technical and vocational education and training (TVET) graduates (World Bank 2014).

With the TVET system moving away from focusing on infrastructure development and increasing the number of students toward improving the content and quality of the curricula it is now important to take advantage of the moment and build on the system's achievements, to ensure that the new programs offered by the TVET system are relevant to the labor market's needs.[8]

Reports by the World Bank (2014) and OECD (2011) highlight the need to modernize the education system and/or upgrade skills to be competitive in the labor market. To monitor and update TVET policies, more data, acquired through tracer studies with graduates, and employer surveys, are needed. Lessons are available from the successful example of rapid TVET expansion in the Republic of Korea (Box 3.1).

3.3.4. Skills development and continued learning and training

Continued vocational education and training (CVET) opportunities are limited in Uzbekistan. Provision of CVET decreased significantly after the dissolution of the Soviet Union when many training centers serving state-owned enterprises closed. With higher demand for skilled workers from the private sector, CVET provision is now predominantly company-based. The public education and training system does not recognize the training delivered by enterprises as it cannot assess the quality of training that does not comply with formal curricula (ETF 2015). The notion of continuing education is largely applied as formal education, mainly for people to upgrade their qualifications

---

[8] The vocational education system is covered by the government's education reforms initiated in 2017. Starting from 2018, professional colleges only accept students who have completed 11 years of secondary education. At the same time, the new initiative was introduced in the compulsory education system: educational and industrial complexes at schools and colleges will provide students in years 10 and 11 with professional training courses in one of 50 specialties. The professional courses will be offered as part of the secondary education curricula with students taking full-day training once a week.

Box 3.1: Use of Data and Research for Tailor-Made Vocational Education and Training Policies: The Republic of Korea's Success

The Republic of Korea has two vocational and education training systems under two Ministries: (i) the Ministry of Education, Science and Technology focuses on pre-employment education, medium-level technician, and technical training; and (ii) the Ministry of Employment and Labor focuses on adults and employed people in various occupational fields, including many vocation training centers, both private and public.

The Republic of Korea collects labor market surveys and uses data and research extensively to tailor-make their vocational and education training policies to current labor market demands, whether they entail skill- or industry-specific needs. The analysis is based on the following data sources (usually collected monthly or quarterly):

- Administrative data are collected from individual schools, colleges, individual training centers, and labor employment offices. One database then connects provinces, municipalities, and schools electronically via the internet. This database is linked to the Korean e-government system.
- Cross-sectional survey data are collected from individuals, households, and companies.
- Longitudinal survey data are collected from students after their graduation. The sampled students are tracked over time to examine the impact of vocational and education training policies on their career path.
- Skills identification survey data are collected from industries (including small and medium-sized enterprises) and provide a useful diagnostic tool to understand skills mismatch.
- Worker supply–demand forecasts are done every 2 years for future education and training planning and manpower needs for specific occupations.

The surveys are usually funded by the government and carried out by private survey companies by phone, e-mail, or in-person interviews.

Source: OECD (2011).

or to requalify. Informal adult education is still in its infancy. In the latest Enterprise Survey (World Bank 2013b), only 11.0% of firms reported providing their permanent staff with any formal training—the lowest share in the whole East and Central Asia region and significantly lower than the regional average of 35.6%.

3.3.5.   Higher education

In 1988/89, there were 43 higher education institutions (HEIs) in Uzbekistan, including 40 specialized institutes and 3 generic universities. About 310,000 students were enrolled in degree courses in the HEIs, of which around 45% were in courses offered in evenings and by correspondence (World Bank 2007). In 2015, the number of HEIs had increased to 72, and the number of full-time students had increased to about 250,000 from about 180,000 in 1988/89. However, higher education offered in evenings and by correspondence courses were gradually phased out by early 2000. In the 2017/18 school year, there were 72 HEIs and about 300,000 students (Figure 3.4). Seven of the institutions are international branch campuses of institutions based elsewhere, with one each affiliated with schools in Italy, the Republic of Korea, Singapore, and the United Kingdom, and three affiliated with schools in the Russian Federation (Box 3.2).

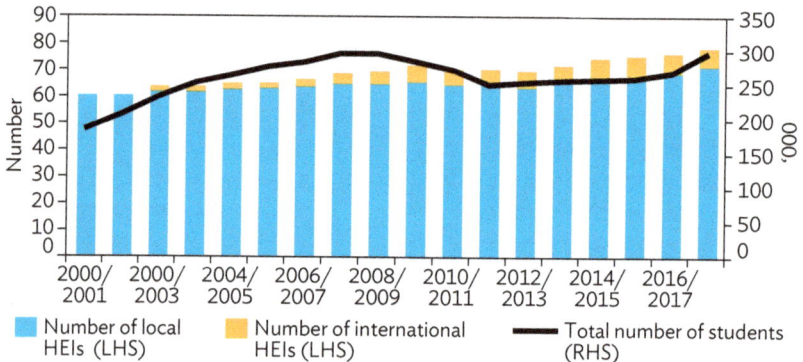

Figure 3.4: Higher Education Institutions and Students, Uzbekistan, 2001–2018

LHS = left-hand scale, HEI = higher education institutions, RHS = right-hand scale.
Source: Uzbekistan Statistics. Higher Educational Institutions. https://stat.uz/en/249-ofytsyalnaia-statystyka-en/sotsyalnaya-sfera-en/obrazovanye-en/4431-special-secondary-professional-educational-institutions-2 (accessed 7 August 2019).

Almost all of Uzbekistan's HEIs have been reorganized to offer 4-year bachelor's degrees, two-year master's degrees, and doctoral programs. The current intake is about 63,000 students and about 25% graduate each year from a university; more than 90% graduate with bachelor's degrees. The majority of students in HEIs are enrolled in full-time courses. The largest number of part-time university students was reported in 2003/04, at

Box 3.2: International Universities in Uzbekistan

The number of international universities in Uzbekistan is growing. These universities do not receive state funding and enroll about 7% of the total undergraduate student intake and 10% of all higher education students. Classes in the international schools are taught exclusively in English or Russian, and entry requirements and all degrees meet international standards. At present, there are seven international universities in Uzbekistan, all in Tashkent.

Westminster International University in Tashkent was the first international university with English as a language of instruction. It was established in 2002 in partnership with the University of Westminster (London, United Kingdom) and the "Umid" Foundation[a] of the President of the Republic of Uzbekistan. In its first year, 120 students were enrolled; and it currently serves close to 3,000 students. The university offers undergraduate courses in business administration, economics (economics with finance), business information systems, and commercial law; and postgraduate courses: master of arts in international business and management, master of law in international commercial law, and a university certificate in special study. In 2016, the university enrolled 14 international students, from Afghanistan, the People's Republic of China, Iran, Israel, Kazakhstan, the Republic of Korea, the Kyrgyz Republic, and Pakistan.

The Management Development Institute of Singapore in Tashkent was established in 2007 in partnership with the Management Development Institute of Singapore. Currently, more than 2,200 students are enrolled in undergraduate courses such as international hospitality and tourism management; accounting; banking and finance; industrial management; and business and economics (management, financial management, and marketing management). The institute is Tashkent's only school that offers a master of business administration (MBA) degree with specialization in finance, marketing, hospitality management, supply chain management, and human resource management.

Turin Polytechnic University in Tashkent was established in 2009 in partnership with Politecnico di Torino (Turin, Italy). It offers technical undergraduate programs in mechanical engineering, energy engineering, industrial and civil engineering and architecture, and information technology and programming in industry. In 2015, the university began offering a master of science in mechanical engineering. The programs collaborate closely with technical industry leaders such as MAN Auto-Uzbekistan, Siemens Uzbekistan, UzCLAAS Agro, Guhring Uzbekistan, Hexagon Metrology, General Motors Uzbekistan, General Motors PowerTrain Uzbekistan, and Samarkand Auto.

Continued on next page

Box 3.2 continued

Inha University in Tashkent was established in 2014 cooperation with Inha University of the Republic of Korea. Inha admits 250 students to its School of Computer and Information Engineering and 80 students are enrolled in its School of Logistics. Inha collaborates closely with local information technology start-ups, industries, and international companies such as Huawei and Samsung. They host events and programs in math and coding.

The Gubkin Russian State University of Oil and Gas branch in Tashkent was established in 2007. The main mission of this branch is to produce highly qualified specialists for Uzbekistan's oil, gas, and petrochemical industry. The curriculum focuses mainly on oil and gas (i.e., geology, exploration, geophysics, and information systems, etc.) and economics and management of the oil and gas industry.

Lomonosov Moscow State University branch in Tashkent was founded in 2006. It trains high-quality specialists in the fields of mathematics, computer science, and psychology.

Plekhanov Russian University of Economics is the oldest international branch institute operating in Uzbekistan. In the 20 years since its foundation, more than 2,800 students have graduated. It offers undergraduate and post-graduate degrees in economics. The university has international students, including from Afghanistan, Armenia, the People's Republic of China, Israel, Kazakhstan, the Kyrgyz Republic, the Russian Federation, Tajikistan, and Turkmenistan.

[a] The Umid Foundation was established in 1997 to help talented Uzbek youth study abroad and was later transformed into the "Iste'dod" Foundation of the President to enhance the professional skills of prospective teachers and scientists.

Source: Authors.

79,800 students in the total cohort of 174,500 higher education students. The number of part-time programs offered was reduced in the following decade, when evening and correspondence courses were phased out, bottoming out in 2014/15 with only 300 part-time students. In 2017/18, however, universities resumed offering part-time programs, and enrollment increased sharply, with over 10,000 students admitted to study part time.

Despite its high primary and secondary enrollment rates, the country's gross enrollment rate remains below 10% at the tertiary level, suggesting that access to higher education remains a challenge for many (Figures 3.5 and 3.6). Student admission quotas and higher education fees are centrally determined in collaboration with ministries, the private sector, and other stakeholders, and universities have little or no say in the matter (World Bank 2014). However, the stakeholders involved have no incentives to provide accurate estimates of the students they need by their specialization areas, and having a centrally determined quota for admissions makes higher education inaccessible (World Bank 2018).

Figure 3.5: Gross Enrollment Rates, Uzbekistan, 2012–2017 (%)

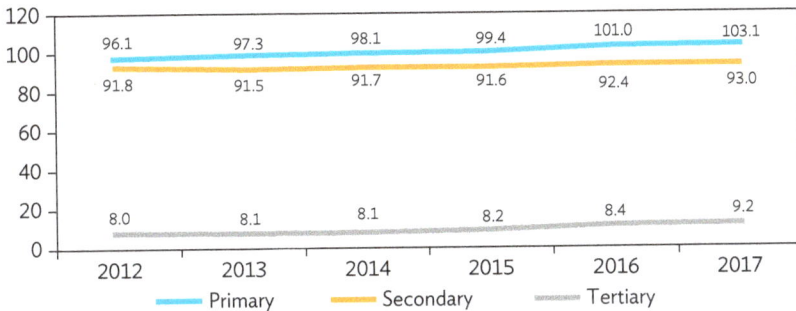

Source: UNESCO Institute of Statistics. http://uis.unesco.org/ (accessed 7 August 2019).

Figure 3.6: Acceptance at Higher Education Institutions, Uzbekistan, 1996–2018

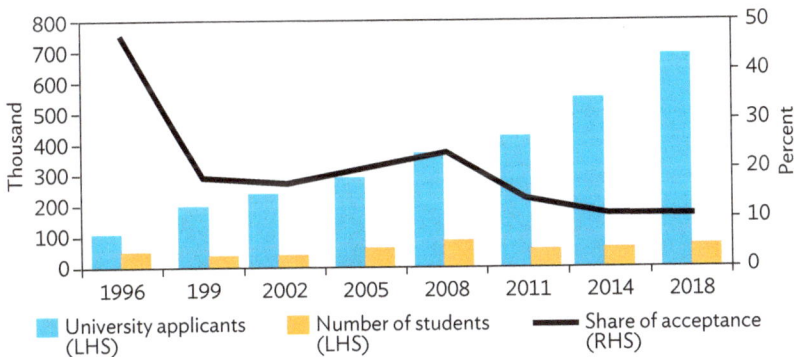

LHS = left-hand scale, RHS = right-hand scale.
Source: Ministry of Higher and Secondary Specialised Education of the Republic of Uzbekistan. Statistics. http://edu.uz/ru/pages/sss (accessed 7 August 2019).

Affordability of tertiary education is another challenge: over 50% of students currently in higher education come from households in the top consumption quintile, which suggests barriers to financial accessibility of higher education (World Bank 2014). Almost 70% of students at the undergraduate level study on a paid-fee basis (through individual contracts),[9] and the share increases to 75% at the graduate level (Bertelsmann Stiftung 2018). From the 2017/18 school year, universities in Uzbekistan are allowed to admit additional students at a higher contract rate called the "super-contract." Additional admission is executed in accordance with the order of applicants who do not have the required number of points (at least 68 points) to be admitted on a regular contract base, and their willingness to pay the higher contract rates. The higher rates are established by the State Commission, depend on the applicant's score, and vary from 1.5 to 10 times the established contract rate depending on the institution. The introduction of the "super contract" raises at least two issues: it undermines the concept of minimum knowledge requirements for university applicants, which negatively affects the quality of higher education; and it will increase the gap in terms of affordability and access to higher education for students from households in the lower consumption quintiles.

With the increased costs of higher education, concerns about quality, and difficulties associated with admission, more students are choosing to study abroad. Since 2012, the number of international students from Uzbekistan has increased from 19,000 to more than 33,000. More than half of the students who studied abroad during 2011–2016 chose the Russian Federation, with Kazakhstan and the Ukraine next (Figure 3.7). This is understandable because Russian is the language of instruction in these countries and proficiency in

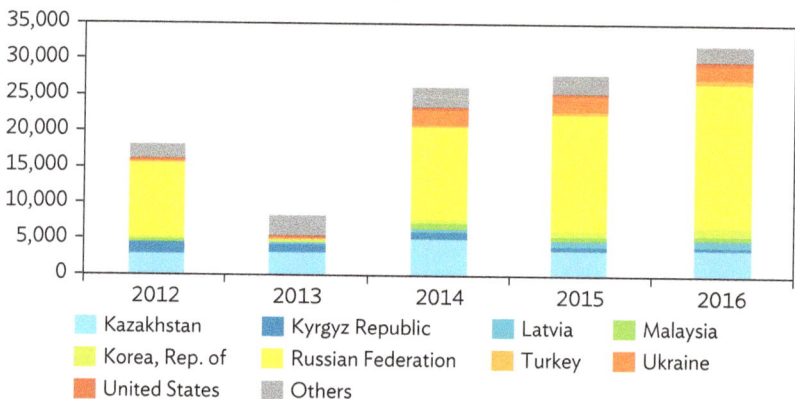

Figure 3.7: International Students from Uzbekistan in Selected Countries, 2012–2016

Note: No data for Malaysia for 2013, Russian Federation for 2013, and Ukraine for 2012 and 2013.
Source: UNESCO Institute of Statistics. http://uis.unesco.org/ (accessed 7 August 2019).

---

9   Students can study at an HEI with fees paid by the government and with 5 years subsequent compulsory employment in the public sector, and through individual contracts that are paid by students' families or private companies.

other languages is not usually required. Also, the cost of education in the three countries is much lower than in other countries, and the possibilities of combining studies with work are greater. More recently, the number of Uzbek students who choose to study in the People's Republic of China and the Republic of Korea has increased significantly.

3.3.6. Gender disparities in tertiary enrollment

Gender parity has been achieved in enrollment rates at primary and secondary levels, but disparities begin at the level of specialized secondary and higher education. The gross enrollment rate of women in tertiary education declined from 11.7% in 1999 to 6.9% in 2017 and the gender parity index fell from 0.8 to 0.6 during the same period (Figure 3.8). There are distinct gender patterns in students' choice of study areas and selection of academic subjects. The overall tendency is that a higher proportion of men than women are receiving higher education and technical training in the fields that are experiencing growth (industry, transport, information and communication technology [ICT], and agriculture), which suggests women may not have equal access to better jobs in the future. Tertiary institutions and the government should consider introducing measures to promote gender balance in the choice of academic subjects and areas of study, such as setting enrollment quotas or providing scholarships, stipends, or other incentives for young women to enter nontraditional educational fields.

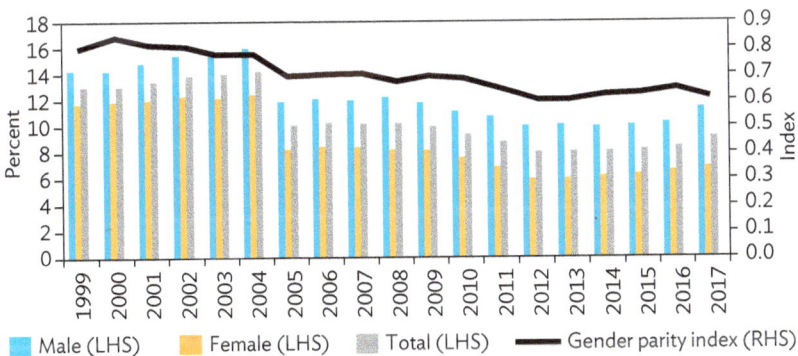

Figure 3.8: Gross Enrollment Rates and Gender Parity Index in Tertiary Education, Uzbekistan, 1999–2017

LHS – left-hand scale, RHS = right-hand scale.
Note: The gender parity index for the gross enrollment ratio in tertiary education is the ratio of women to men enrolled at the tertiary level in public and private schools.
Source: World Bank. World Development Indicators. http://datatopics.worldbank.org/world-development-indicators/ (accessed 7 August 2019).

International evidence suggests that HEIs' degree of autonomy is positively linked to the management of human and financial resources, research performance, and the ability to adapt to a rapidly changing environment (World Bank 2014). The current management structure of HEIs in Uzbekistan, with several levels of guiding and controlling bodies, is rigid and impedes adjustments in the provision of higher education services in response to changing needs of the market economy and to particular skill demands in the labor market.

HEIs in Uzbekistan have very limited freedom in choosing the curriculum: 95% of the HEIs are under the control of the Ministry of Higher and Secondary Special Education, which sets state education standards and thus limits the level of flexibility (World Bank 2014). The lack of freedom results in lower creativity and innovation in teaching, research, and academic processes, and limits students' abilities to gain additional qualifications and have double major programs.

Even with the government as regulator, HEIs should be given greater autonomy in designing programs they offer, more flexibility in curriculum management, more choice of student enrollment numbers, and greater control of their management. Such autonomy is necessary to encourage and support the development of a competitive environment in the higher education sector, with players competing for the best staff, students, and projects that generate extra-budgetary income (e.g., research and development projects, training programs, etc.). Considering the growing mismatch between the demand for and supply of tertiary education services, initiatives to support private sector entry into the sector should be considered, provided the government retains its regulation, supervision, and quality oversight roles.

One-fourth of the universities in the 2019 nonacademic ranking of all HEIs in Uzbekistan are international universities (Table 3.2). This may signal a high demand for education in English as the language of instruction, and for subjects such as ICT and business, finance, management, and economics. The majority of universities listed below do not offer majors in science, technology, engineering, and mathematics (STEM).

Furthermore, analysis of the webometrics ranking of universities by Cybermetrics Lab (Table 3.3) shows that only the National University of Uzbekistan was in the world's top 5,000 universities, indicating that much more can still be done to strengthen the state of higher education in the country and make it globally competitive and recognizable.

Table 3.2: Top Universities Based on UniRank, Uzbekistan, 2019
(of the total 65 universities)

Rank	University
1	Tashkent University of Information Technologies
2	Westminster International University in Tashkent[a]
3	Tashkent Financial Institute
4	Tashkent State Pedagogical University
5	National University of Uzbekistan
6	Inha University in Tashkent[a]
7	University of World Economy and Diplomacy
8	Karakalpak State University
9	Termez State University
10	Namangan Engineering-Technological Institute

[a] International universities.
Notes: The ranking is based on the popularity of the universities' official websites (web-metrix). The current uniRank University Ranking™ is based upon an algorithm including 5 unbiased and independent web metrics extracted from 4 different web intelligence sources: Moz Domain Authority, Alexa Global Rank, SimilarWeb Global Rank, Majestic Referring Domains and Majestic Trust Flow.
Source: uniRank. 2019 Uzbekistani University Ranking. http://www.4icu.org/uz/ (accessed 8 August 2019).

Table 3.3: Webometrics Ranking of Universities in Uzbekistan, 2019

	World Rank	University	Presence Rank	Impact Rank	Openness Rank	Excellence Rank
1	4,071	National University of Uzbekistan	6,868	10,264	4,427	3,455
2	6,647	Tashkent University of Information Technologies Muhammad Al Khwarizmi	2,897	5,922	7,263	6,115
3	7,657	Tashkent Pediatric Medical Institute Nukus Branch	11,360	4,705	8,602	6,115
4	9,606	Karakalpak State University	1,678	8,341	8,602	6,115
5	9,634	Tashkent Medical Academy	1,887	14,014	4,146	6,115
6	10,852	Westminster International University in Tashkent	4,473	12,095	7,263	6,115
7	11,148	Uzbekistan State University of World Languages	9,228	13,020	6,479	6,115
8	11,715	Uzbek State Institute of Arts and Culture Nukus Branch	21,189	9,220	8,602	6,115
9	11,816	Tashkent Financial institute	3,355	13,686	7,208	6,115
10	12,233	Andijan Agricultural Institute	16,404	10,274	8,602	6,115

Note: Cybermetrics Lab is a research group belonging to the Consejo Superior de Investigaciones Científicas, the largest public research body in Spain.
Source: Cybermetrics Lab. Ranking Web of Universities: Uzbekistan. http://www.webometrics.info/en/Asia/Uzbekistan (accessed 8 August 2019).

Low enrollment and little association between private sector employers and universities also negatively impact the economy's capacity for innovation, technology adoption, and value creation. Universities need to be adequately equipped to better address the requirements of a developing economy and reduce the skills and supply–demand mismatch of graduates. The employability of graduates remains a priority of higher education policymakers. While data on employability of graduates are not available on the websites of universities operating in Uzbekistan, findings of the World Bank (2014) show that graduates often do not enter employment related to their area of study. For example, only 57% of graduates working in education pursued this field in university, and graduates of various disciplines fill over 75% of all graduate-level jobs in the construction industry.

While broadening access to education, Uzbekistan should also improve the matching of skills and jobs, a challenge that is common to most developing countries and that requires a responsive approach to education and skills development, involving collaboration between education institutions and the private sector. To meet the challenge requires developing a stronger knowledge base on jobs and skills, and greater adaptability among both entrepreneurs and the youth (Jagannathan 2012).

As Uzbekistan develops, the need for workers with specialized skill sets and training, and with higher education degrees, will be more pronounced. Tertiary education should pay attention to the quality of education and have the right tool set to monitor labor markets and outcomes of higher education programs. Box 3.3 provides some examples of recent initiatives that focus on the interactions between higher education and the labor market in several countries.

3.3.7. Governance of the education sector

No single actor can ensure proper governance of the education sector, because many actors have overlapping responsibilities. Under the current education sector reforms initiated by the government, several significant changes concern the sector's management. Education is now managed by three ministries: the Ministry of Higher and Secondary Specialized Education (formerly the Center for Secondary Special and Vocational Education), the Ministry of Public Education, and the Ministry of Preschool Education.

Currently no single national qualification framework in Uzbekistan is analogous to the European understanding of the notion. Various systems potentially

Box 3.3: Higher Education Outcomes and Labor Market Relevance

European Union: In 2017, the European Union commissioned a study on the relevance of higher education, focusing on three objectives for the teaching function of higher education: personal development, sustainable employment of graduates, and active citizenship. The report is Promoting the Relevance of Higher Education: Trends, Approaches and Policy Levers.

Canada: The Conference Board of Canada (with support from the Government of Canada, provincial and territorial governments, higher education institutions, and business partners) launched the Centre for Skills and Post-Secondary Education. This is a 5-year initiative that examines the advanced skills and education challenges facing Canada. The Centre published Aligning Skill Development to Labor Market Needs in May 2016.

Poland: In 2014, the National Centre for Research and Development conducted research on the competencies and qualifications needed for the labor market. The final report, The Analysis of Key Competencies and Qualifications for Increasing the Chances of University Graduates in the Labour Market, examines the types of skills that lead to strong labor market outcomes, and provides recommendations for how to better align the skills developed in Polish higher education with the needs of employers.

New Zealand: The New Zealand Productivity Commission has recently undertaken an inquiry into new models of tertiary education. The inquiry focuses on how various trends, including changing skills demand, may drive change in business models and delivery models in the tertiary education sector. It is examining how new models of higher education can deliver the skills required by graduates in the 21st century.

Sources: OECD (2017) and Vossensteyn et al. (2018).

serve that role (ETF 2015). Instead, Uzbekistan has separate sets of centrally regulated standards, the State Educational Standards among them, and qualifications for individual specialties and education areas. The introduction of a single framework would make education in Uzbekistan comparable to that of other countries, and would simplify the process of developing and modifying the qualifications structure. Although the majority of State Educational Standards are openly accessible in Uzbek, having them available in English and Russian would allow for easier international comparison and better regional integration, such as developing and enhancing university exchanges and credit transfer processes.

With technical support, and credit from the World Bank worth $42.2 million, the government is now implementing its 2017–2021 policy program for improving the country's higher education system (Box 3.4). The program aims to gradually increase student intake and raise the quality of education based on international benchmarks.[10] It includes long-term higher education reform plans such as sending faculty members to PhD and research training abroad through the Iste'dod Fund, and bringing prominent scientists from abroad for scholarly exchange and professional development.

Box 3.4: Uzbekistan's Higher Education Policy for 2017–2021

Raising the quality of education and making it more inclusive is crucial for developing relevant skills. Uzbekistan's Higher Education Policy for 2017–2021 focuses on pursuing measures that will upgrade the country's higher education system, particularly the system's managerial capacity and its relevance to the labor market. The policy is implemented under the Ministry of Higher and Secondary Special Education and its main directions are as follows:

- forging close partnerships between each higher education institution (HEI) and leading international scientific and educational institutions, and implementing advanced pedagogical technologies, educational programs and materials, and attracting highly qualified international scholars into teaching and research activities;
- establishing target parameters for developing human resources with higher education, and optimizing course specializations in tertiary education, bearing in mind the development needs of industries, regions, and economic sectors;
- developing and using modern teaching aids in higher education;
- ensuring a steady growth in the level and quality of skills of academic staff, including staff professional training and further education abroad of academic staff at master's and PhD levels;
- strengthening the scientific and research potential of HEIs and increasing the research capacity of faculty, involving talented students in the research process;
- upgrading university buildings, science laboratories, and sports facilities and equipping university facilities with modern educational instruments and research tools;
- equipping the HEIs with modern information and communication technology and expanding the access of students, faculty, and young researchers to the global educational resources, databases, electronic journals, and books; and
- increasing higher education admission rates gradually to 18% by 2021.

Sources: UzReport. 2017. The President approved measures to develop the system of higher education. 21 April. http://news.uzreport.uz/news_3_r_150952.html (accessed 25 November 2018); and World Bank (2016c).

---

[10]   For more information, see Gazeta.uz (2017a).

In September 2018, the Strategy for Innovative Development of the country for 2019–2021 and the road map for its implementation was approved by a Presidential Decree. The strategy's main goal is "the development of human capital as the main factor determining the level of a country's competitiveness in the global market and its innovative progress." Among the strategy's main objectives is that by 2030 Uzbekistan will be among the top 50 countries according to the Global Innovation Index rating. Other objectives include an improved quality and coverage of education at all levels and the development of the system of continuing education. Measures will also be taken to strengthen the scientific potential and effectiveness of research and development. Effective mechanisms will be created for integrating education, science, and entrepreneurship for the widespread introduction of the results of research and development. Increased investment of public and private funds in innovation, research, development, and technological work is planned.

3.4. Employment Structure and Job Quality

As in all other countries, Uzbekistan is being affected by technological change that is displacing unskilled labor with skilled workers and capital. The growth in skilled labor demand and a rise in labor productivity is a global phenomenon, and countries that adopt global technology will face the challenge of a low employment intensity of economic growth. On a business-as-usual scenario, these trends may lead to higher unemployment of basic labor and an increased wage premium for skilled labor, which will jeopardize inclusive growth if focused policies that address both the demand and supply sides of the labor market are not adopted.

The structure of employment is moving toward greater industry and services shares. In the 1990s, agriculture, particularly cotton production, constituted the largest share of GDP—over 30%. Since then, the government has adopted an industrialization strategy that facilitated transformation and a shift toward a market-based economy while ensuring self-sufficiency in energy and food. Between 1991 and 2018, the shares of modern industry and services in the country's output and employment expanded, while the share of agriculture fell (Figure 3.9). The robust employment growth in services outpaced the growth in both industry and agriculture, leading to services accounting for the top share of employment. This is typical of a growing open economy, especially a resource-rich one (see, e.g., Anderson and Ponnusamy 2018).

The biggest employer in the Uzbek economy is thus now the service sector, which employs 36% of the labor force and accounted for 32% of Uzbekistan's GDP in 2018. The sector now accounts for almost 80% of all newly created jobs in the country. Also, the structure of the service sector is continually changing. For example, due to the tourism development program, the share of accommodation and food services in total employment increased from 1.1% in 2010 to 3.3% in 2016. Judging by these trends, a large proportion of jobs created in the labor market in the near future will be in services. A large number of the newly created jobs will require cognitive and noncognitive skills, which will benefit graduates who follow education paths in the appropriate fields.[11]

Figure 3.9 shows that while the industry sector adds more value to the economy than the agriculture sector, the latter still accounts for more employment. This implies higher output per worker in industry than in farming. Thus, the industry sector can play an important role in catalyzing growth, generating more high-value jobs, and employing more skilled workers. Built on this potential, the government's 2018 Government Employment Promotion Program focuses on generating more jobs in industry (Box 3.5).

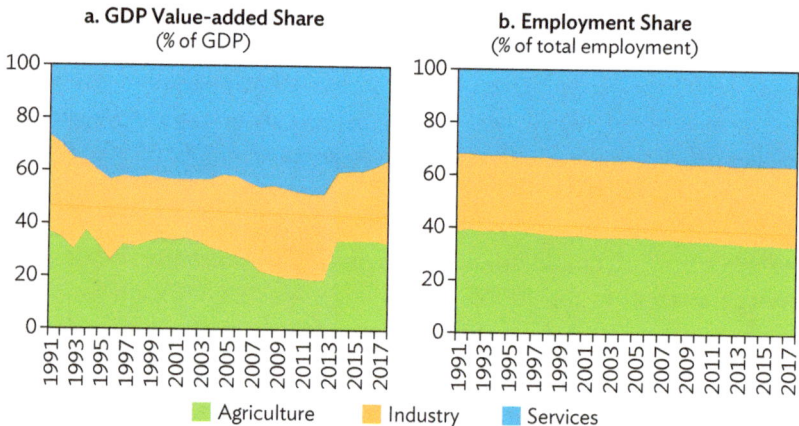

Figure 3.9: Sectoral Shares of GDP and Employment, Uzbekistan, 1991–2018

GDP = gross domestic product
Source: World Bank. World Development Indicators. http://datatopics.worldbank.org/world-development-indicators/ (accessed 7 August 2019).

---

[11] A separate strand of the literature argues that noncognitive skills are particularly valued in certain sectors (e.g. services). In addition, some recent evidence in the context of high-income countries suggests that employers value noncognitive abilities more than cognitive ability or independent thought (Ajwad et al. 2014).

The government's reform program continues to focus on liberalizing the economy and contains relevant socioeconomic policies—such as growth of the private sector and a reduced role of state enterprises in rural production, manufacturing, trade, and finance. The aim is to ensure a more favorable investment and business climate. Employment in the nonstate sector has been increasing continually, from 77.2% in 2005 to 82.7% in 2017 (Figure 3.10). Industry and construction show the largest growth in employment, by 3% in 2017 compared to 2015. At the same time, growth in employment in agriculture, forestry, and fisheries (2.3%) is higher than that in services (1.5%). The share of people employed in SMEs increased in 2017 to 78.3% from 77.9% in 2015 (Uzbekistan Statistics 2018).

Figure 3.10: Shares of Employment in State and Nonstate Sectors, Uzbekistan, 2005–2017

(%)

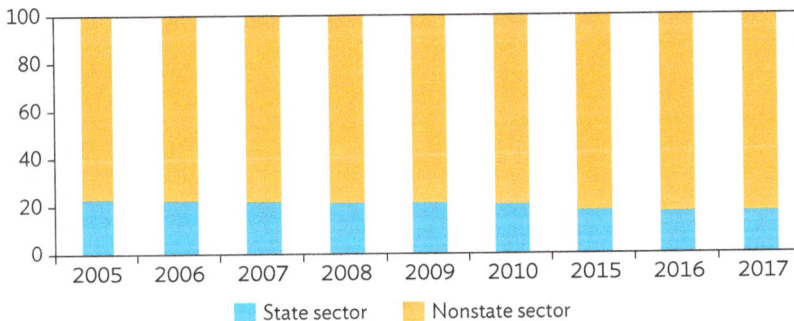

Sources: Based on data from Uzbekistan Statistics (2018) and CER and UNDP (2013).

The sectoral distribution of SMEs is unchanged since 2003. About 60% of small businesses work in services and the rest are in agriculture, industry, and construction. There have been no overall changes in the employment structure of SMEs by sector. Agriculture, industry, and construction employ about 60% of the total small business labor force, and SMEs in the service sector provide jobs to the remaining 40%.

Participation of women in the labor force remains low. Despite the large economic adjustments and ongoing reforms, labor participation rates in Uzbekistan are still relatively low, and the female labor participation rate is a particular challenge. With only a slight improvement since independence, Uzbekistan's labor force participation, at 69.2% in 2018, remains below the

71.2% average for European and Central Asian countries.[12] The gap between the labor force participation rates of males and females has yet to be narrowed. On the contrary, from 1995 to 2018 the gap widened by almost 2 percentage points to 24.6 percentage points, reflecting the lack of improvement in the labor participation rate among females and the slight improvement among males during the period (Figure 3.11). An important factor that impacts women's labor force participation is the low coverage of kindergartens and nurseries, which prevents women from relinquishing time spent on childcare.

Box 3.5: Government Employment Promotion Program for 2018

Employment especially among young people is the most serious problem in Uzbekistan, according to data from a sociological survey by the Izhtimoiy Fikr Center (*Regnum.ru* 2018). The government's Employment Promotion Program for 2018 gives priority to job creation across all sectors. The development of small businesses and private enterprises, as well as support for craftsmanship, remains very important. The Employment Promotion Program aims to boost employment through mobilizing resources to create more (*Gazeta.uz* 2018)

- permanent jobs (346,000 jobs) by implementing regional road maps and investment projects and stimulating the growth of private enterprises; and
- seasonal and temporary jobs (169,500 jobs) in agriculture and construction, including public works and overseas employment.

Jobs in permanent workplaces are to be created by setting up new capacities and expanding existing ones including those in industry, services, agriculture, rural construction, and infrastructure. Seasonal and temporary employment through public works programs in agriculture include jobs in (i) agricultural processing, crop growing and harvesting, silk-worm breeding, and construction of housing and other infrastructure; and (ii) placements abroad through the Agency for External Labor Migration. Public works will mainly benefit individuals from socially vulnerable sectors of the population.

To achieve this, the Employment Promotion Program plans to (i) establish a regional road map of jobs; (ii) use modern information technology and programs to make job search easier (e.g., college.mehnat.uz); and (iii) conduct on-site and online job fairs in different cities and districts together with potential employers, businesses, and organizations.

Sources: *Gazeta.uz* (2018) and *Regnum.ru* (2018).

---

[12] World Bank. World Development Indicators. http://datatopics.worldbank.org/world-development-indicators/ (accessed 7 August 2019).

Figure 3.11: Labor Force Total and Participation Rate, Uzbekistan
(ages 15–64, and 15–24 modeled ILO estimate)

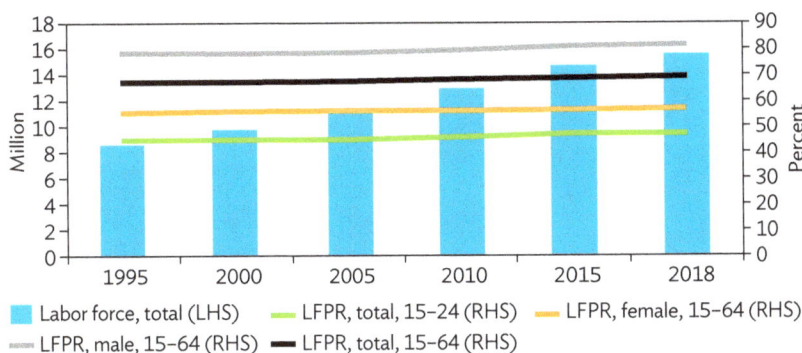

Labor force, total (LHS) ■   — LFPR, total, 15–24 (RHS)   — LFPR, female, 15–64 (RHS)
— LFPR, male, 15–64 (RHS)   — LFPR, total, 15–64 (RHS)

ILO = International Labour Organization, LFPR = labor force participation rate, LHS = left-hand scale, RHS = right-hand scale.
Source: World Bank. World Development Indicators. http://datatopics.worldbank.org/world-development-indicators/ (accessed 7 August 2019).

As expected, labor force participation rates are higher among people with university degrees (77.5%) and secondary special and/or technical degrees (68.4%) than those with either a secondary general education (57.6%) or less (48.3%). The gap is more pronounced among women. Men with less than secondary education have a broadly similar participation rate (79.9%) to men with tertiary education (83.2%). In contrast, women holding a university degree are nearly three times more likely to participate in the labor market (69.4%) than are women with less than secondary education (25.1%).

After controlling for individual and family characteristics, labor force participation is positively related with cognitive skills (as proxied by memory literacy scores) but inversely related to having an overseas migrant worker in the family (Table 3.4).[13] While workers with high cognitive skills are more likely to work, those with a migrant family member working abroad are less likely to work. In addition, the level of cognitive skills has a differential effect on labor supply decisions of members of migrant and nonmigrant households. Females and divorcees are also less likely to work. Women divorcees are most likely to return to their parents' home and stay supported by their families' income. Household-level analysis in 2013 validates that being female is negatively associated with the probability of being in the labor force (Table 3.4).

---

[13] Information in this paragraph is from World Bank (2013a). Labor force participation is based on the results of a probit model fitted over the Central Asia's Labor and Skills Survey (CALISS) 2013 data. The CALISS collects data from a nationally representative household and individual survey on migration, remittances, and cognitive skills conducted in Uzbekistan by the World Bank and the German Society for International Cooperation (GIZ) in 2013.

Table 3.4: Factors Affecting Labor Force Participation, Aged 25–55, 2013

Variables	Probit Estimates	Marginal Effects
female	-0.960[a]	-0.322[a]
	(0.120)	(0.0364)
migrant_hh	-0.235[b]	-0.0787[b]
	(0.104)	(0.0345)
rural	0.458[a]	0.153[a]
	(0.0985)	(0.0320)
MemoryRaw	0.0715[a]	0.0240[a]
	(0.0234)	(0.00773)
LiteracyRaw	-0.0401	-0.0134
	(0.0291)	(0.00972)
NumeracyRaw	0.0270	0.00903
	(0.0348)	(0.0117)
DweckScore	-0.0313	-0.0105
	(0.0531)	(0.0178)
age30_34	-0.0370	-0.0124
	(0.147)	(0.0494)
age35_39	0.110	0.0367
	(0.171)	(0.0574)
age40_44	0.350[b]	0.117[b]
	(0.178)	(0.0592)
age45_49	0.380[b]	0.127[b]
	(0.172)	(0.0571)
age50_55	0.115	0.0386
	(0.170)	(0.0570)
hh_head	0.0289	0.00968
	(0.142)	(0.0475)
hh_child6	0.129[c]	0.0433[c]
	(0.0749)	(0.0250)
hh_child6_18	0.0830	0.0278
	(0.0563)	(0.0188)
hh_elderly65	0.0171	0.00573
	(0.0792)	(0.0265)
hhsize	-0.0559	-0.0187[c]
	(0.0340)	(0.0114)
divorced	-0.473[a]	-0.158[a]
	(0.162)	(0.0536)
widow	-0.110	-0.0368
	(0.245)	(0.0820)
uzbek	0.359[a]	0.120[a]
	(0.138)	(0.0459)
Fergana Valley	-0.333[a]	-0.112[a]
	(0.123)	(0.0408)
CentralRegion	-0.838[a]	-0.281[a]
	(0.144)	(0.0458)
SouthRegion	-0.0305	-0.0102
	(0.131)	(0.0437)
Observations	965	965

[a] p<0.01, [b] p<0.05, [c] p<0.1
Notes: Dependent variable: Worked in last 14 days (labor force participation); standard errors in parentheses.
Source: Author's calculations based on World Bank (2013b).

Men dominate high-paying jobs. The relatively low female participation rate is a reflection of the fact that many women are involved in unpaid home and care work, and are discouraged from looking for work outside the home (Ajwad et al. 2014).[14] Female workers who are in the labor market are mostly concentrated in professional and service occupations—although proportionately slightly less women than men are in managerial positions (including legislators and senior officials). Even in sectors where women constitute the majority of employees, the proportion of women in managerial positions is insignificant—the gender gap in the education sector is illustrative: 70% of schoolteachers, but only 36% of principals are female. Table 3.5 shows the occupational and sectoral distribution of jobs by gender. In technical fields, such as technicians and plant and machine operators, men are the majority. Almost one-third of employed women are in the service sector followed by 20% in agriculture. Women still work predominantly in low-paid sectors such as education, health, and agriculture, while men dominate in better-paying jobs and sectors (such as construction, manufacturing, transport and logistics, and information and communication).

The share of people engaged in high-tech industries and science is trivial. Only 1.5% of all employed people are in high-tech industries[15] and science (CER and UNDP 2013), thus inhibiting the activation of innovative factors of economic growth. The current employment policy model does not create the prerequisites for the emergence of high-quality outputs: growth of labor productivity and the flow of labor resources into the sectors and industries that have a good potential to become new drivers of economic growth.

Informal employment remains substantial, posing a key challenge to both firms and workers. Informal employment rates vary across a number of factors but the informally employed are usually males, rural residents, and less educated, and they work mostly in agriculture, construction, retail, and transport.

In 2016, an estimated 21.1%[16] of the total employed population (18–64 years old) was engaged in informal employment (Table 3.6), which shows a positive (declining) trend from 42% in 2013 and 38% in 2009. However, the structure and gender-related tendencies of informal employment remain the same, with

---

[14] The ILO defines discouraged workers as persons who are not in the labor force and, although they are available to work, are no longer seeking employment because they do not believe they will find any.

[15] High-tech industries include mechanical engineering, the pharmaceutical and microbiology industry, and information technology services.

[16] There are no reliable estimates of the size of the informal sector, but it is believed to be large. The National Scientific Center for Employment provides a higher estimation of informality, at 59.8% of the working age population based on a sociological study conducted in 2018 (Tashkenttimes.uz 2018).

Table 3.5: Occupational and Sectoral Distribution by Gender, Aged 25–55, Uzbekistan, 2013

(%)

Occupation and Industry	Men	Women
Occupation Group		
Professionals	16.8	22.6
Unskilled workers	18.2	11.6
Service workers, shop or market sales workers	9.7	12.6
Skilled agricultural and fishery workers	11.9	9.7
Technicians and associate professionals	4.9	1.9
Craft and related trades	4.4	2.4
Armed forces	2.4	0.2
Clerks	1.1	1.3
Plant and machine operators and assemblers	1.3	0.3
Legislators, senior officials and managers	0.7	0.7
None	7.4	21.3
Don't know / missing	21.1	15.4
Number of observations	1,750	1,735
Industry*		
Agriculture	18.2	19.4
Industry	8.0	2.7
Construction	25.7	0.6
Services	37.9	30.1
Don't know / missing	10.2	47.7
Number of observations	1,750	1,735

Note: Agriculture includes fishing; industry includes mining, manufacturing, energy, and water; services include trade and repair, hotels and restaurants, transport and communications, finance, public administration, education, health and social work, utilities, social and personal services, private households with employed persons, and extra-territorial organizations.
Source: Author's calculations based on World Bank (2013a).

men being employed informally more often than women in general (26.2% of men and 12.5% of women age 18–64), and especially in seasonal work (Table 3.6). At the same time, more women have informalities in employment within the permanent jobs. The shortage of jobs in the formal sector is one of the main causes of informal employment.

Informal jobs usually offer lower wages and imply lower labor productivity than formal jobs, and are often temporary and not covered with employment benefits. Informal workers also usually have fewer opportunities for training, have greater exposure to risks, and are more vulnerable to labor exploitation (e.g., receiving wages below the minimum and working longer hours). For employees in the informal sector, capacity development is not available or extremely limited.

Table 3.6: Formal and Informal Employment, Uzbekistan, 2016
(%)

	Men	Women	Total
Employed as permanent employees			
Formal	69.4	85.2	75.2
Informal	10.0	6.9	8.9
Employed as part-time employees			
Formal	2.5	1.0	1.9
Informal	1.2	0.7	1.0
Employed in seasonal jobs			
Formal	1.9	1.3	1.7
Informal	8.1	1.3	5.6
Casual/daily workers	5.8	3.0	4.7
Others	1.2	0.7	1.0
Total			
Informally employed	26.2	12.5	21.1

Note: Informal employment is defined as working without a formal contract or unpaid family work.
Sources: CER and UNDP (2018), based on the data from the European Bank for Reconstruction and Development and World Bank survey, Life in Transition III (EBRD and World Bank 2016)

Factors contributing to the high level of informal employment in Uzbekistan include the low level of education among the population;[17] a complex and uncertain tax system; and a high tax burden on larger businesses, which discourages entrepreneurs from expanding and growing their businesses. High personal income tax rates and a single social payment lead to underreporting of wages, a cash-based payment, and double accounting.

A high incidence of informality usually indicates that other factors hinder firm entry, growth, and exit in the formal private sector and is a symptom of challenges to both firms and workers. The Enterprise Surveys (World Bank 2013b) show that the top business environment obstacles firms in Uzbekistan face are electricity issues, followed by practices of competitors in the informal sector, and then tax rates (Figure 3.12). These findings are robust regardless of firm size. A flourishing informal sector is a major obstacle for starting a new business in the formal sector given the perceived unfair competition brought about by the presence of informal firms. Informal enterprises have an average operating life of 2 years without a formal registration.

---

[17] The higher the taxpayer's level of education, the higher the tax literacy, and therefore the higher the incentive to work formally. For example in 2016, informal employment among people with higher education was one-third the level of people with only secondary education (CER and UNDP 2018).

Informality and time-related underemployment is especially common among young people. Almost half (43%) of youth aged 15–24 in Uzbekistan and almost 41% of people aged 25–34 are employed informally, and 85% of young people are underemployed. The data on the relation between informal employment and level of education suggest a strong correlation between the level of education and type of employment. In 2016, only 7.5% of the people with higher education were employed informally, and informal employment of people with higher education was 3 times lower than among those with secondary and professional education (CER and UNDP 2018).

Figure 3.12: Major or Severe Obstacles to Operations as Reported by Businesses, Uzbekistan, 2013
(%)

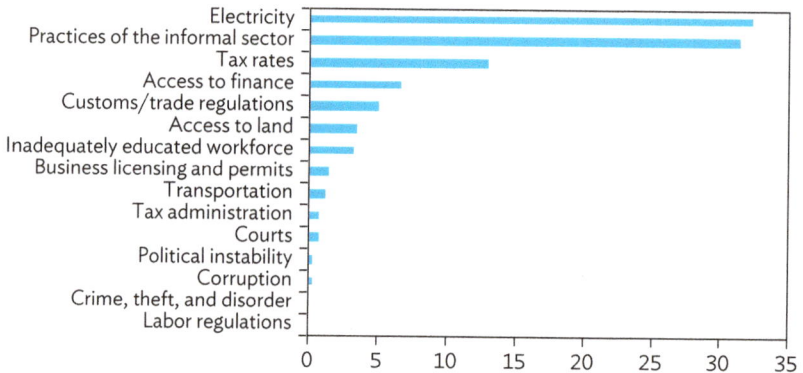

Source: World Bank (2013b).

There is a mismatch between skills supply and employment opportunities. Addressing the current and future mismatch of skills demand and supply in Uzbekistan is critical to accelerating labor productivity and long-term economic growth. Currently, education and skills are not linked to market needs. This is especially true of the industry sector, where 1 in every 2 firms encounters difficulty filling jobs; skills shortage is also prevalent in construction, transport and communications, and other services (Figure 3.13). The academic qualifications of graduates, especially those from vocational institutions, do not match the needs of available jobs.

The status of competition in the job market is characterized by the Head Hunter Index, which measures the shortage of specialists in the labor market. The index is calculated as the ratio of the number of candidates (proxied by resumes submitted) to the number of open positions for a certain period of time. Values from 1 to 4 (i.e., 1–4 resumes submitted per job) usually illustrate normal market competition, values of 5–6 indicate increased competition and a possible oversupply of candidates, and values of more than 6 indicate an oversupply to severe oversupply of workers.

Data show that competition has significantly increased among young specialists in the beginning of their career and for jobs in the mining and extraction sectors, as well as among top management specialists and for public sector jobs (Figure 3.14). The Head Hunter Index shows that the highest demand for labor in 2018 was for specialists in sales (40% of the total number of vacancies), medicine and pharmaceuticals (25%), and ICT (10%). In spite of the initiatives in new production capacities, the demand for technical specialists remains low (5.4%).

Figure 3.13: Share of Firms Reporting Difficulty Hiring Sufficient Qualified Specialists with Higher Education and Training, Uzbekistan, 2016
(%)

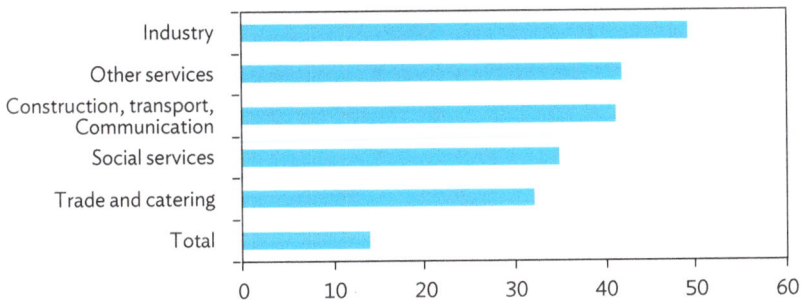

Source: World Bank (2016d).

Figure 3.14: Head Hunter Index, Uzbekistan, 2017 and 2018

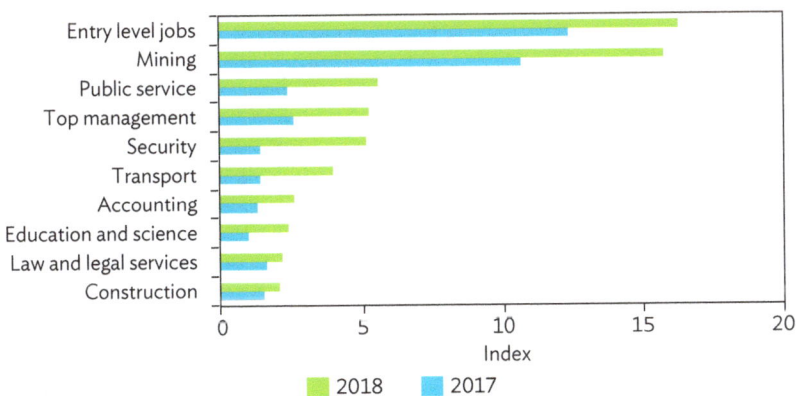

Source: *Infocom.uz* (2018).

Many employers find that many workers lack important cognitive skills, such as languages, i.e., proficiency in English and Russian, and analytical thinking, and noncognitive skills, including accountability, self-motivation, and creativity (World Bank 2014). While foundation skills are learned at the early stages of life, these transferable cognitive and noncognitive skills are mostly developed at the secondary and post-secondary levels, both in and outside of school.

Labor force discouragement is a barrier to worker productivity. The International Labour Organization defines "discouraged" workers as those who are unemployed but not seeking work due to specific labor market-related reasons, such as the belief that no work is available to or suitable for them given their qualifications, or lack of information on where to look for work (ILO 2014 and 2016). Labor discouragement is highest among male workers 20–24 and 55–59 years old, and among females 16–24 years old (Figure 3.15). The presence of discouraged workers indicates that, in addition to a lack of jobs in the market, the matching of skills with jobs is also weak due to a lack of or an inefficient labor market information system (i.e., an "information failure"). In the current online labor market information systems, which are run by private job agencies (e.g., uzjobs.com and olx.uz) or state job agencies (e.g., mehnat. uz), job advertisements are often limited or not updated regularly.

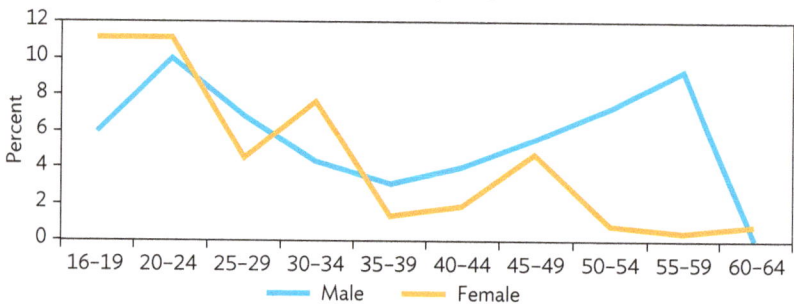

Figure 3.15: Labor Force Discouragement Across Age Groups, Uzbekistan, 2013

Note: The graph depicts the share of unemployed individuals (people looking for work) and discouraged individuals (people who are unemployed but not seeking work due to a specific labor market-related reason) in the total population by age cohort.
Source: World Bank and GIZ (2013).

Another cause of labor discouragement is the lack of formal skills training in schools and in the workplace, which leads to perceptions of skill inadequacy. Causes of labor discouragement, especially among women, include their disadvantaged situation in the labor market and the need to take care of young and old family members, which is not a common practice for men (Ajwad et al. 2014).

3.5. Labor Migration and Remittances

Economic difficulties have driven migration. More than 2 million Uzbeks reside abroad, mostly in the Russian Federation, and chiefly to seek better employment opportunities. A typical migrant is 31 years old, comes from a rural area, is male, married,[18] and has completed at least secondary education (Table 3.7).

Table 3.7: Profile of a Typical Migrant, Uzbekistan, 2013

Characteristic	Mean/Share
Age (mean)	30.84
Male (%)	89.8
Married (%)	62.9
Education completed	
Basic or less (%)	9.8
Secondary (%)	85.0
University (%)	5.2
From a rural area (%)	74.6
Sample size	645

Note: Only migrants aged 15 and over are considered.
Source: Author's calculations based on World Bank (2013b).

The Russian Federation hosts over half of the migrants—about 1.15 million—while Kazakhstan and Ukraine host a fourth of them—about 0.5 million migrants (Figure 3.16).[19] The majority of Uzbek migrants stay in these countries because of a liberal visa regime; a common language; and/or established business, family, and other connections (Maksakova 2006).[20]

As of 2016, Uzbeks obtained more than half of the work permits issued by the Commonwealth of Independent States to migrant workers (Figure 3.17). A large number of migrant workers are without formal work contracts and/or social insurance. The pattern of migration has become less seasonal, and the usual duration is increasingly becoming long term.

---

[18] Although a large majority of migrant workers are male, some studies have pointed to the gradual feminization of migration (e.g., Ahunov et al. 2015).

[19] With 1.15 million Uzbek citizens living in the Russian Federation in 2017, Uzbeks are the third-largest minority group in the Russian Federation. About 1 in 10 migrants in the Russian Federation is an Uzbek (UNDESA, Population Division 2017). Figures from the Russian Federation's Federal Migration Service for January 2015 report a higher estimate at 2.2 million, of which 81% are of working-age (cited in Parpiev 2015).

[20] Since the signing of a bilateral agreement between Uzbekistan and the Republic of Korea in 2007, the number of Uzbek migrants residing in the Republic of Korea has expanded, from only 10,000 in 2005 to about 50,000 in 2015. The number is expected to increase further with the signing of a memorandum of agreement in 2015/2016, which intends to intensify the economic partnership between the two countries (Romanova 2016).

Figure 3.16: Stock of Migrant Uzbek Citizens in Selected Countries, 1990 to 2017

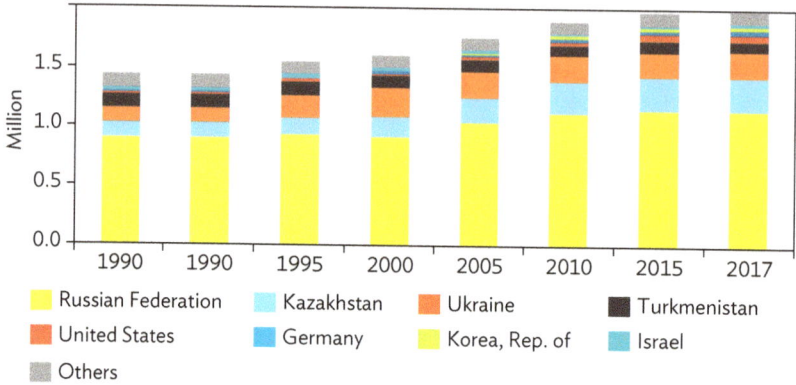

Note: The dataset presents estimates of the international migrant Uzbek citizens at mid-year, based on official statistics on the foreign-born or the foreign population.
Source: UNDESA, Population Division (2017).

Figure 3.17: Uzbek Labor Migration to the Russian Federation, 2006–2016

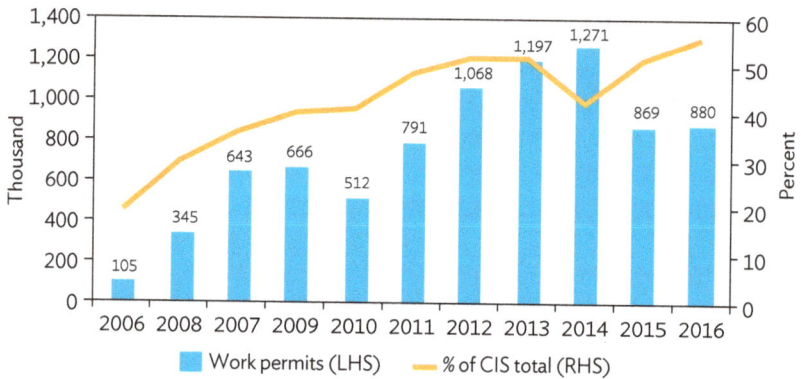

CIS = Commonwealth of Independent States (excluding Georgia), LHS = left-hand scale, RHS = right-hand scale.
Notes: The Ministry of Internal Affairs of the Russian Federation indicates that since 2015 citizens of Armenia, Kazakhstan, and the Kyrgyz Republic are not required to have permits or "patents" to work. Work permits are issued to foreign nationals who have arrived in the Russian Federation with a visa, including highly qualified specialists. "Patents" are issued to foreign nationals who entered the Russian Federation without visa requirements and are subject to work registration.
Source: Russian Federal State Statistics Service (Rosstat). http://www.gks.ru/wps/wcm/connect/rosstat_main/rosstat/en/main/ (accessed 20 March 2017).

Remittances have contributed to economic growth but the recent poor economic outlook in migrant host countries has caused remittances to decline, prompting the return of some migrants. With millions of Uzbeks working and living abroad, remittances are a major contributor to economic growth, but levels have been declining in recent years. As the majority of migrants are from rural areas, remittances from migrant workers tend to be spent mainly on consumption and family welfare in rural areas. In 2013, personal remittances peaked at around $6.7 billion, equivalent to 12% of the country's GDP (Figure 3.18). However, remittances declined to $2.5 billion in 2016, or about 40% of its 2013 level, as the number of migrants fell by about 26% due to the weak economy and stricter migration policies in the Russian Federation (Box 3.6). The stricter labor requirements in the Russian Federation also made it difficult for foreign workers to find a job and cover their living costs.

Data from the Russian Federation's Migration Service indicates that in the second half of 2014, about 365,000 Uzbeks left the country (cited in Farber 2015) because the Russian ruble had devalued more than 50% against the United States dollar between July and December 2014. In addition, the average remittance by Uzbek workers in the Russian Federation to the families at home has also declined, from an average remittance of $581 per transaction in 2010 to only $279 in 2016 (Figure 3.19). For a country with a minimum monthly wage of $21, a reduction of $302 is very substantial.[21]

In light of the recent economic crisis in the Russian Federation, along with the collapse of the Russian ruble, more Uzbek migrants are expected to return (UNDP and CIS 2015). Returning migrants will likely rejoin the labor market and raise the unemployment rate, thus creating both a challenge and an opportunity for policymakers. The challenge is to accommodate the influx of people into the local labor force to avoid repeated out-migration. The opportunity is the possibility that the returnees could use their acquired skills and savings to start their own businesses or invest in entrepreneurial activities.[22]

---

[21] The minimum wage is set at SUM172,240/month ($21/month), compared with the Russian Federation's $163/month as of 10 February 2018.

[22] There is very limited analytical work done on the occupational choice of returning migrants in Central Asian countries. Using 2013 CALISS data, Khikmetov et al. (2016) find that returning female migrants are more likely to stay out of the labor market than males with similar demographic characteristics. A study by Hausmann and Nedelkoska (2017) shows that following the 2009 Greek economic crisis, the return of more than 100,000 migrants to Albania did not reduce the wages of nonmigrant workers. Instead, returning migrants started engaging in entrepreneurial activities such as commercial farming, using their savings and technical know-how.

Figure 3.18: Personal Remittance Receipts, Uzbekistan, 2006–2016

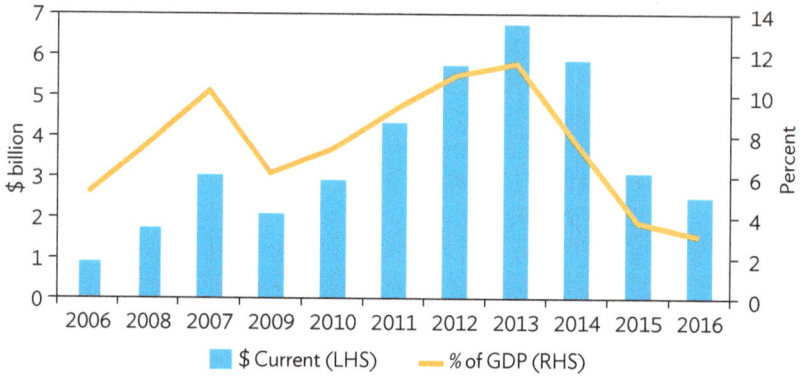

LHS = left-hand scale, GDP = gross domestic product, RHS = right-hand scale.
Notes: Personal remittances comprise personal transfers and compensation of employees. Personal transfers consist of all current transfers in cash or in kind made or received by resident households to or from nonresident households. Personal transfers thus include all current transfers between resident and nonresident individuals. Compensation of employees refers to the income of border, seasonal, and other short-term workers who are employed in an economy where they are not resident and of residents employed by nonresident entities (World Bank. World Development Indicators Metadata).
Source: World Bank. World Development Indicators. http://datatopics.worldbank.org/world-development-indicators/ (accessed 7 August 2019).

Figure 3.19: Average Value of Remittance Transactions, Uzbekistan, 2010–2017

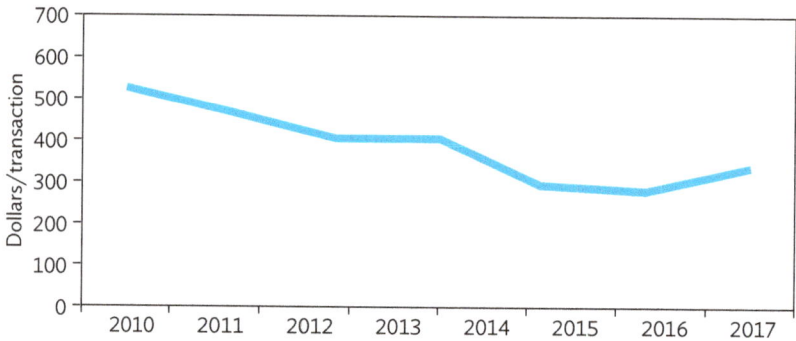

Source: Central Bank of Russia. Cross-border Transfers of Individuals. https://www.cbr.ru/eng/statistics/macro_itm/svs/ (accessed 8 August 2019).

Box 3.6: New Labor Policies for Migrant Workers in the Russian Federation

On 24 November 2014, the Russian government amended Federal Law No. 115-FZ of 25 July 2002 (*On the Legal Status of Foreign Nationals in the Russian Federation*). Under the revised policy, employers are no longer required to obtain quotas for employing visa-free foreign nationals.[a] Instead of applying for work permits, migrant workers buy "patents," which are valid for 1–12 months.

Unlike a work permit, a patent allows workers to move from one employer to another if the work falls within the position, specialization, and type of labor activity specified in the patent, and within the specified region only. Workers who intend to move to another region must secure another patent that will allow them to do so. A patent costs at least ₽1,200 ($18.40), but the actual cost varies across regions, depending on a region's demand for foreign workers.[b]

Applicants must (i) provide a medical insurance policy contract valid in the Russian Federation for the period of their labor activity or a copy of an agreement on the provision of paid medical services signed with an insurance company or a medical institution; (ii) prove that they are fit for work by submitting documents showing they are not addicted to illegal substances and they have not contracted any contagious diseases that may pose a threat to the public, including HIV, skin diseases, and tuberculosis; and (iii) submit a document certifying their command of the Russian language and knowledge of Russian history and basic legislative principles.[c]

In addition to the Uzbekistan consulates in Moscow, Uzbekistan is planning to open consular offices in five major Russian cities: Ekaterinburg, Kazan, Roston-on-Don, Saint-Petersburg, and Vladivostok, as well as another consular office in Almaty, Kazakhstan.

[a] Nonvisa countries, or visa-free foreign nationals include citizens of most Commonwealth of Independent States, in particular Armenia, Azerbaijan, the Kyrgyz Republic, Moldova, Tajikistan, the Ukraine, and Uzbekistan.
[b] ₽1 = $0.015 as of 10 August 2019.
[c] Passing the Russian language test became a requirement for applying for a work visa starting in 2012, as mandated by Federal Law No. 185 (amended).
Sources: PwC (2014) and *Gazeta.uz* (2017b).

Migration has led to a loss of skilled workers and, while it has helped families escape poverty, the majority of remittances are used for unproductive spending. If the remittances were to be invested, they would support long-term economic growth, rather than just short-term expenditure. Studies suggest that workers' migration can create both positive and negative impacts (Table 3.8). Remittances of migrant Uzbek workers contribute to the country's overall economic development by boosting expenditure and improving the housing and living conditions of remaining families. However, recent work suggests that migrants' remittances are most often spent on household improvements, which are seen to increase the social status of a family, rather than on productive investments or their children's education, which would have a greater effect on longer-term growth (Ahunov et al. 2015).

Table 3.8: Positive and Negative Outcomes of Migration

Positive	Negative
• Remittances stimulate consumption spending on health, durable goods, weddings, and home improvements. • Remittances may improve household welfare and human capital, and reduce poverty; • Remittances may improve household food security and nutrition (especially for poor households). • Remittances may promote financial sector development. • Migrant workers in receiving countries spur economic growth by filling vacant jobs and addressing labor shortages. • Migrant workers may learn new skills. • Migration may ease the burden on public transfer programs.	• Loss of labor force (e.g., negative effect on crop income). • Socio-psychological problems (e.g., deterioration of the family, depression, broken families, etc.). • Abuse (forced labor, low wage compared to locals) and lack of access to social security measures and free medical services. • Greater exposure to sexually transmitted and other diseases. • Reduced labor supply of family members left behind. • Remittances may not improve the human capital of children left behind. • Strong remittance inflows may cause appreciation of the real exchange rate and damage the competitiveness of sectors producing tradables such as manufactures. • Large swings in remittance inflows may bring macroeconomic volatility. • Remittances may reduce the government's incentive to stay fiscally healthy and increase public debt.

Sources: Malyuchenko (2015); Somach and Rubin (2010); Smolak, et al. (2015); Ahunov, et al. (2015); Danzer and Ivaschenko (2010); Betti and Lundgren (2012); Justino and Shemyakina (2012); Kroeger and Anderson (2014); Chakraborty, Mirkasimov, and Steiner (2014); Atamanov and Van den Berg (2012).

Similarly, Irnazarov (2015) points out that a majority of remittances are spent on "unproductive" items. Expenditures on traditional rites (e.g., weddings and funerals) are the third highest category (of seven) for remittance expenditure, after food and housing. Other categories include clothing, education, health, and debt repayment. Furthermore, that the majority of remittances are transmitted via money transfer operators implies that the remittances are more likely to be spent quickly than money sent through the banking sector, which is more likely to be retained in the form of deposits and therefore possesses a greater potential for economic development by funding investment (Kakhkharov and Akimov 2014).[23]

Receiving countries, such as the Russian Federation, benefit from the skills of migrant workers, and their willingness to perform jobs that are often refused by locals but are important for economic growth. For example, the Russian Federation's construction industry grew largely due to the use of cheap labor from abroad (Ryazantsev 2016).

Migrant workers usually have higher levels of cognitive and noncognitive skills than nonmigrants, and high-skilled workers are in general four times more likely to migrate abroad than low-skilled ones (Kerr et al. 2016). Although skill-biased migration increases global welfare, an excessive "brain drain" poses a threat to the migrants' home country (Biavaschi et al. 2016). For example, monitoring of the Asian Development Bank's water and sanitation projects in Uzbekistan suggests that in some project areas, insufficient working-age males are available to take part in community planning and priority setting (ADB 2014). On the positive side, returning migrant workers are more capable of contributing to their home country's labor force after gaining experience and enhancing their skills in foreign countries (Ajwad et al. 2014). Rahmatullaevich (2012) finds that 2 in 10 migrants claim that they gained a new skill while working abroad.

3.6. Policy Recommendations

The government is pursuing new ideas and principles to sustain the country's development through its Action Strategy for Five Priority Areas of the Republic of Uzbekistan 2017–2021 (Government of Uzbekistan 2017a).

---

[23] In 2016, Uzbekistan received $2.48 billion in remittances, of which $1.89 billion (or 76% of total remittances) was sent from the Russian Federation alone through money transfer operators (World Bank. World Development Indicators. http://datatopics.worldbank.org/world-development-indicators/ [accessed 7 August 2019] and Central Bank of Russia. Cross-Border Transfers of Individuals. https://www.cbr.ru/eng/statistics/macro_itm/svs/ [accessed 8 August 2019]).

Creating jobs and promoting employment, especially among the youth, is among the strategy's priorities. Investing in skills development, if effective, can improve employability of graduates, promote the quality of available jobs, help improve the competitiveness of sectors of the economy, and reduce socioeconomic inequality.

Uzbekistan is at an early stage of its demographic transition. To generate high-quality jobs for the labor market entrants, it needs to expand the levels of physical capital per worker and develop human capital. The government's priority now is to improve productivity and raise wages to transition into upper-middle-income country status by 2030 while maintaining social stability and transforming the economy. It seeks to do so by (i) moving manufacturing from primary goods to products with more added value and a higher degree of processing, (ii) promoting effective agriculture to ensure food security and enable sound employment, and (iii) transition to production of higher-quality services using higher-quality human capital.

The accumulation of human capital is considered an important determinant in the process of economic growth. Uzbekistan needs to overcome several labor market challenges and harness the economic growth opportunities associated with having a high population growth rate, low dependency ratio, and rapid urbanization. The government's plans for job creation need to address both the demand-side and supply-side labor market challenges. This will involve (i) focusing on supporting private sector growth and productivity, particularly of SMEs; (ii) enhancing workers' employability and addressing the skills gap; and (iii) ensuring that labor market interventions are inclusive.

3.6.1. Improve policy making and implementation practices and support evidence-based and responsive education policy by investments and public–private partnerships

Reassess labor policies and regulations. It is important to eliminate distortive regulations that inhibit rather than promote entrepreneurship and development of human resources. The definition of the "employment contract" should be clarified and extended to "daily" workers in rural areas. The definition of the key concepts such as "hired labor," "external labor migration," "internal labor migration," and "informal employment" need to be adopted in accordance with international standards. Adjustments of part-time and temporary contracts are needed to promote formalization of the jobs available in the labor market.

Invest more in data-driven policy implementation approaches such as reforming institutions can reap large benefits. The current lack of evidence-based policymaking leads to issues in policy formulation and measures for enhancing the system, and difficulties in monitoring the policies' implementation. Regular collection and analysis of labor market data and business trends to identify skills gaps and needs, and forecasts of labor market trends need to be supported by the government and can be implemented through public–private partnership initiatives.[24]

Develop policies that integrate education, skills, and human capital development with entrepreneurship, SME development, research, and innovation.[25] Multilevel governance and coordination mechanisms need to be established between ministries, government agencies, and stakeholders for effective policy formulation and implementation. Legislative changes need to be in place to ensure active participation of private stakeholders in policy formulation for education and skills development. At the same time the coordination of efforts and implementation practices to support the pace of education reforms needs to be encouraged and supported.

Improve sector governance and institutional efficiency. The government needs to introduce a public administration sector reform that will improve the governance of the education sector, reduce overlapping of responsibilities between state actors, ensure a holistic approach in the development of the education system, effectively plan and use the financial resources, and coordinate activities of development partners. More autonomy needs to be given to universities in areas such as student enrollment and curricula development, and the election process for rectors needs to be transparent and competitive. A modern higher education management information system needs to be deployed to reduce information discrepancies.

Adopt a national qualifications framework and harmonize it with the national occupational classification. A single national qualification framework is needed to ensure comparability with European and other foreign equivalents for easier knowledge transfer and skills training at national and

[24] There is an information gap between employers that lack information on workers, available qualifications and skills, and workers who seek information on education opportunities and jobs. Institutions and private and public sector career centers can address this gap by collecting relevant data, for example, the recently launched *zarplata.uz* provides the average and maximum salary information in different sectors to those who are registered on the website.

[25] A recent good example of a systematic approach in government strategy development was the government's approval of its *Strategy for Innovative Development of the Republic of Uzbekistan* (Government of Uzbekistan 2018b). It is extremely important that the targets in such documents be based on baselines to provide a rationale for realistic expectations and for planning the actions and investments to achieve the strategic goals.

international levels, and a policy document defining the process for creating and adopting the framework needs to be developed. The framework should be harmonized with the national occupational classification so as to enable a full analysis of employment opportunities and ensure the recognition and validation of nonformal and informal learning, along with the compulsory introduction of a quality assurance system and assessment procedures. A properly structured national qualifications framework could help to reduce the mismatch between the labor market demand and learner qualifications, and incentivize learners to seek nonformal and lifelong learning.

3.6.2. Enhance skills development for employability and job creation

Prioritize investments aimed at increasing the number and qualifications of teachers and TVET instructors. Public finance allocation for education needs to prioritize investments to improve education quality and learning outcomes (e.g., infrastructure versus teacher training, development of learning materials, and new education methods). Furthermore, a system of regular training to equip teachers and TVET instructors with up-to-date knowledge and skills, as well as capacity building of school managers should be emphasized.

Ensure the development of high-quality basic skills among students at all levels and in all subsystems of education and training. Include key skills for employability such as reading, numeracy, science, and technology in primary education, and integrate 21st century skills (critical thinking, problem solving, communications skills, research skills, teamwork, leadership, and language proficiency, etc.) in tertiary education.

Ensure social partnerships for TVET for the development, updating, and implementation of curricula. Update training curricula regularly to match current labor market demands and keep up with technology to help reduce skill mismatches. A strong partnership with the private sector could help to introduce a "matching skills" approach providing the skills needed in the labor market and supporting economic growth to create new jobs. Encourage work-based learning as an integral part of all TVET programs, and introduce apprenticeships and workplace training to support young and unemployed people to gain useful work-related skills. Support TVET instructors to update their knowledge and develop competencies through regular exposure to companies.

Design and implement public incentives to encourage active participation of large companies and SMEs in TVET. With the right incentives, industry players can take part in designing and implementing competency-based training programs for creating the skills that industry requires. Encouraging stronger public–private partnerships in developing critical technical skills could help accelerate technological convergence, entrepreneurship, and innovation. Outsource parts of educational services to the private sector, and integrate digital competencies into blended learning curricula.

Develop an affordable and functional labor market information system to facilitate the training and matching of skills with employers' demands. A system that can store and connect data from institutions, employers, and job seekers is needed. It will enable accountability and skills development and improve the governance of the labor market sector. To further align skills with demand, harmonize job and skill classifications according international standards. Provide electronic systems to ensure efficient data collection.

Create effective learning pathways between TVET and higher education. Address the job–skill mismatch through a flexible education and training system with efficient skills recognition processes. An effective and efficient TVET system that generates relevant skills can play an essential role in creating sustainable jobs and promoting inclusive growth and can serve as an entry point for higher education opportunities for people with TVET qualifications or practitioner backgrounds. This could be done through a system for recognizing prior learning, which assesses an individual's overall learning experience. Establish credit transfer arrangements between institutions regionally and nationally.

Ensure that TVET and tertiary education become demand-driven and increase tertiary enrollment rates especially in science, technology, engineering, and mathematics. Science, technology, engineering, and mathematics (STEM) should be substantially developed to focus on the "21st century skill set." 21st century skills are abilities that today's students need to succeed in their careers during the Information Age. These are quantitative and qualitative analytical skills, computation and data processing, experimental design, language skills, critical thinking, and creativity and social skills. Because global demand for skills is changing toward nonroutine and socio-emotional skills, increase the dialogue between employers and education institutions about STEM skills and needs in the labor market. To improve employability, promote the international and regional mobility of students to develop their STEM skills. Special measures to encourage and support girls in entering STEM need to be designed and implemented.

Ensure that ICT-based learning opportunities are effectively integrated and used in education and training. Building up-to-date labs and broadening access to ICT infrastructure, particularly in rural areas, would facilitate the development of relevant skills. Funding for this could be raised from multiple sources, including employers, donors, and governments. Outsourcing of government services also could be considered. Related issues that need to be addressed on a high priority basis include schools' power supply, especially in the rural areas, and school budgets to support costs associated with the use of new technologies.

Create new jobs by enhancing regional cooperation in labor markets and education. Matching labor demand and supply through regional labor information systems can create new employment and entrepreneurship opportunities. Common qualifications and unified certification standards are needed for technical and vocational education, as are supporting faculty and student exchanges, and launching new productivity-enhancing technologies at the regional level.

References

Ahunov, M., J. Kakhkharov, Z. Parpiev, and I. Wolfson. 2015. Socio-Economic Consequences of Labor Migration in Uzbekistan. *Griffith Business School Discussion Papers*. 2015-07. Southport: Griffith University.

Ajwad, M., I. Abdulloev, R. Audy, S. Hut, J. de Laat, I. Kheyfets, J. Larrison, Z. Nikoloski, and F. Torrachi. 2014. *The Skills Road: Skills for Employability in Uzbekistan*. Washington, D.C.: World Bank.

Aliyeva, K. 2017. Uzbekistan Reforms its Cotton, Textile Industries. *Azernews*. 15 December. https://www.azernews.az/region/124018.html (accessed 3 December 2018).

Anderson, K. and S. Ponnusamy. 2018. Structural Transformation to Manufacturing and Services: The Role of Trade. *Working Papers in Trade and Development*. No. 2018/26. Canberra: Australian National University.

Asian Development Bank (ADB). 2014. *Uzbekistan: Country Gender Assessment*. Manila.

_____. 2019. *Basic Statistics 2019*. Manila.

Atamanov, A. and M. Van den Berg. 2012. Heterogeneous Effects of International Migration and Remittances on Crop Income: Evidence from the Kyrgyz Republic. *World Development*. 40(2). pp. 620–30.

Bertelsmann Stiftung. 2018. *Country Report: Uzbekistan*. Gütersloh: Bertelsmann Stiftung.

Betti, G. and L. Lundgren. 2012. The Impact of Remittances and Equivalence Scales on Poverty in Tajikistan. *Central Asian Survey*. 31(4). pp. 395–408.

Biavaschi, C., M. Burzynski, B. Elsner, and J. Machado. 2016. The Gain from the Drain: Skill-Biased Migration and Global Welfare. *Centre for Research and Analysis of Migration Discussion Paper*. 1624. London: University College London.

Center for Economic Research (CER) and United Nations Development Programme (UNDP). 2013. *Employment in Uzbekistan: Challenges and Opportunities* (in Russian). Tashkent.

Central Bank of Russia. Cross-Border Transfers of Individuals. https://www.cbr.ru/eng/statistics/macro_itm/svs/ (accessed 8 August 2019).

Chakraborty, T., B. Mirkasimov, and S. Steiner. 2014. Transfer Behavior in Migrant Sending Communities. *Journal of Comparative Economics*. 43(3). pp. 690–705.

Cybermetrics Lab. Ranking Web of Universities: Uzbekistan. http://www.webometrics.info/en/Asia/Uzbekistan (accessed 8 August 2019).

Danzer, A. and O. Ivaschenko. 2010. Migration Patterns in a Remittances Dependent Economy: Evidence from Tajikistan During the Global Financial Crisis. *Migration Letters*. 7(2). pp. 190–202.

European Bank for Reconstruction and Development (EBRD) and World Bank. 2016. Life In Transition III. London: EBRD. https://www.ebrd.com/publications/life-in-transition-iii

European Training Foundation (ETF). 2015. *Torino Process 2014: Uzbekistan*. Turin.

Farber, G. 2015. One-Way Ticket to Dushanbe: Russia Sees Exodus of Migrant Workers. *The Moscow Times*. 5 Feb. https://themoscowtimes.com/articles/one-way-ticket-to-dushanbe-russia-sees-exodus-of-migrant-workers-video-43627 (accessed 17 February 2017).

Gazeta.uz. 2017a. Admission to Universities by 2021 Will Increase by 18%. 20 April. https://www.gazeta.uz/ru/2017/04/20/edu/ (accessed 29 December 2018).

_____. 2017b. Uzbekistan Opens Consulates in Five Cities of Russia. 24 April. https://www.gazeta.uz/ru/2017/04/24/council/ (accessed 15 April 2018).

_____. 2018. Uzbekistan Employment Program for 2018 Is Approved. 8 February. https://www.gazeta.uz/ru/2018/02/08/labor/ (accessed 25 November 2018).

Government of Uzbekistan. 2017a. Action Strategy for Five Priority Areas of the Republic of Uzbekistan, 2017–2021. Tashkent.

_____. 2017b. Presidential Decree No. PP-2829. On Measures to Further Improve the Activities of Educational Institutions of Secondary Special and Vocational Education. 14 March 2017.

_____. 2018a. Presidential Decree No. UP-3651. On Measures for Promoting and Developing Preschool Education System. 5 April 2018.

_____. 2018b. Presidential Decree No. UP-5544. About Approval of Strategy of Innovative Development of the Republic of Uzbekistan 2019-2021. 21 September 2018.

_____. 2018c. Regulation On Measures to Improve the Public Education System (Russian). https://regulation.gov.uz/document/43 (accessed 25 November 2018).

Hausmann, R. and L. Nedelkoska. 2017. Welcome Home in a Crisis: Effects of Return Migration on the Non-Migrants' Wages and Employment. *Harvard Kennedy School Working Paper*. RWP17-015. Cambridge, MA. http://dx.doi.org/10.2139/ssrn.2939702

Holzhacker, H. 2018. *Assessing Progress and Challenges in Unlocking the Private Sector's Potential and Developing a Sustainable Market Economy*. London: European Bank for Reconstruction and Development.

Infocom.uz. 2018. The Main Trends in Supply and Demand in the Labor Market of Uzbekistan. 10 August. http://infocom.uz/2018/08/10/osnovnye-tendencii-sprosa-i-predlozheniya-na-rynke-truda-uzbekistana/ (accessed 25 November 2018).

International Labour Organization (ILO). 2014. *Key Indicators of the Labour Market. 8th Edition*. Geneva.

———. 2016. *Key Indicators of the Labour Market. 9th Edition*. Geneva.

International Monetary Fund (IMF). 2015. IMF Executive Board Concludes 2015 Article IV Consultation with Uzbekistan. https://www.imf.org/en/News/Articles/2015/09/14/01/49/pr15414. News release. 15 September.

Irnazarov, F. 2015. *Labor Migrant Households in Uzbekistan: Remittances as a Challenge or Blessing? The Central Asia Fellowship Papers*. Washington, D.C.: George Washington University. https://app.box.com/s/j5dmyvkpxjjythysuwphnocd78lghfbu

Jagannathan, S. 2012. *Skills for Inclusive and Sustainable Growth in Developing Asia and the Pacific*. Manila: Asian Development Bank.

Justino, P. and O. Shemyakina. 2012. Remittances and Labor Supply in Post-Conflict Tajikistan. *IZA Journal of Labor and Development*. 1(1). pp. 1–28.

Kakhkharov, J. and A. Akimov. 2014. Estimating Remittances in the Former Soviet Union: Methodological Complexities and Potential Solutions. *Griffith Business School Discussion Papers in Finance*. 2014(03). Southport: Griffith University.

Kerr, S., W. Kerr, C. Ozden, and C. Parsons. 2016. Global Talent Flows. *Journal of Economic Perspectives*. 30(4). pp. 83–106.

Khikmetov, N., O. Saidmamatov, K. Yusupov, and N. Yusupov. 2016. Return Migration and Self-Employment in Uzbekistan. In *Inclusive and Sustainable Economic Growth: Current Issues*. Tashkent: Central Bank of Uzbekistan and Westminster International University in Tashkent.

Korea Times, The. 2018. The Present and Future of Preschool Education of the Republic of Uzbekistan. 31 August. https://www.koreatimes.co.kr/www/nation/2019/05/176_254720.html (accessed 11 December 2018).

Kroeger, A. and K. Anderson. 2014. Remittances and the Human Capital of Children: New Evidence from Kyrgyzstan during Revolution and Financial Crisis, 2005–2009. *Journal of Comparative Economics*. 42(3). pp. 770–85.

Kupets, O. 2016. Education–Job Mismatch in Ukraine: Too Many People with Tertiary Education or Too Many Jobs for Low-Skilled? *Journal of Comparative Economics*. 44(1). pp. 125–47.

Kwon, Dae-Bong. 2009. Human Capital and Its Measurement. Proceeds of the 3rd OECD World Forum on Statistics, Knowledge, and Policy. http://www.academia.edu/24595168/ (accessed 11 December 2018).

Maclean, R., S. Jagannathan, and J. Sarvi. 2013. Skills Development Issues, Challenges, and Strategies in Asia and the Pacific. In R. Maclean, S. Jagannathan, and J. Sarvi, eds. *Skills Development for Inclusive and Sustainable Growth in Developing Asia-Pacific*. Dordrecht: Springer.

Maksakova, L. 2006. Feminization of Labour Migration in Uzbekistan. In Rodriguez Rios, R., ed. *Migration Perspectives: Eastern Europe and Central Asia*. Vienna: International Organization for Migration.

Malyuchenko, I. 2015. Labour Migration from Central Asia to Russia: Economic and Social Impact on the Societies of Kyrgyzstan, Tajikistan, and Uzbekistan. *Central Asia Security Policy Briefs*. 21.

Ministry of Higher and Secondary Specialised Education of the Republic of Uzbekistan. Statistics. http://edu.uz/ru/pages/sss (accessed 7 August 2019).

Organisation for Economic Co-operation and Development (OECD). 2011. *Developing Skills in Central Asia through Better Vocational Education and Training Systems*. https://www.oecd.org/global-relations/VocationalEducation.pdf (accessed 25 November 2018)

————. 2017. *In-Depth Analysis of the Labour Market Relevance and Outcomes of Higher Education Systems: Analytical Framework and Country Practices Report: Enhancing Higher Education System Performance*. Paris: OECD.

Parpiev, Z. 2015. Who is Behind Remittances? A Profile of Uzbek Migrants. Blog. 6 March. http://www.uz.undp.org/content/uzbekistan/en/home/ourperspective/ourperspectivearticles/2015/03/05/who-is-behind-remittances--a-profile-of-uzbek-migrants.html (accessed 25 November 2018).

PricewaterhouseCoopers (PwC). 2014. *Russia: Administrative Procedure for Nationals from Visa-Free Countries Working under Patents*. https://www.pwc.ru/en/legal-services/news/assets/flash27_eng.pdf (accessed 15 April 2018).

Rahmatullaevich, A. J. 2012. *Labor Migration from Uzbekistan: Social and Economic Impacts on Local Development*. Doctoral Thesis. http://eprints-phd.biblio.unitn.it/805/

Regnum.ru. 2018. The Most Acute Problems of Uzbekistan Named. 19 January. https://regnum.ru/news/2369950.html (accessed 25 November 2018).

Romanova, M. 2016. Labor Migrants from Russian Siberia and Former Soviet Republics to Contribute to the South Korea's Racial Make-Up Change. *Russian Briefing*. 11 July. https://www.russia-briefing.com/news/labor-migrants-russian-siberia-former-soviet-republics-contribute-south-koreas-racial-make-change.html/ (accessed 1 November 2018).

Russian Federal State Statistics Service (Rosstat). http://www.gks.ru/wps/wcm/connect/rosstat_main/rosstat/en/main/ (accessed 3 March 2017).

Ryazantsev, S. 2016. Labour Migration from Central Asia to Russia in the Context of the Economic Crisis. *Russia in Global Affairs.* 31 August (accessed in 3 March 2017).

Sabyrova, L. 2017. Take Gini Coefficient with a Grain of Salt. Blog. May. https://blogs.adb.org/blog/take-gini-coefficients-grain-salt (accessed 25 November 2018).

Smolak, A., N. El-Bassel, A. Malin, A. Terlikbayeva, and S. Samatova. 2015. Sex Workers, Condoms, and Mobility Among men in Uzbekistan: Implications for HIV Transmission. *International Journal of STD & AIDS.* 27 (4). pp. 268–72.

Somach, S. and D. Rubin. 2010. *Gender Assessment: USAID/Central Asian Republics.* Washington, D.C: United States Agency for International Development.

State Committee of the Republic of Uzbekistan on Statistics (Uzbekistan Statistics). 2017. *Analysis of the Development of Living Standards and Welfare of the Population in the Republic of Uzbekistan.* https://stat.uz/en/435-analiticheskie-materialy-en1/2078-analysis-of-the-development-of-living-standards-and-welfare-of-the-population-in-the-republic-of-uzbekistan

_____. 2018. *Employment and the Labor Market: January–December 2017 (preliminary data) (Russian).* https://stat.uz/uploads/docs/8.Trud-ekspresska-12-2017.pdf

_____. Higher Educational Institutions. https://stat.uz/en/249-ofytsyalnaia-statystyka-en/sotsyalnaya-sfera-en/obrazovanye-en/4431-special-secondary-professional-educational-institutions-2 (accessed 7 August 2019).

Tashkenttimes.uz. 2018. Nearly 60% of Uzbekistan's Employed Population are in the Informal Economy. October 5. https://tashkenttimes.uz/national/2988-nearly-60-of-uzbekistan-s-employed-population-are-in-the-informal-economy (accessed 12 August 2019).

United Nations, Department of Economic and Social Affairs (UNDESA). 2011. *Country Study: Assessing Development Strategies to Achieve the MDGs in the Republic of Uzbekistan.* https://www.un.org/en/development/desa/policy/capacity/output_studies/roa87_study_uzb.pdf

United Nations, Department of Economic and Social Affairs (UNDESA), Population Division. 2017. Trends in International Migrant Stock: The 2017 Revision. https://www.un.org/en/development/desa/population/migration/data/estimates2/estimates17.asp

_____. 2019. World Population Prospects: The 2019 Revision. https://population.un.org/wpp/Download/Standard/Population

United Nations Development Programme (UNDP). 2018. *Human Development Indices and Indicators: 2018 Statistical Update*. New York: UNDP.

United Nations Development Programme (UNDP) Regional Bureau for Europe and the Commonwealth of Independent States (CIS). 2015. *Labour migration, remittances and human development in Central Asia (Central Asia Human Development Series)*. http://www.eurasia.undp.org/content/dam/rbec/docs/CAM&RHDpaperFINAL.pdf (accessed 21 January 2018).

United Nations Educational, Scientific and Cultural Organization (UNESCO) Institute of Statistics. http://uis.unesco.org/ (accessed 7 August 2019).

uniRank. 2019 Uzbekistani University Ranking. http://www.4icu.org/uz/ (accessed 8 August 2019).

Uzbekistan Authority for Foreign Investment (UZAFI). 2017. This is the Right Time to Invest in Uzbekistan. PowerPoint Presentation. https://www.chuhai.edu.hk/sites/default/files/MrKhamraevUZAF.pdf (accessed 25 November 2018).

UzReport. 2017. The President Approved Measures to Develop the System of Higher Education. 21 April. http://news.uzreport.uz/news_3_r_150952.html (accessed 25 November 2018).

Vossensteyn, H., J. Huisman, K. Muehleck, R. Kolster, M. Seeber, C. Gwosc, and Y. Ayalew. 2018. *Promoting the Relevance of Higher Education: Annex 3: Country Fiches*. European Union. https://doi.org/10.2766/952691

World Bank. 2007. Higher Education in Central Asia: The Challenges of Modernization (English). Washington, DC: World Bank. http://documents.worldbank.org/curated/en/266211468235483571/Higher-education-in-Central-Asia-the-challenges-of-modernization

_____. 2013a. Enterprise Surveys. http://www.enterprisesurveys.org (accessed 28 December 2018).

_____. 2013b. Central Asia's Labor and Skills Survey (CALISS) Dataset (accessed 17 January 2017).

_____. 2014. *Uzbekistan Modernizing Tertiary Education*. Report No. 88606. http://www.worldbank.org/content/dam/Worldbank/document/eca/central-asia/Uzbekistan-Higher-Education-Report-2014-en.pdf

_____. 2016a. *Country Partnership Framework for Uzbekistan, 2016–2020*. Washington, D.C.: World Bank.

_____. 2016b. Uzbekistan: On the Path to High-Middle-Income Status by 2030. News release. 13 April. https://www.worldbank.org/en/results/2016/04/13/uzbekistan-on-the-path-to-high-middle-income-status-by-2050 (accessed 25 November 2018).

_____. 2016c. *Uzbekistan: Modernizing Higher Education Project (English)*. Washington, D.C.: World Bank. http://documents.worldbank.org/curated/en/823401467999690136/Uzbekistan-Modernizing-Higher-Education-Project

_____. 2016d. *Uzbekistan: Systematic Country Diagnostic*. Washington, D.C.: World Bank.

_____. 2018. *Uzbekistan: Education Sector Analysis*. Washington, D.C.: World Bank.

_____. World Development Indicators. http://datatopics.worldbank.org/world-development-indicators/ (accessed 7 August 2019).

_____. World Development Indicators Metadata. http://datatopics.worldbank.org/world-development-indicators/ (accessed 7 August 2019).

World Bank and German Society for International Cooperation (GIZ). 2013. *Uzbekistan Jobs, Skills, and Migration Survey*. Quoted in Ajwad, M.I., I. Abdulloev, R. Audy, S. Hut, J. de Laat, I. Kheyfets, J. Larrison, Z. Nikoloski, and F. Torrachi. 2014. *The Skills Road: Skills for Employability in Uzbekistan*. Washington, D.C.: World Bank.

World Economic Forum (WEF). 2017. *The Global Human Capital Report. Preparing People for the Future Work*. Geneva: World Economic Forum.

Wu, T. 2013. Constraints to Human Capital Investment in Developing Countries: Using the Asian Financial Crisis in Indonesia as a Natural Experiment. *Bulletin of Indonesian Economic Studies*. 49 (1). pp. 113–4.

CHAPTER 4

Private Sector Development and Access to Finance

Shigehiro Shinozaki

Uzbekistan has experienced relatively stable growth since its independence from the former Soviet Union, with limited influence from the 2007–2008 global financial crisis and the 2014–2015 Russian financial crisis. The country's economic growth has been supported by the expansion of private sector businesses, and has been accelerated by government efforts to transition to a market-based economy. The liberalization of foreign exchange markets in September 2017 brought increased opportunities for private businesses in Uzbekistan, which will encourage more foreign investment. Also, ongoing tax reforms, including unified tax payments, will reduce the administrative burden for private sector activities.

However, several remaining concerns affect the country's economic growth. In general, economic development entails structural change (McMillan and Rodrik 2011), but the sectoral and employment structures of Uzbekistan's economic activities have not changed for more than a decade. Labor mobility between low and high productive activities has stagnated, and the country's economy still relies on labor-intensive agriculture, industry, and construction. This raises the question of how Uzbekistan could develop a sustainable economic growth model.

Private sector development acts as an engine of growth. However, strategically important sectors such as banking, mining, gas, electricity, water supply, and transport are still controlled by state-owned enterprises (SOEs). Uzbekistan classifies SOEs as enterprises that are directly state owned or are 100% state owned through direct plus indirect state shares. All other enterprises are classified as privately owned, even if the state has a majority share. Some goods and services are not yet subject to market-based pricing but instead use prices set by the Ministry of Finance. Privatization of SOEs is ongoing, but privatized enterprises with partial state ownership often dominate the market, making it harder for new private sector entrants to boost competition.

The World Bank (2018) analyzed the growth pattern of Uzbekistan and noted "jobless growth"—growth not accompanied by satisfactory job creation. This is not a sustainable and resilient growth model that creates good quality jobs. Small businesses have led the expansion of private sector business. The role of small businesses and their entrepreneurs is critical to promote a more tangible shift from state-driven to private sector-led economic growth. Such a shift will promote job creation and accelerate economic diversification by competitive businesses. Among several factors affecting the development of small businesses, their access to affordable finance is essential to encourage their growth and entrepreneurships.

This chapter reviews private sector and financial sector development, and especially focuses on small business development and financial inclusion. The chapter discusses government efforts to expand the private sector, and then draws the policy implications.

4.1. Private Sector Development for Economic Diversification

Private sector-led economic growth is one of the high priority areas of the national development strategy that Uzbekistan adopted in 2017. The business climate has been improving gradually, backed by a multitude of government measures to promote a liberalizing market-based economy. Uzbekistan's Ease of Doing Business ranking has risen from 147th in 2007 to 69th in 2020, with improvements in "starting a business" from 70th to 8th and "getting credit" from 159th to 67th (World Bank various years). The introduction of an electronic application and payment system has facilitated trading across borders and improved the investment climate.

4.1.1. Enterprise landscape

This section focuses on three periods of private sector development in Uzbekistan:

(i)   transformation during 2003–2008 (period I);

(ii) after the global financial crisis, 2009–2013 (period II); and

(iii) the Russian Federation's financial crisis and Uzbekistan's administrative change in 2014–2017 (period III).

Throughout the three periods, private sector businesses have been expanding steadily, led by small businesses (Figure 4.1 and Table 4.1). The number of small businesses has grown rapidly, in the 5%–7% range annually, and they comprise more than 70% of all enterprises across all periods. As of the third quarter (Q3) of 2018, Uzbekistan had 316,668 registered enterprises, 81% of which (257,127) were small businesses. The number of small businesses has increased 168% since 2003.

The majority of operating commercial enterprises are limited liability companies (57% of enterprises in 2017), followed by private companies (not state owned, 33%).[1] Due to the progress of privatization, only 1% of enterprises are fully state-owned, but joint-stock companies are still fewer, at only 0.3% (Uzbekistan Statistics 2017a).

Enterprises employed 13.5 million people as of 2017, of which 78% (10.5 million people) worked in small businesses (Figure 4.2). Although the growth pace is slowing, the aggregate number of people employed by small businesses has gradually increased, accounting for 66% in period I, 75% in period II, and 78% in period III, with no serious influence from external factors such as the global and the Russian financial crises. By contrast, the number employed by medium and large enterprises has been shrinking: by 6% in period I and 0.3% in period II, although it grew by 0.5% in period III. Against the increase of aggregate employment, however, the number of workers employed per small business (employment size) has been decreasing, from 61 on average in period I to 52 in period II and 49 in period III.

Despite weak job creation in enterprises, gross value added (GVA) by all enterprises has expanded sharply: by 313% in period I, 149% in period II, and 58% in period III, although the pace is slowing (Figure 4.3). As of Q3 2018, GVA amounted to SUM210,905 billion ($26 billion),[2] half of which was generated by small businesses. GVA growth was driven by small businesses during periods I and II but was led by other businesses during period III.

---

[1]   The data exclude farmers and dekhkan (family) farms.

[2]   The exchange rate refers to domestic currency per U.S. dollar, end of period. International Monetary Fund, International Financial Statistics (IFS).

Figure 4.1: Number of Enterprises, Uzbekistan, 2003–2017

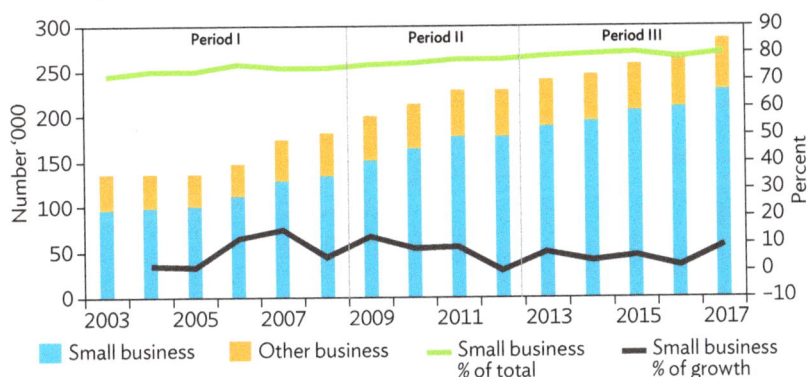

Note: Data collected on forms specially designed by the author.
Source: Data received from Uzbekistan Statistics on 3 October 2018.

Table 4.1: Number of Enterprises, Employment, and Gross Value Added, Uzbekistan, 2003–2017

Item	Period I: 2003–2008	Period II: 2009–2013	Period III: 2014–2017
Enterprises			
Change in the number of small businesses (%)	38.5	24.7	17.2
Change in the number of other businesses (%)	18.3	5.4	10.2
Average share of small businesses in total enterprises (%)	73.8	77.3	79.7
Average growth in number of small businesses (%)	6.9	7.0	4.9
Average growth in number of other businesses (%)	3.8	2.3	2.4
Employment			
Change of employment by small businesses (%)	48.5	14.7	5.9
Change of employment by other businesses (%)	-28.6	-1.3	3.9
Average share of small business in total employment (%)	66.0	75.1	77.9
Average growth of employment in small businesses (%)	8.4	3.5	2.4
Average growth of employment in other businesses (%)	-6.1	-0.3	0.5
Average number of employed people per small business	61	52	49
Average number of employed people per other business	89	59	54
Gross Value Added (GVA)			
Change of small businesses' GVA (%)	469.0	177.0	60.9
Change of other businesses' GVA (%)	229.3	120.3	68.9
Small businesses' average share of total GVA (%)	40.8	53.4	55.7
Average growth of small businesses' GVA (%)	40.2	29.6	18.1
Average growth of other businesses' GVA (%)	27.4	21.9	19.5

Note: Data collected on forms specially designed by the author.
Sources: Author's calculations based on data received from Uzbekistan Statistics on 3 October 2018.

Figure 4.2: Employment, Uzbekistan, 2003–2017

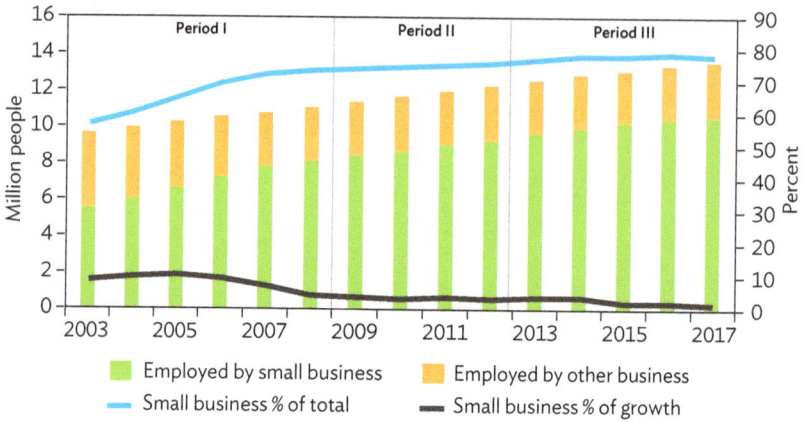

Note: Data collected on forms specially designed by the author.
Source: Data received from Uzbekistan Statistics on 3 October 2018.

Figure 4.3: Gross Value Added, Uzbekistan, 2003–2017

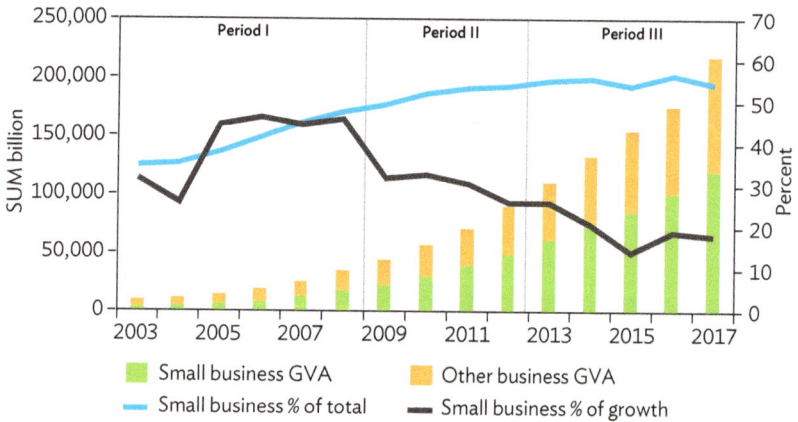

GVA = gross value added.
Note: Data collected on forms specially designed by the author.
Source: Data received from Uzbekistan Statistics on 3 October 2018.

The expansion of private businesses, driven by small businesses, has contributed to increasing the country's GVA, but as the employment size in enterprises diminishes, the speed of productivity growth has decelerated in Uzbekistan. Given the growth of small businesses with no serious influence from the external environment during the three periods, most small business would be domestically focused with limited operating areas. The shrinking employment size of small businesses indicates that they have not supported satisfactory job creation in Uzbekistan. This suggests that structural change of enterprises is needed to sustain economic growth in the country. The next subsection reviews Uzbekistan's small businesses in detail and discusses what structural changes will be needed.

4.1.2. Small business and entrepreneurship development

Effective January 2019, the government redefined the categories of small businesses, adding a new category of medium enterprises. The new definition has four categories: (i) an individual entrepreneur, (ii) a microenterprise as a legal entity with an annual average of up to 25 employees, (iii) a small enterprise as a legal entity with an annual average of 26–100 employees, and (iv) a medium enterprise as a legal entity with an annual average of 101–250 employees. This important reform enables the government to target a group of firms that seek growth of innovative businesses in its national growth strategies, but the new classification is yet to be reflected in national statistics. Thus, data analyzed in this chapter follow the definition of small businesses applied until the end of December 2018.[3]

The sectoral structure of small businesses did not change between 2003 and Q3 2018. About 60% of small businesses are in services and the rest are engaged in agriculture, industry (manufacturing), and construction (Figure 4.4a). Retail trade and catering services accounted for the largest share of small businesses (34%) in Q3 2018. Agriculture is the fourth-largest sector of small businesses but would be the third-largest if food processing were included in the sector. Food processing however, is considered part of industry, and accounts for a quarter of manufacturing production (24% in 2016).

Small businesses concentrate in the capital city, Tashkent (Figure 4.4b). The number of small businesses in Tashkent city trebled from 2003 to Q3 2018, and comprised 22.6% of all small businesses in Q3 2018, a 5 percentage point rise since 2003.

---

[3]   Until the end of December 2018, small businesses were legally classified into three categories: (i) microenterprise, (ii) small enterprise, and (iii) individual entrepreneur. The categories were defined as follows: a microenterprise has any form of ownership and employs up to 20 persons in manufacturing and up to 5 persons in services and other industries per year on average; a small enterprise has any form of ownership and up to 200 employees in manufacturing and up to 100 employees in services and other industries; an individual entrepreneur is a person with a certificate of state registration as an individual entrepreneur, with the right to hire up to 3 persons.

Figure 4.4: Small Businesses, Uzbekistan, 2003 and 2018

a. By Sector (% of total)

2003

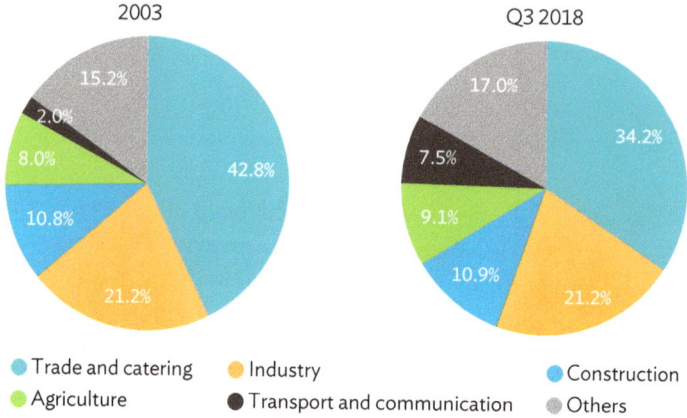

15.2%
2.0%
8.0%
10.8%
21.2%
42.8%

Q3 2018

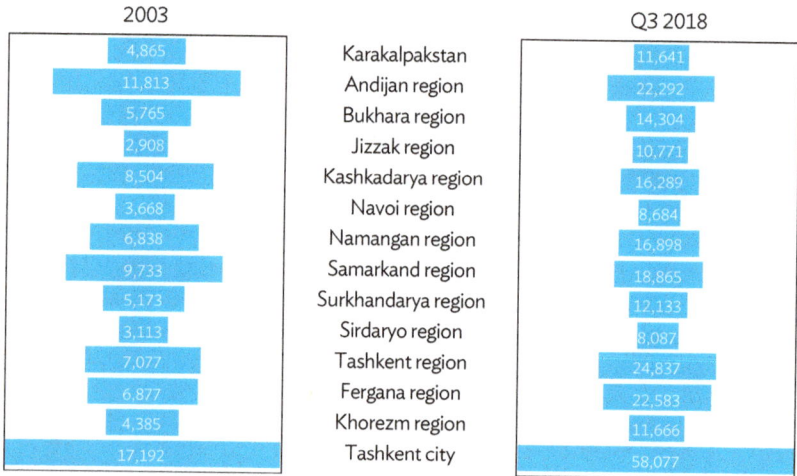

17.0%
7.5%
9.1%
10.9%
21.2%
34.2%

● Trade and catering   ● Industry   ● Construction
● Agriculture   ● Transport and communication   ● Others

b. By Area (number of enterprises)

2003		Q3 2018
4,865	Karakalpakstan	11,641
11,813	Andijan region	22,292
5,765	Bukhara region	14,304
2,908	Jizzak region	10,771
8,504	Kashkadarya region	16,289
3,668	Navoi region	8,684
6,838	Namangan region	16,898
9,733	Samarkand region	18,865
5,173	Surkhandarya region	12,133
3,113	Sirdaryo region	8,087
7,077	Tashkent region	24,837
6,877	Fergana region	22,583
4,385	Khorezm region	11,666
17,192	Tashkent city	58,077

Note: Data collected on forms specially designed by the author.
Source: Data received from Uzbekistan Statistics on 3 October 2018.

The employment structure of small businesses by sector also did not change during 2005 and 2017. Three sectors—agriculture, industry, and construction—absorbed about 60% of small business employment (Figure 4.5a). In particular, agriculture-related small businesses, with 9% of total small businesses, employed 34% of the total small business labor force. Meanwhile, services-related small businesses, with 60% of total small businesses, employed only 40% of the total small business labor force.

Figure 4.5: Employment by Small Businesses, Uzbekistan, 2003, 2005, and 2017

a. By Sector (% of total)

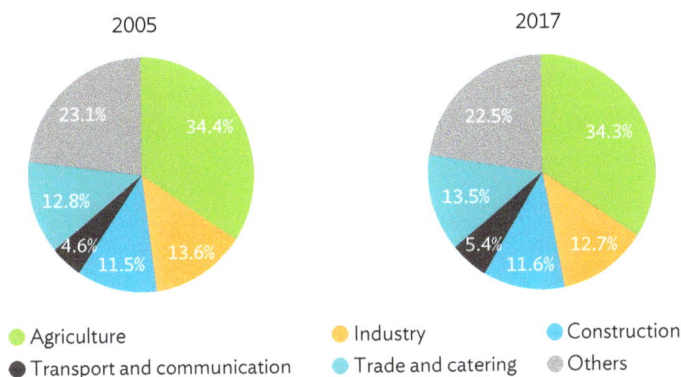

2005

- 34.4%
- 13.6%
- 11.5%
- 4.6%
- 12.8%
- 23.1%

2017

- 34.3%
- 12.7%
- 11.6%
- 5.4%
- 13.5%
- 22.5%

- Agriculture
- Industry
- Construction
- Transport and communication
- Trade and catering
- Others

b. By Area ('000 people)

Region	2003	2017
Karakalpakstan	287	486
Andijan region	518	1,110
Bukhara region	356	649
Jizzak region	218	379
Kashkadarya region	429	974
Navoi region	159	251
Namangan region	363	864
Samarkand region	593	1,287
Surkhandarya region	330	803
Sirdaryo region	177	278
Tashkent region	538	969
Fergana region	655	1,229
Khorezm region	273	599
Tashkent city	541	664

c. Employment per Small Business by Area (average number of people)

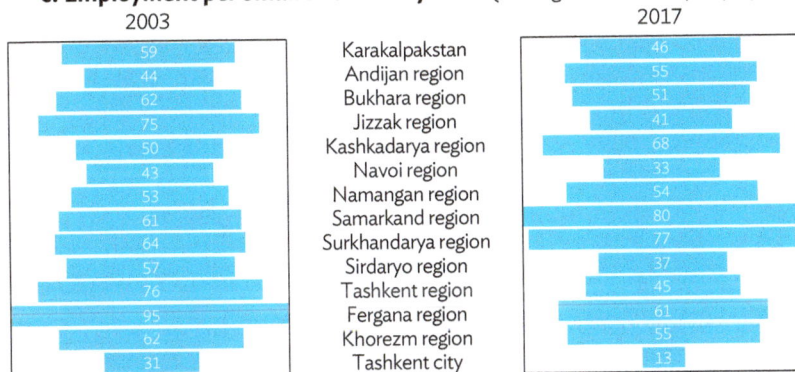

Region	2003	2017
Karakalpakstan	59	46
Andijan region	44	55
Bukhara region	62	51
Jizzak region	75	41
Kashkadarya region	50	68
Navoi region	43	33
Namangan region	53	54
Samarkand region	61	80
Surkhandarya region	64	77
Sirdaryo region	57	37
Tashkent region	76	45
Fergana region	95	61
Khorezm region	62	55
Tashkent city	31	13

Note: Data collected on forms specially designed by the author.
Sources: Author's calculations based on data received from Uzbekistan Statistics on 3 October 2018.

The top two regions where small business workers live are Samarkand and Fergana, both accounting for 12% of the total small business labor force (Figure 4.5b). Tashkent city hosts the largest number of small businesses but absorbed only 6% of total small business workers in 2017, 4 percentage points less than in 2003. Figure 4.5c shows the average number of employees per small business by area. The number of employees per small business diminished in 9 of the 14 regions between 2003 and 2017, with the largest decline in Tashkent city (60% less in 2017 than in 2003), followed by Jizzak region (a 46% decrease), and Tashkent region (a 41% decrease). Small businesses based in Tashkent city employ 13 people on average, a size that is generally in the microenterprise category.

Uzbekistan does not have a large base of viable small and medium-sized enterprises (SMEs) to create jobs, especially in the capital city and its neighboring regions. More space for job creation could be made in highly productive services-related SMEs (not retail trade and catering services but capital-intensive technology-based services) by promoting labor mobility into such SMEs from less productive sectors. Agriculture-related SMEs could also create more jobs if they became more productive by using technology that could be obtained through participating in agricultural value chains.

The sectoral trend of small businesses' output follows that of small business employment. Agriculture, industry, and construction combined contribute about 60% of small businesses' GVA (Figure 4.6a). Services-related small businesses generate the remaining 40%. Agriculture-related small businesses generate the largest share of GVA among all small businesses, at 34%.

Tashkent city is the largest contributor to small businesses' GVA, accounting for 21% of their total GVA in Q3 2018, a 5.8 percentage point rise from 2003. This is followed by Tashkent region at 10.4% and Samarkand at 9.8% (Figure 4.6b). Figure 4.6c shows the labor productivity of small businesses by area, denoted by their GVA per worker. The labor productivity in Tashkent city is by far the highest, at SUM36.5 million ($4,492) per worker in 2017.

By sector, although transport and communication services are small in scale, they have the highest labor productivity of small businesses, with an increasing trend, at SUM21.6 million ($2,659) per worker (Figure 4.6d). Next are industry (SUM16.2 million or $1,998), trade and catering (SUM13.7 million or $1,690), agriculture (SUM11.9 million or $1,466), and construction (SUM8.5 million or $1,047). Overall, Uzbekistan's economy is led by labor-intensive agriculture, industry, and construction, supported by small businesses' labor forces.

Figure 4.6: Gross Value Added by Small Businesses, Uzbekistan, 2003, 2015, 2017, and 2018

a. By Sector (% of total)

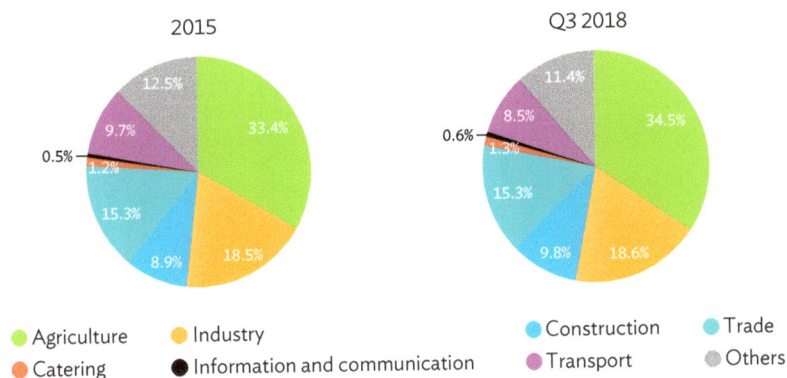

2015

Q3 2018

- ● Agriculture
- ● Catering
- ● Industry
- ● Information and communication
- ● Construction
- ● Transport
- ● Trade
- ● Others

b. By Area (SUM billion)

	2003	Q3 2018
Karakalpakstan	135.5	3,957.6
Andijan region	260.7	8,618.3
Bukhara region	224.3	7,422.9
Jizzak region	177.1	4,135.4
Kashkadarya region	283.1	8,284.4
Navoi region	109.8	4,326.3
Namangan region	212.6	6,105.4
Samarkand region	386.1	11,045.4
Surkhandarya region	211.1	7,145.9
Sirdaryo region	131.6	2,962.3
Tashkent region	363.6	11,715.4
Fergana region	365.0	8,750.6
Khorezm region	151.7	5,150.0
Tashkent city	521.5	23,295.1

c. Labor Productivity of Small Business by Area (SUM million per worker)

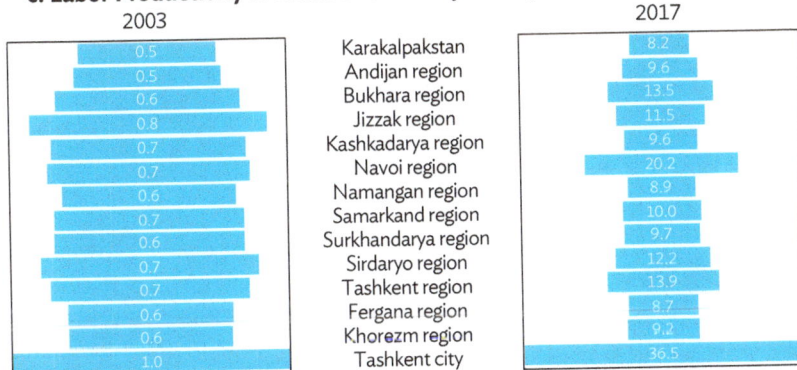

	2003	2017
Karakalpakstan	0.5	8.2
Andijan region	0.5	9.6
Bukhara region	0.6	13.5
Jizzak region	0.8	11.5
Kashkadarya region	0.7	9.6
Navoi region	0.7	20.2
Namangan region	0.6	8.9
Samarkand region	0.7	10.0
Surkhandarya region	0.6	9.7
Sirdaryo region	0.7	12.2
Tashkent region	0.7	13.9
Fergana region	0.6	8.7
Khorezm region	0.6	9.2
Tashkent city	1.0	36.5

Note: Data collected on forms specially designed by the author.
Sources: Author's calculations based on data received from Uzbekistan Statistics on 3 October 2018.

Figure 4.6 continued

d. Labor Productivity of Small Business by Sector (SUM million per worker)

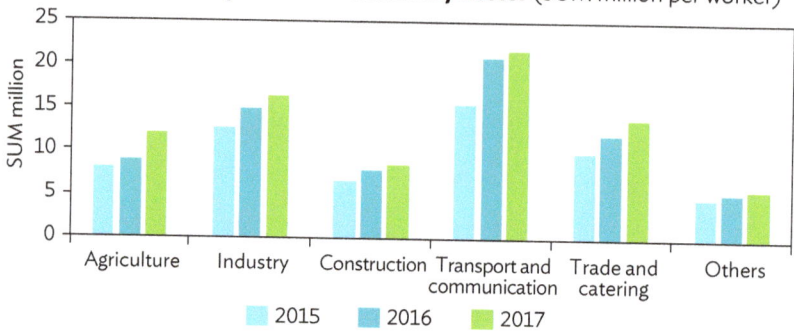

Note: Data collected on forms specially designed by the author.
Sources: Author's calculations based on data received from Uzbekistan Statistics on 3 October 2018.

Given that small business development is a key policy priority toward sustainable economic growth in Uzbekistan, a strategic approach is required to realize the growth potential of small businesses and young entrepreneurs. Services-related businesses (60% of small businesses) employ 40% of small business workers and produce 40% of small business GVA. Three labor-intensive sectors (40% of small businesses—agriculture, industry, and construction) employ 60% of small business workers and produce 60% of small business GVA. Services-related businesses, especially knowledge-intensive and capital-intensive industries such as education, health, transport, tourism, and information technology, have good potential to create more good quality jobs in the country and help boost national productivity. Small businesses are concentrated in the capital city, and they contribute a large share of GVA but employ only 6% of small business workers. Tashkent city has yet to become a hub of growth-oriented SMEs, but has the potential to create a base of good quality jobs by encouraging the development of innovative small businesses and entrepreneurs, including those in high-tech service industries.

Small businesses have influenced Uzbekistan's international trade. They accounted for 28% of the total value of exports and 57% of the total value of imports in Q3 2018: 10 times and 8 times more, respectively, than in 2003 (Figure 4.7). While small business imports are trending upward, their exports are on a declining trend. Internationalization can help vitalize small businesses and encourage structural changes in their business models, moving from being domestically focused and import-competing to being export-focused and globally competitive.

Figure 4.7: Small Business Exports and Imports, Uzbekistan, 2003–2018

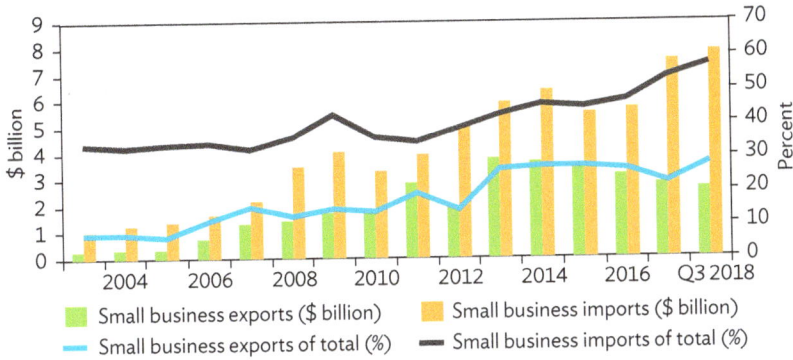

Note: Data collected on forms specially designed by the author.
Source: Data received from Uzbekistan Statistics on 3 October 2018.

Uzbekistan's exports are concentrated in raw materials, especially gas and metals, cotton, and fruits and vegetables. The major destinations of exports include the People's Republic of China, Kazakhstan, and the Russian Federation (OECD 2017). The export structure has changed from a heavy reliance on cotton and natural resources to a basket including a more diverse range of processed products and services. The latter offers more opportunities for small businesses, especially by participating in global value chains. Developing agricultural value chains can help promote the country's agribusinesses, led by innovative small businesses and entrepreneurs, and provide good potential to boost the productivity of agricultural labor.

SMEs play a critical role of promoting private-sector-led economic growth with satisfactory job creation. However, they need a support mechanism to fulfill that role. By participating in global value chains, SMEs could reap benefits such as achieving increased competitiveness through vertical linkages with multinational lead firms, enhanced product quality through technology transfer, and resultant business expansion to overseas marketplaces, with associated job creation (Shinozaki 2015). SMEs involved in value chains (such as in agriculture, food processing, automotive, and electronics processing) have the advantage of offering products at a competitive price and geographical positioning to access their customers, but they face difficulties meeting international quality standards for products, managerial constraints, and insufficient financial resources. To surmount these issues requires institutional policy support measures.

4.1.3. Technology, innovation, and business competitiveness

The rapidly changing global business environment, accelerated by the fourth industrial revolution,[4] will create diverse opportunities for small businesses, but appropriately designed policy support is needed for such opportunities to materialize. In 2018, the Government of Uzbekistan established its Strategy for Innovative Development of the Country for 2019-2021, supported by the United Nations Development Programme (Government of Uzbekistan 2018). The strategy promotes the use of global best practices in scientific and innovative achievements, including in areas of infrastructure development, green energy, public health care, agribusiness, and information technology.

New technology, as an enabler of innovation, is a key survival tool for growth-oriented SMEs, including seed and start-up companies. But the fourth industrial revolution will also have negative impacts on some of the workforce. It may affect large and established firms by reducing their workforce while generating more tech-based SMEs that create good quality jobs. Tech-based SMEs can play an important role in increasing national productivity with innovation, by benefiting from foreign direct investment and active participation in global value chains.

However, tech-based SMEs face challenges to achieving that role: research and development (R&D), product quality control, skilled labor, market access, logistics, business literacy, networking, and access to finance. In particular, financial constraints directly and negatively affect innovation capability and business development. Thus, tech-based SMEs are seeking long-term financing options to invest in R&D, raise the quality of their human capital, and transfer and commercialize technologies to maximize their ability to innovate. Some successful innovative SMEs could obtain finance from the lead firm of a relevant global value chain, venture capital firms, and business angels; but most early stage firms unavoidably use their own funds or retained profits to develop their business.

In Uzbekistan, the number of enterprises producing innovative goods and services is still small but has been increasing sharply, from 289 in 2010 to 2,373 in 2016 (Uzbekistan Statistics 2017b). However, most of the costs of technology adoption and innovation are financed by the firms' own funds, which amounted to SUM1,180 billion ($365 million) in 2016 or 46% of the total financing for innovations.

---

[4]   The fourth Industrial revolution is "an age in which scientific and technological breakthroughs are disrupting industries, blurring geographical boundaries, challenging existing regulatory frameworks, and even redefining what it means to be human." Schwab (2017).

Figure 4.8 shows the extent to which SME categories in Uzbekistan have engaged in product and process innovation and the level of their access to bank credit.[5] The number of SMEs that introduce new products and services is small compared to the number of large enterprises that introduce them. Few SMEs have access to technology licensed from foreign companies, and some SMEs are still state owned, which may impede their active involvement in innovation.

Limited access to finance is a structural problem for business development in SMEs. The World Bank's Enterprise Surveys identified a relatively high rejection rate of loan applications from small businesses in Uzbekistan (World Bank 2013). Also, no SME spending on R&D is evident in the surveys (even large enterprises spent little on R&D). Such investments were mostly self-financed by SMEs. The limited use of external finance or a lack of available sources of long-term finance contribute to SMEs' dearth of investment in R&D. It is therefore not surprising that only a small number of SMEs introduce new products and services. Diversification of finance sources beyond traditional bank credit is vital for SMEs, especially tech-based start-ups and ventures. An appropriate government support framework is needed to remedy the situation. The next section reviews the country's financial sector development in detail.

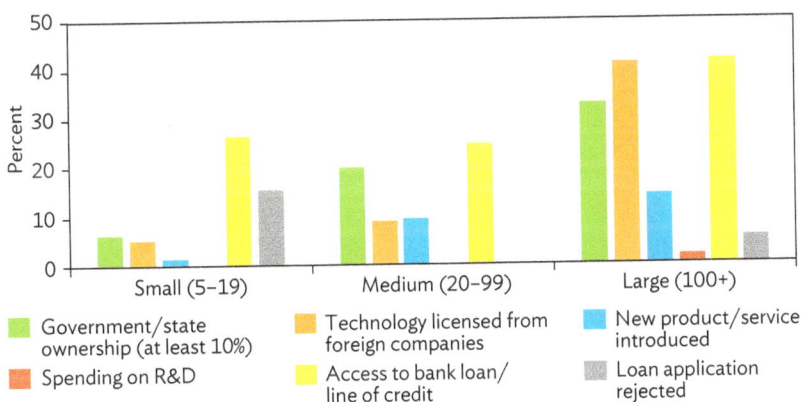

Figure 4.8: Business Innovation and Finance, Uzbekistan, 2013

R&D = research and development.
Note: Data as a percent of firms.
Source: World Bank. 2013. Enterprise Surveys. Uzbekistan (2013). http://www.enterprisesurveys.org/data/exploreeconomies/2013/uzbekistan.

---

5   The latest World Bank Enterprise Survey in Uzbekistan was in 2013. The survey's classification of SMEs follows the World Bank's standardized definition, with a threshold of fewer than 100 employees.

4.2. Financial Sector Development: Trends and Challenges

Sound development of a stable financial sector is essential to promote private sector development, associated job creation, and sustainable economic growth. In Uzbekistan, a bank-centered financial system has been established, with commercial bank credit as a key source of funding for enterprises' working and investment capital. The nonbank finance industry and capital market have yet to be a source of funding for private businesses, especially SMEs. Financial infrastructure such as a credit bureau and a collateral registry need to be improved and strengthened before they can effectively reach out to the private sector. The following subsections review the financial sector in Uzbekistan and discuss key challenges.

4.2.1. Banking sector

That the credit market expands as the economy grows is empirically recognized. Central and West Asia follow this trend, as shown by the positive correlation between gross domestic product (GDP) per capita and bank credit with GDP (Figure 4.9). Uzbekistan also generally follows this trend, but shows some volatility due to complex external and internal factors including the currency devaluation that was triggered when the country liberalized its foreign exchange markets.

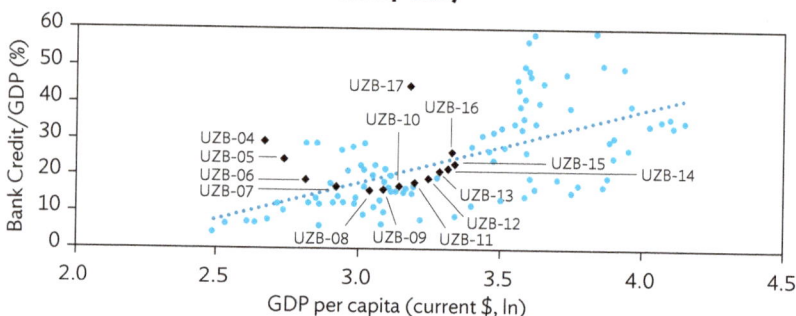

Figure 4.9: Bank Credit and GDP per Capita, Central and West Asia, 2004–2017

GDP = gross domestic product.
Notes: Bank credit/GDP (%) refers to bank loans outstanding as a percent of GDP for Uzbekistan and domestic credit to private sector by banks as a percent of GDP for other countries. For Uzbekistan, data collected on forms specially designed by the author. Central and West Asia is Armenia, Azerbaijan, Georgia, Kazakhstan, the Kyrgyz Republic, Pakistan, Tajikistan, and Uzbekistan.
Sources: Author's estimates based on data received from the Central Bank of Uzbekistan on 2 October 2018, and World Bank. World Development Indicators. http://www.databank.worldbank.org/ (accessed 20 September 2018).

Figure 4.10 shows the positive correlation between credit supply and the opening of new businesses in Central and West Asia: increased bank credit delivery correlates with increases in new business density, denoted by the number of new business registrations per 1,000 people aged 15–64 years old. However, Uzbekistan does not follow this trend well, suggesting its credit supply may not suffice to promote new businesses, including start-ups and other SMEs.

Figure 4.10: Bank Credit and New Business, Central and West Asia, 2006–2016

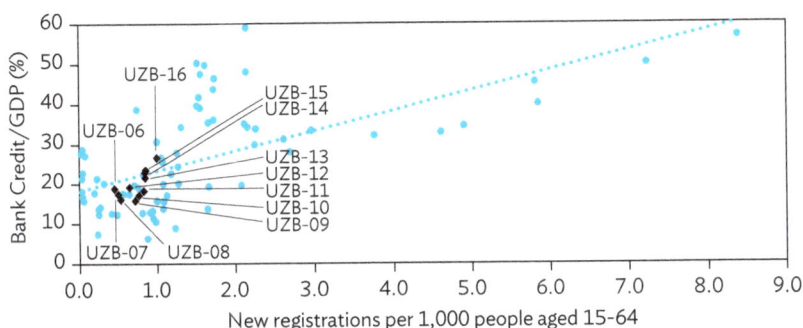

GDP = gross domestic product.
Notes: Bank credit/GDP (%) refers to bank loans outstanding as a percent of GDP for Uzbekistan and domestic credit to private sector by banks as a percent of GDP for other countries. For Uzbekistan, data collected on forms specially designed by the author. Central and West Asia is Armenia, Azerbaijan, Georgia, Kazakhstan, the Kyrgyz Republic, Pakistan, Tajikistan, and Uzbekistan.
Sources: Author's estimates based on data received from the Central Bank of Uzbekistan on 2 October 2018, and World Bank. World Development Indicators. http://www.databank.worldbank.org/ (accessed 20 September 2018).

Commercial banks are dominant players in Uzbekistan's financial system. As of Q3 2018, 28 commercial banks, including 11 state-owned banks, are active in Uzbekistan. Total bank assets accounted for 67% of GDP at the end of 2017 and amounted to SUM195 trillion ($24 billion) in Q3 2018. Bank capital as a share of risk-weighted assets has been improving and was 19.55% as of Q1 2018 (Figure 4.11). The return on assets was 2.01% in Q1 2018. The return on equity has been decreasing since the currency devaluation in late 2017, but was at the moderate level of 15.57% in Q1 2018. The liberalization of foreign exchange markets in September 2017 had some negative impacts on the banking sector, but the soundness of the sector has been maintained as it was backed by the government's capital injection into nine state-owned banks. The injection amounted to $500 million from the Uzbekistan Fund for Reconstruction and Development and SUM500 billion ($62 million) from the Ministry of Finance.

Outstanding loans have been expanding sharply in value, increasing 40-fold between 2004 and 2017. That increase has been led by the growth of local currency loans, which have risen by 75 times in nominal SUM terms. As of Q3 2018, commercial banks' total loans outstanding amounted to SUM151 trillion ($18.7 billion), of which 45% were local currency loans and 55% were foreign currency loans. Due to the currency devaluation associated with the liberalization of foreign exchange markets, the amount of foreign currency loans almost doubled in September 2017 (Figure 4.12). The loan-to-deposit ratio (local and foreign currency combined) was high at 225% as of Q3 2018. Meanwhile, the ratio of gross nonperforming loans to total loans has been low, and was 1.3% in Q3 2018.

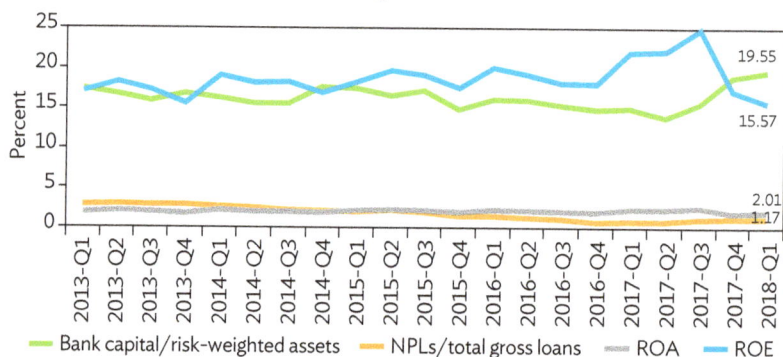

Figure 4.11: Financial Soundness in the Banking Sector, Uzbekistan, 2013–2018

NPL = nonperforming loan, ROA = return on assets, ROE = return on equity.
Source: Compiled from the Central Bank of Uzbekistan Statistics (https://www.cbu.uz) data as of end of period (accessed 15 October 2018).

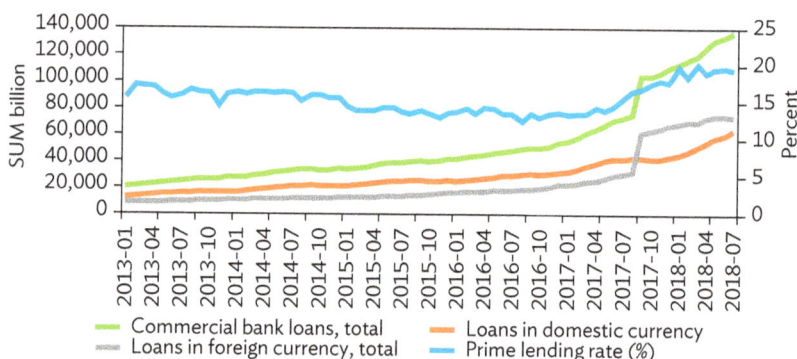

Figure 4.12: Commercial Bank Lending, Uzbekistan, 2013–2018

Source: Compiled from the Central Bank of Uzbekistan Statistics (https://www.cbu.uz) data as of end of period (accessed 15 October 2018).

Credit markets have expanded but small businesses may not be benefiting from this. The average annual lending rate has risen for local and foreign currency loans since 2016, by 20.45% and 6.26%, respectively as of Q3 2018. This has limited small businesses' access to bank credit. The Central Bank of Uzbekistan (CBU) has introduced Basel III (the international standard for banking supervision), which requires tighter risk management as well as greater capital and liquidity for commercial banks than was previously required. The Basel III standard may also negatively affect the banks' attitude to lending to small businesses, which are typically considered high-risk borrowers. Given the financial soundness of the banking sector, commercial banks should be able to take more risks in financing small businesses, including start-ups and young entrepreneurs.

4.2.2. The nonbank finance industry and capital market

Uzbekistan's nonbank finance industry is at an early stage of development and has yet to be a funding source for private businesses. As of Q3 2018, 89 nonbank finance institutions, comprising 36 microcredit organizations and 53 pawnshops, were active under the supervision of the CBU (Figure 4.13). The total assets of microcredit organizations and pawnshops were increasing and amounted to SUM349 billion ($43 million) in Q3 2018, but was equal to only 0.18% of commercial bank assets (Figure 4.14). Until 2010, there were 116 credit unions, but the credit union system was abolished due to systematic defects. There are also some leasing companies, which are supervised by the Ministry of Finance. The government has discussed the possibility of creating a new financial authority for regulating and supervising all nonbank finance institutions including microcredit organizations, pawnshops, leasing companies, and the securities market, to add to the CBU's supervision of the banking sector.

The capital market is underdeveloped and has yet to be a source of long-term funding for private businesses. The Tashkent Stock Exchange was established to promote privatization of SOEs, and 186 companies were listed as of the end of 2017. However, the stock market is small in scale and with low trading liquidity (Figure 4.15). Market capitalization accounts for about 6% of the country's GDP, and the total value of stocks traded accounts for only 0.1% of GDP. Stocks are normally traded over-the-counter. High turnover stocks, mainly banks, are owned by the government or by SOEs. The liberalization of foreign exchange markets in 2017 has allowed investors to convert capital gains from domestic currency to foreign currency, attracting more foreign investors to the securities market. At the end of 2017, 43% of the investors in the Tashkent Stock Exchange were foreign. Uzbekistan has strict regulatory barriers for issuing corporate bonds, but the government is drafting a new regulation to relax the bond issuance requirements. Due to the high reference ratio (16% as of October 2018), bond issuance is costly (bond yields will be 18%–20%).

Figure 4.13: Nonbank Finance Industry, Uzbekistan, 2004–2018

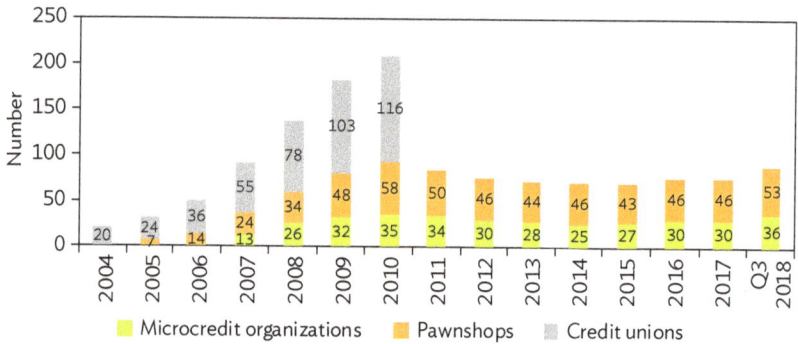

Note: Data collected on forms specially designed by the author.
Source: Data received from the Central Bank of Uzbekistan on 2 October 2018.

Figure 4.14: Nonbank Finance Institutions' Total Assets, Uzbekistan, 2017–2018

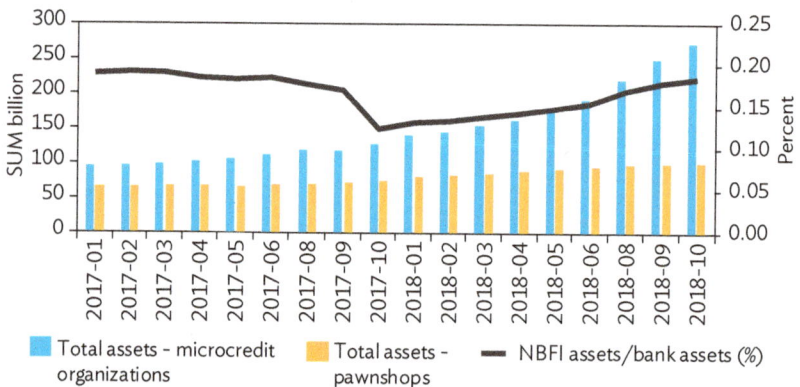

NBFI = nonbank finance institution.
Note: Nonbank finance institutions' assets are the sum of assets of microcredit organizations and pawnshops.
Source: Compiled from the Central Bank of Uzbekistan (https://www.cbu.uz), accessed 15 October 2018.

Figure 4.15: Securities Markets, Selected Countries, 2017

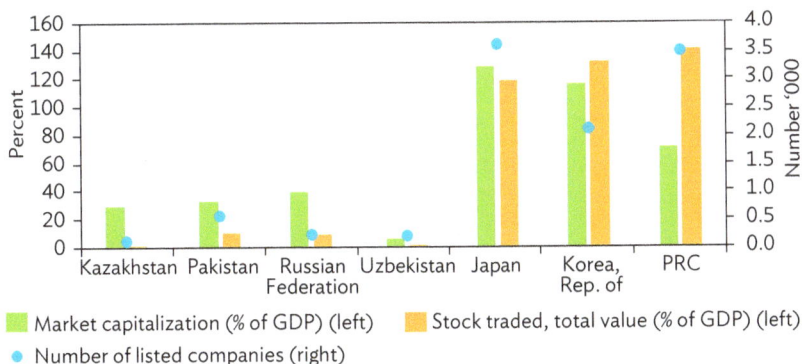

Market capitalization (% of GDP) (left)   Stock traded, total value (% of GDP) (left)
Number of listed companies (right)

GDP = gross domestic product, PRC = People's Republic of China.
Data for Pakistan: listed domestic companies (2014); market capitalization and stock traded (2016).
Sources: Republican Stock Exchange Tashkent. http://www.uzse.uz/; World Bank. World Development
Indicators. http://www.databank.worldbank.org/; JETRO (2018).

4.2.3. Financial infrastructure and legal frameworks

Sound financial systems require high-quality financial infrastructure to effectively reduce supply–demand gaps in finance, especially for SMEs. The essential infrastructure needed (Figure 4.16) includes (i) a credit data platform (a credit bureau), (ii) a secured lending legal system (a collateral registry), and (iii) credit guarantees. These are key components of the financial infrastructure needed to support financial institutions' credit enhancement. The three components should be supplemented by a financial education system to facilitate active use of the infrastructure. To help close SMEs' knowledge gaps about financial products and services, a systematic approach to financial education is needed, including digital finance literacy programs and e-learning platforms.

Credit bureau. Many developing Asian countries have made significant efforts to develop a national credit bureau. In Uzbekistan, a private sector credit bureau, the Credit Information Analytical Center (CIAC), was established in 2012 and licensed by the CBU. The CIAC holds data on more than 9 million individuals and 620,000 organizations with a 5-year credit history, totaling more than 2 billion records (half the data pertain to small businesses). The data are collected through the credit information exchange system from 28 banks, 29 microcredit organizations, 45 pawnshops, and a leasing company. The CIAC is trying to expand its data sources to utility companies and the tax

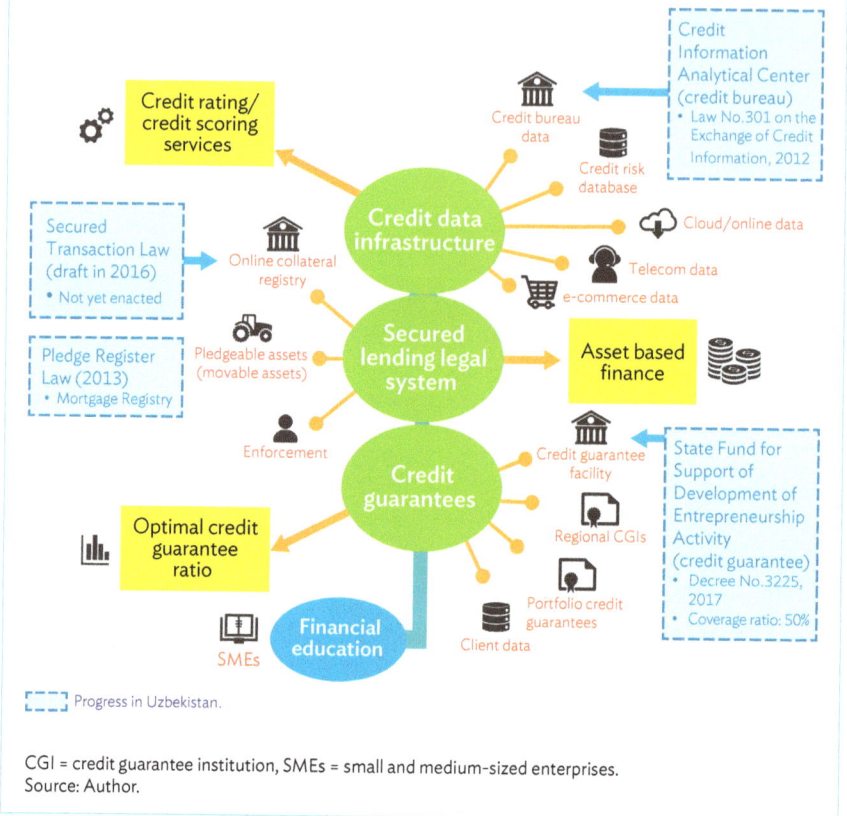

Figure 4.16: Financial Infrastructure Development, Uzbekistan

CGI = credit guarantee institution, SMEs = small and medium-sized enterprises.
Source: Author.

authority. The CIAC sells credit reports and provides credit ratings and scoring services, but user financial institutions are concerned about the high cost of purchasing data, the narrow range of data coverage, and the sometimes low data quality. Further improvements of the credit bureau system are needed.

In general, the data collected through a credit bureau are expected to contribute to developing a national credit rating system. Low quality and a limited range of data are often major impediments to developing such a system in many countries. But modern digital technology allows various types of alternative data on bank borrowers, including SMEs to be stored easily through the internet, telecommunication companies, and e-commerce platforms, which enable a country to develop a comprehensive credit risk database. Use of such alternative data can help develop a sophisticated credit rating system, especially for SMEs, in developing Asia including in Uzbekistan.

Collateral registry. A secured lending legal system can help private businesses to use movable assets as collateral for loans. Such a system includes creating an online collateral registry. Many developing Asian countries still lack a legal framework for secured transactions or movable asset financing. Broadening the range of "pledgeable" assets, including machinery, equipment, inventory, receivables, and intellectual property rights, will enhance enterprises' access to finance. This is especially important for SMEs, which typically do not have real estate to use as security for loans. In Uzbekistan, a mortgage registry exits under the Pledge Register Law (2013). The pledge register is a single information database containing records on the rights of creditors to debtors' property. The Pledge Register Law does not specify pledgeable movable assets, and this law is to be replaced with the rules of the international agreement once it is established (Article 2). The Secured Transaction Law was drafted in 2016, supported by the International Finance Corporation, but it had yet to be enacted as of March 2019. Thus a collateral registry has yet to be created in Uzbekistan.

Credit guarantees. Credit guarantees support SMEs' access to finance. Public credit guarantees are provided through various channels including a specialized guarantee facility (as in the Philippines), regional credit guarantee institutions (as in Indonesia), and portfolio guarantee schemes (as in Thailand). Credit guarantee institutions have the advantage of being able to store SME client data for assessment. Based on such data, an optimal credit guarantee ratio can be developed, a flexibly adjusted rate according to the level of a bank's financial soundness and the macroeconomic environment.

In Uzbekistan, the State Fund for Support of Development of Entrepreneurship Activity was established in 2017. It provides 50% partial credit guarantees not exceeding $250,000, targeting small businesses as part of public financial support. Because the organization is relatively new, credit guarantees have yet to be well disseminated across the country. The World Bank suggested principles for public credit guarantee schemes for SMEs, including the need for a comprehensive enterprise risk management framework and a transparent risk-based pricing policy (World Bank 2015). These are needed for sustainable credit guarantee operations but have yet to be developed in country's credit guarantee system.

The credit market has been expanding in Uzbekistan, but small businesses are not yet able to enjoy the full benefits of the expanded market due to high interest rates and collateral requirements. Credit enhancement schemes supported by a credit bureau, a collateral registry, and credit guarantees have yet to function fully for small businesses to access appropriate financial services. Tightened risk management in the banking sector may make it even more difficult for small businesses to access bank credit. The nonbank finance industry and the capital market have yet to be a viable substitute for bank lending for SMEs. This forces small businesses to use their own funds and/or informal financing to survive. In particular, tech-based SMEs that are expected to lead sustainable economic growth in the country have failed to realize business opportunities due to the lack of access to appropriate long-term funding options. Balanced development of banking and the nonbank finance industry, including market-based instruments, is needed to hasten private sector development in Uzbekistan. That requires a comprehensive policy framework for financial sector development, providing more financial inclusion or enhancing SMEs' access to finance. The next section expands on accessible financial inclusion for future growth.

4.3. Financial Inclusion for Future Growth

Promoting financial inclusion is critical for the country to grow sustainably and resiliently while creating sufficient good jobs. Segments of the economy such as SMEs that are traditionally underserved by financial institutions often forego growth opportunities due to a lack of capital; hence, the opportunity cost for economic growth will increase unless SMEs' access to finance is enhanced. In Uzbekistan, financial inclusion will reduce the extent of jobless growth and strengthen private sector business competitiveness. This section reviews small businesses' access to finance in Uzbekistan and possible solutions for promoting financial inclusion.

4.3.1. Financing gap and constraints on businesses

The International Finance Corporation (2017) estimates that the financing gap that formal micro, small, and medium-sized enterprises experience in developing economies amounts to $5.2 trillion or 19% of global GDP (Figure 4.17). The Asia and Pacific region accounts for 46% of the total financing gap, or $2.4 trillion. Europe and Central Asia, including Uzbekistan, has the third-largest gap, accounting for 15% of the global gap, or $776 billion. The financing gap that Uzbekistan's micro, small, and medium-sized enterprises face was estimated at $11.8 billion or 17% of country's GDP in 2016.

Figure 4.17: Financing Gap Faced by Micro, Small, and Medium-Sized Enterprises, Developing Economies, 2016

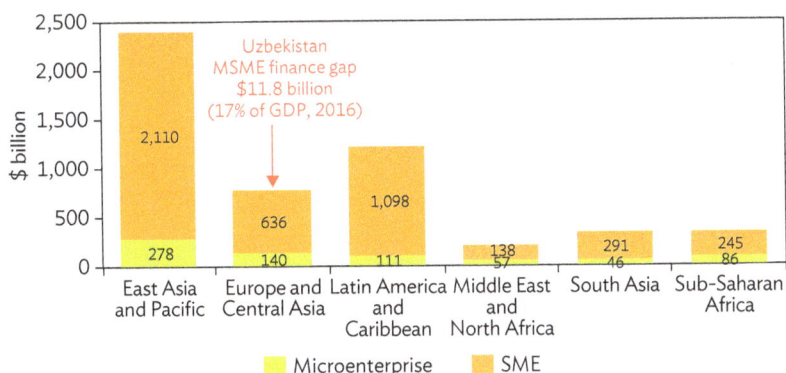

GDP = gross domestic product, MSMEs = micro, small, and medium-sized enterprises; SMEs = small and medium-sized enterprises.
Source: Adapted from IFC (2017).

SMEs' limited access to finance is a structural problem in developing economies. Factors constraining SMEs' access to finance have a common feature in most countries. SME surveys by the Asian Development Bank identified the common supply- and demand-side factors constraining SMEs' access to finance.[6] The key barriers SMEs identified were collateral and guarantee requirements for loans, followed by high lending rates and complicated procedures for borrowing from financial institutions. SMEs also recognized their lack of knowledge about available financial services and their inadequate management and human resources.

Interviews by the author at the chamber of commerce, private sector commercial banks, and government authorities in October 2018[7] identified similar constraints for small businesses' access to finance. The Institute of Forecasting and Macroeconomic Research of the Ministry of Economy recognized that limited access to financial services is the most critical challenge for SME development in Uzbekistan, followed by a lack of skilled labor, product quality control, and legal protection issues. Due to commercial banks' high lending rates (24%–28% per annum) and collateral requirements (real estate and vehicles), SMEs have difficulty accessing bank credit. Land

---

[6] SME surveys were conducted in India, Kazakhstan, Malaysia, Papua New Guinea, the People's Republic of China, the Philippines, the Republic of Korea, and Sri Lanka during 2013 and 2015.

[7] Interviewed by the author on 2–5 October 2018, Tashkent.

is not utilized as collateral for loans as its ownership is basically held by the government. The American Chamber of Commerce reported that a lack of proper financial reporting (based on the International Financial Reporting Standards) is a major challenge for SMEs seeking access to formal financial services. Private sector commercial banks (Ipak Yuli Bank, Hamkorbank, and Davrbank) raised common demand-side issues behind limited access to finance for small businesses: a lack of transparency in their business records, inaccurate financial reporting, insufficient cash flow and collateral, and low financial literacy. They also noted that the difficulty of obtaining information on borrowers from external sources impedes loan processing to small businesses, and that the country's financial infrastructure, including the credit bureau system and collateral registry, are in the early stage of development.

4.3.2.　Small business access to finance

Data on commercial bank loans to small businesses are available from January 2017. Small business loans disbursed during the first half of 2018 amounted to SUM15,403 billion ($1,957 million), of which 89% were loans to legal entities and the remaining 11% went to individual entrepreneurs (Figure 4.18a). Lending to small businesses is increasing, but accounted for only 2.1% of the total commercial bank loans disbursed in the first half of 2018. Thus, the access of small businesses to bank credit is quite limited.

Small business loans are concentrated in Tashkent city, accounting for 35% of the total small business loans disbursed in the first half of 2018 (Figure 4.18b). Nationally, three sectors combined—agriculture, industry, and construction— accounted for 54% of the total small business loans disbursed in that period, of which industry (manufacturing) had the largest share, at 33% (Figure 4.18c). The remaining 46% went to services-related small businesses, of which trade and catering services had the largest share, at 19%.

Recall from section 4.1 that services-related businesses comprise 60% of small businesses in number but absorb only 40% of small business workers and provide only 40% of small business GVA. As a whole, insufficient credit supply to services-related small businesses may be dampening their employment and GVA. However, given that the delivery of small business loans was concentrated in the capital city, small businesses based in Tashkent city could have a relatively good environment for accessing bank loans, which may be contributing to the relatively large GVA in the capital city; however, the credit supply seems not to have created many jobs in the city, as small businesses there employ only 6% of all small business workers.

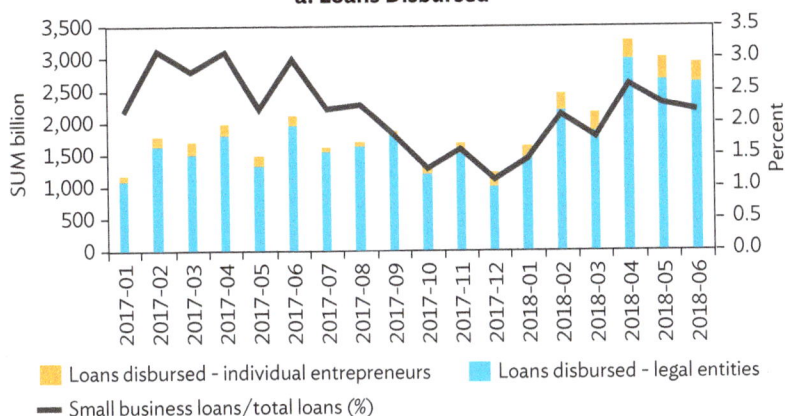

Figure 4.18: Commercial Bank Loans to Small Businesses, Uzbekistan, 2017–2018

a. Loans Disbursed

Loans disbursed - individual entrepreneurs   Loans disbursed - legal entities
Small business loans/total loans (%)

b. By Area

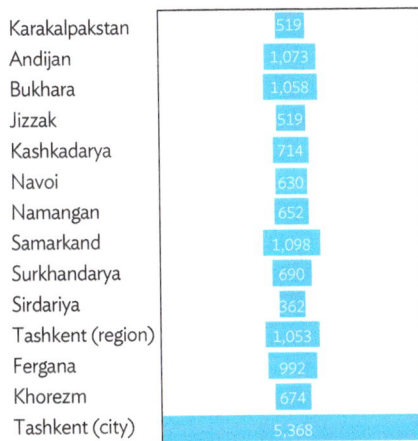

Karakalpakstan	519
Andijan	1,073
Bukhara	1,058
Jizzak	519
Kashkadarya	714
Navoi	630
Namangan	652
Samarkand	1,098
Surkhandarya	690
Sirdariya	362
Tashkent (region)	1,053
Fergana	992
Khorezm	674
Tashkent (city)	5,368

c. By Sector

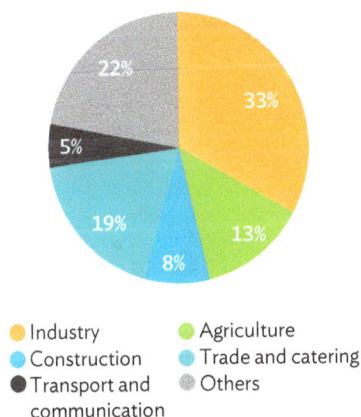

Industry 33%   Agriculture 13%   Construction 8%   Trade and catering 19%   Transport and communication 5%   Others 22%

Unit = SUM billion.
Note: Data collected on forms specially designed by the author. For figure a, author's calculation. For figures b and c, data for the first half of 2018.
Sources: Data received from the Central Bank of Uzbekistan on 2 October 2018, and author's calculations.

Access to finance is critical for creating jobs and boosting productivity, but services-related small businesses, especially knowledge-intensive and capital-intensive industries, have yet to obtain enough credit to expand their businesses and enhance job creation. Tech-based SMEs, most of which are in the service sector, seek access to long-term finance to maintain their quality of innovation, but commercial bank credit has yet to meet their financing demand.

Given that the limitations of bank lending for SMEs are exacerbated by the Basel III-based tighter risk management in the banking sector, the nonbank finance industry needs to be more competitive to diversify financing options for SMEs. At present, microcredit organizations are not a major source of funding for small businesses. As of Q3 2018, financing from microcredit organizations amounted to SUM247 billion ($30.6 million) for 55,476 borrowers (Figure 4.19a). The ratio of gross nonperforming loans to total loans was low at 0.4% in the same period, but annual lending rates were high: 60.6% for individuals and 26.5% for legal entities (Figure 4.19b). Thus, less than 5% of the microcredit organizations' lending portfolio covered small businesses.

Figure 4.19: Microcredit Organizations, Uzbekistan, 2004–2018

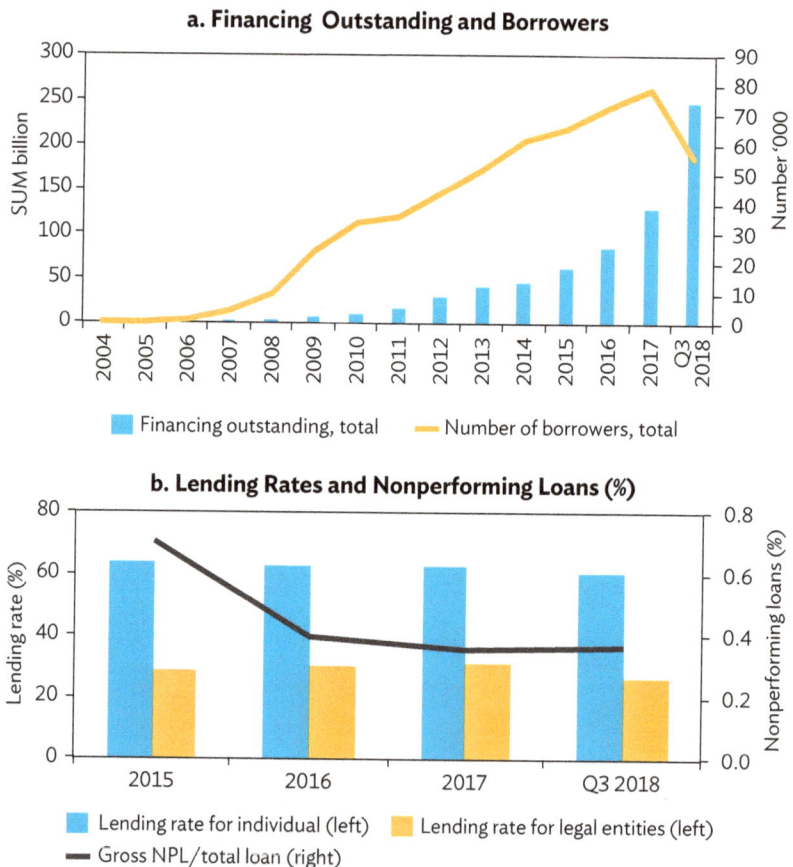

a. Financing Outstanding and Borrowers

Financing outstanding, total — Number of borrowers, total

b. Lending Rates and Nonperforming Loans (%)

Lending rate for individual (left)   Lending rate for legal entities (left)
— Gross NPL/total loan (right)

NPL = nonperforming loan.
Note: Data collected on forms specially designed by the author.
Source: Data received from the Central Bank of Uzbekistan on 2 October 2018.

The leasing market has considerable potential as a nonbank financing option for SMEs. Uzbekistan's leasing market has been growing rapidly. Total leasing transactions amounted to SUM780 billion ($99 million) in the first half of 2018, a 9.7% increase from the same period of 2017 (Figure 4.20a). More than 70% of the customers are small businesses with strong demands for leasing. The leasing business is concentrated in Tashkent city, which accounted for 31% of total leasing operations in the first half of 2018 (Figure 4.20b). Major lease-financed products are agricultural machinery, vehicles, real estate and property complexes, and technological equipment, through hire-purchase arrangements (Figure 4.20c). As of October 2018, 130 leasing companies were active, 80% of which were private sector companies.

Figure 4.20: Leasing Market, Uzbekistan, 2012–2018

a. Values and Transaction

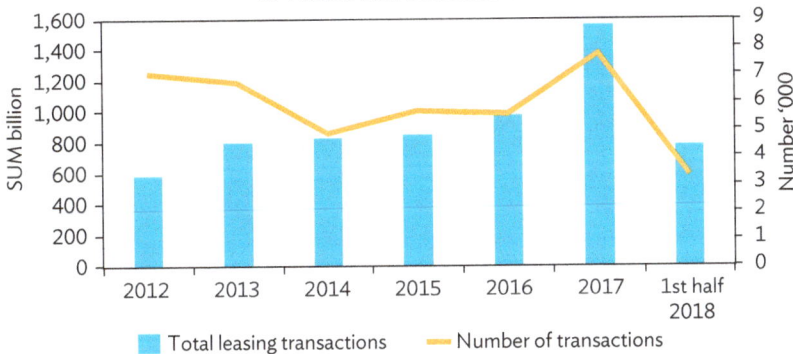

b. By Area

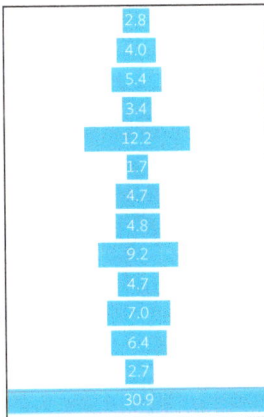

c. By Type

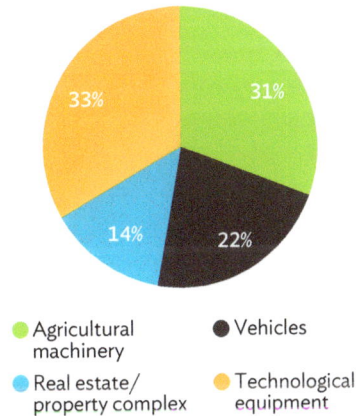

For figures b and c, share of total leasing operations; data for the first half of 2018.
Sources: Uzbekistan Lessors Association (2018) and data received from Asaka Trans Leasing on 5 October 2018.

To provide public financial support, the government established in 2017 the State Fund for Support of Development of Entrepreneurship Activity, offering two measures for small businesses: (i) 50% partial credit guarantees not exceeding $250,000; and (ii) an interest rate subsidy of 5% for loans to specific sectors, mainly for agriculture. As of Q3 2018, the State Fund's total guaranteed loans outstanding amounted to SUM281 billion ($35 million), of which 32% were local currency loans and the remaining 68% were foreign currency loans, with 111 small business beneficiaries (Figure 4.21). In the same period, subsidized loans outstanding amounted to SUM161 billion ($20 million), of which 48% were local currency loans and the remaining 52% were foreign currency loans, with 152 small business beneficiaries (Figure 4.22). Since the State Fund started operating in January 2018, it has supported 1,200 small businesses with a total of SUM1,300 billion ($160 million) in guarantees and interest rate subsidies.

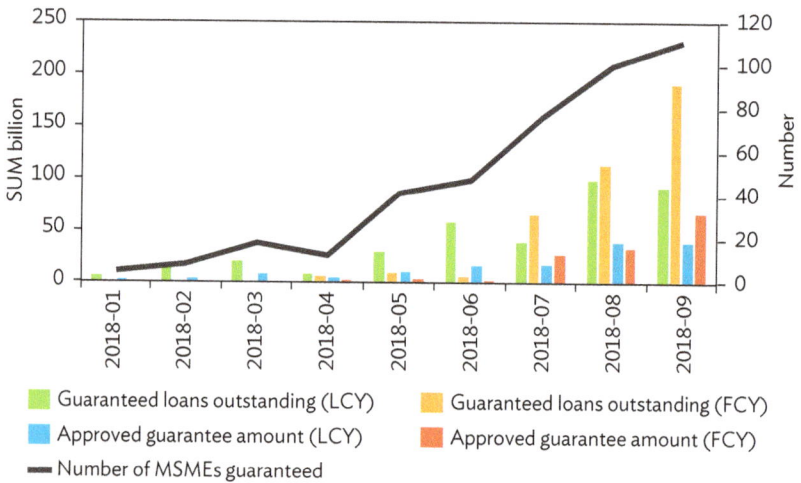

Figure 4.21: Credit Guarantees for Small Businesses, Uzbekistan, 2018

FCY = foreign currency; LCY = local currency; MSMEs = micro, small, and medium-sized enterprises.
Note: Data collected on forms specially designed by the author.
Source: Data received from the State Fund for Support of Development of Entrepreneurship Activity on 5 October 2018.

Figure 4.22: Subsidized Loans for Small Businesses, Uzbekistan, 2018

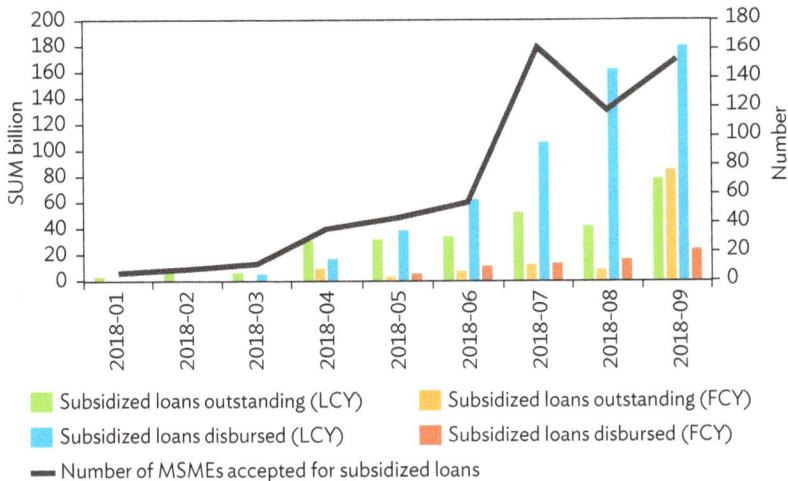

FCY = foreign currency; LCY = local currency; MSMEs = micro, small, and medium-sized enterprises.
Note: Data collected on forms specially designed by the author.
Source: Data received from the State Fund for Support of Development of Entrepreneurship Activity on 5 October 2018.

4.3.3.   Fintech and digital financial services solutions

The fourth industrial revolution, represented by emerging technologies such as artificial intelligence, robotics, and the "Internet of Things," has been dramatically changing the business environment, including for SMEs. The advent of financial technology (fintech) has also been sharply changing the financial sector's architecture and landscape. Given the structural problem with traditional lending models, SMEs may be key beneficiaries of fintech. Fintech can help them survive and grow, offering fast, easy, safe, and low-cost financing to support their innovative business models. New players such as telecommunication companies, mobile network operators, and cash-in/cash-out agents have been emerging in financial markets, bringing new and alternative finance products and services such as marketplace or peer-to-peer lending, e-commerce finance, online supply chain finance, and equity crowdfunding. Peer-to-peer lending generally refers to lending flexible amounts of money to borrowers without going to physical bank branches or requiring collateral. Peer-to-peer lending is very active in the People's Republic of China. E-commerce platforms such as Amazon, eBay, and Alibaba are now offering working capital loans for SMEs that use their platforms for selling goods.

A study of four Asian economies (Cambodia, Indonesia, Myanmar, and the Philippines) indicated that digital finance significantly increases access to finance for low-income households, women, and SMEs (ADB 2017). For example, in Indonesia, unmet demand for payments, credit, and savings amounted to 65%, 36%, and 26%, respectively, of each category; and digital financial services (DFS) solutions could contribute to closing gaps by 37%, 20%, and 35% in payments, credit, and savings, respectively. Mckinsey Global Institute (2016) estimates that digital finance can create $2.1 trillion in new credit and $4.2 trillion in new deposits globally (Figure 4.23). This involves new credit of $197 billion and new deposits of $376 billion created by digital finance for Eastern Europe and Central Asia, including Uzbekistan.

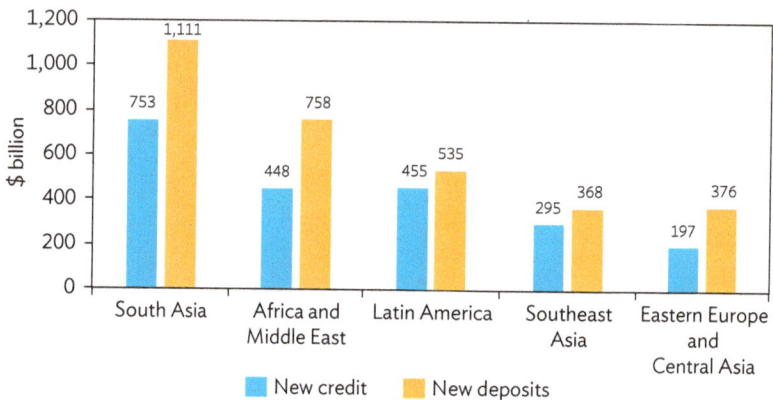

Figure 4.23: Digital Finance Impact on the Financial Sector, Developing Economies, 2016

Source: Author, based on Mckinsey Global Institute (2016).

The introduction of DFS solutions will help encourage financial inclusion in Uzbekistan. The Global Findex Database (World Bank 2017) indicates that in Uzbekistan, the share of people using the internet to pay bills or to buy something online has been increasing sharply, from 0.6% of people over 15 years old in 2014 to 7.1% in 2017 (Figure 4.24). None were using a mobile phone or the internet to access a financial institution account in 2014, but 6.7% of people over 15 years old had done so as of 2017, and 34% of people over 15 years old had made or received digital payments in the past as of 2017.

Online supply chain finance, which provides short-term financing for SME suppliers of goods and services by using an online platform, is a promising DFS solution that is applicable in Uzbekistan (Figure 4.25). This DFS solution offers prompt payment of invoices at a discount for SME suppliers. The SME supplier first uploads its invoice to a specialized online platform through accounting software (e.g., QuickBooks). When the buyer approves the invoice via the online platform, the supplier requests finance through the platform. After the supplier's identity is verified based on the analysis of alternative data or cloud data, the investor (individual and institutional) or the financier provides finance at a discount to the supplier via the platform before the maturity date; then the platform collects the face value of the invoice from the buyer at maturity. If this scheme is combined with a smart contract, financing will be much faster as the smart contract can immediately verify and settle a contract between a seller and a buyer without a third-party intermediary by using

Figure 4.24: Digital Penetration, Uzbekistan, 2014 and 2017

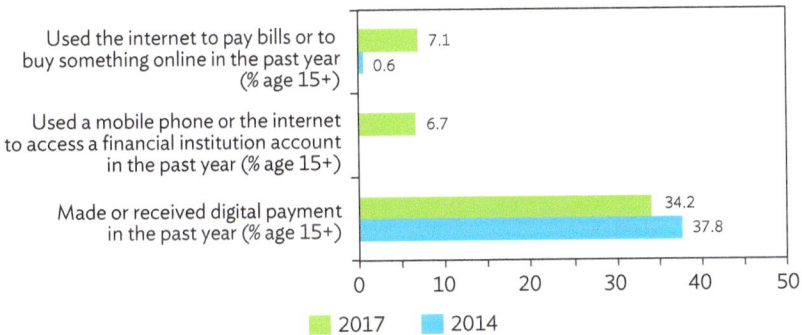

Used the internet to pay bills or to buy something online in the past year (% age 15+): 2017 = 7.1, 2014 = 0.6

Used a mobile phone or the internet to access a financial institution account in the past year (% age 15+): 2017 = 6.7

Made or received digital payment in the past year (% age 15+): 2017 = 34.2, 2014 = 37.8

Source: Author based on World Bank. Global Findex Database 2017.

Figure 4.25: Online Supply Chain Finance

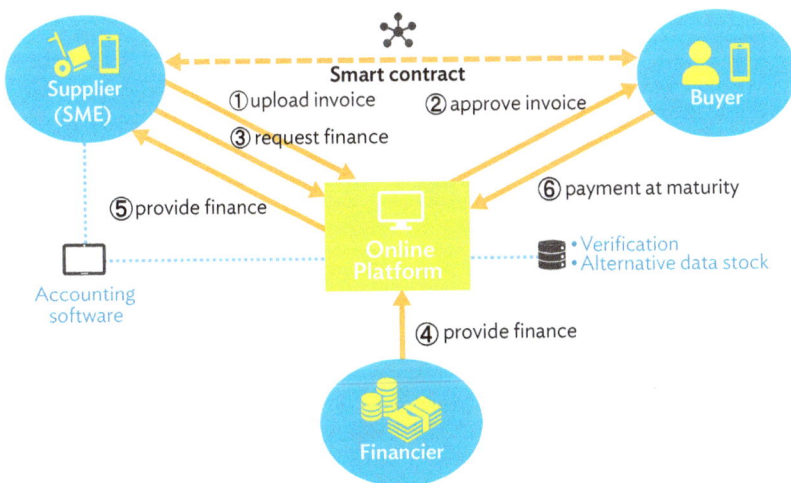

Smart contract. Supplier (SME), Buyer, Online Platform, Financier, Accounting software, Verification, Alternative data stock. ① upload invoice ② approve invoice ③ request finance ④ provide finance ⑤ provide finance ⑥ payment at maturity

Source: Author's compilation.

blockchain technology. DFS can thereby contribute to reducing the financing gap in Uzbekistan. Because DFS is relatively new in the country, efforts will be required to enhance SMEs' financial (digital) literacy so they can use DFS.

4.4. Government Efforts Toward Inclusive and Private Sector-led Growth

4.4.1. Review of private sector development and financial sector reforms

Since the new government administration started in December 2016, Uzbekistan has launched a multitude of policy measures that accelerate the liberalization of the market-based economy. In February 2017, Presidential Decree No. 4947, About the Strategy of Actions for Further Development of the Republic of Uzbekistan, includes a national development strategy comprising five policy priorities: (i) governance and public administration; (ii) rule of law and the judicial system; (iii) economic development; (iv) social development; and (v) security, tolerance, and foreign policy (Table 4.2).

Table 4.2: Priority Areas Under the 2017 National Development Strategy, Uzbekistan

Priority Area	Action
Governance and public administration	• Strengthen the role of Parliament and political parties • Reform the governance system (e-government) • Improve public management system
Rule of law and judicial system	• Improve the judicial and legal system • Guarantee protection of rights and freedoms of citizens • Improve the administrative, criminal, civil, and commercial law
Economic development	• Strengthen macroeconomic stability • Improve the competitiveness of the economy • Intensively develop agriculture • Introduce institutional and structural reforms to reduce the state's presence • Develop small business and private entrepreneurship • Enhance the socioeconomic development of provinces, districts, and cities
Social development	• Increase real incomes and create jobs • Improve social security, health care, housing, education, and youth policy
Security, tolerance, and foreign policy	• Provide measures to ensure security, inter-ethnic harmony, and religious tolerance • Have a balanced and constructive foreign policy

Source: Government of Uzbekistan (2017).

Small business and private entrepreneurship development are clearly incorporated in the third pillar of the national development strategy (economic development). In line with the strategy's five priority areas, several reforms are being implemented, including foreign exchange market liberalization and tax reforms. Related to small business and private entrepreneurship development, a new SME definition has been effective since January 2019, including a new category of medium enterprises, which enables the government to target viable SMEs in implementing its growth strategies.

Ongoing tax reforms are bringing some benefits to SMEs. SMEs are benefiting from the simplified business income tax regime, which offers a unified tax payment of 5% for wholesale trade, 1%–4% for retail trade, 10% for public catering services, and the unified social tax of 15% (Table 4.3). In this scheme, SMEs are exempted from corporate income tax, property tax, mandatory contribution to state funds, value-added tax, and other local taxes and duties. In 2017, 141,965 enterprises (94% of all enterprises) enjoyed the simplified tax regime (IMF 2018). However, requirements of the current simplified regime will need to be adjusted to the new SME definition, as the standard regime may be applied for medium enterprises under the new definition due to the employment threshold. This means that corporate income tax, property tax, mandatory contribution to state funds, and a 20% value-added tax will be levied on medium enterprises.

Table 4.3: Tax on Business Income, Uzbekistan, 2017

Tax Regime	Requirements	Components	Conditions
Standard	• Legal entities with more than 200 employees	• Corporate income tax: 14% (profit based) • Property tax: 5% (asset value based) • Mandatory contribution to state funds: 3.2% (turnover based)	• 9,592 enterprises (6% of the total legal entities, 2017) • Corporate income tax: 0.6% of GDP (2017) • Property tax: 0.9% of GDP (2017) • Mandatory contribution to state funds: 9.3% of GDP (2017)
Simplified	• Legal entities with 200 or fewer employees • Trade and catering firms	• Unified tax payment: (i) wholesale trade 5%, (ii) retail trade 1%, 2%, or 4%, and (iii) public catering 10% • Unified social tax: 15%	• 141,965 enterprises (94% of the total legal entities, 2017) • Designed for micro and small enterprises • Exempt from corporate income tax, property tax, mandatory contribution, value-added tax, and other local taxes/duties

GDP = gross domestic product.
Source: Based on Michielse et al. (2018).

The national development strategy prioritizes SME development but no concrete strategic action plans have been prepared. A comprehensive policy framework for SME development and financial inclusion have yet to be established. The Cabinet of Ministers will play the leading role of coordinating SME policy discussions with line ministries and the CBU, and in setting an SME development master plan covering financial and nonfinancial issues.

4.4.2. Role of state-owned enterprises and banks

ADB (2018) assessed the engagement and reform of SOEs in Uzbekistan and came up with several important findings. Based on these findings, this section discusses the role of SOEs, especially state-owned banks.

Issues arising from SOEs. The business environment in Uzbekistan has been partly controlled by enterprises that are fully or partly state owned. In Uzbekistan, all enterprises that are not directly or indirectly fully state-owned are considered to be not state-owned. Thus, for example, enterprises with state ownership of more than 50% but less than 100% are legally classified as private sector businesses. Privatization of SOEs is moving forward, but privatized enterprises with partial state ownership often dominate private sector markets, potentially crowding out new private sector entrants. Moreover, strategically and socially important enterprises remain SOEs, especially in banking, mining, gas, electricity, water supply, and transport. Some designated goods and services do not rely on market-based pricing but use the Ministry of Finance's set pricing mechanism. This can limit the competitiveness of private sector business and risk market distortions, impeding private sector-led economic growth. The government is aware of this issue, and the national development strategy incorporates SOE reform as a key policy action under the pillar of economic development.

Government reform efforts affecting SOE performance. A multitude of government reform measures have had a mixed impact on SOE performance. For example, the currency devaluation caused by the liberalization of foreign exchange markets in September 2017 negatively affected SOEs' financial positions. In particular, it hit major state-owned banks and negatively affected the banking sector. To recover soundness in the banking sector, the government injected a large amount of capital ($562 million) into nine state-owned banks. Also, the corporate governance reforms of 2015 and ongoing public financial management reforms have increased costs of SOEs, as have the switch to using the International Financial Reporting Standards, replacements of chief operating officers, implementation of the budget accounting standard (2016), and so on. These measures will facilitate the competitiveness of private business, but may risk bloating the national budget. Further reform efforts will be needed, especially for loss-making SOEs. Meanwhile, two government initiatives will benefit both private sector firms and SOEs, creating joint business opportunities: (i) a centralized information portal among the government, SOEs, and other enterprises under the planned master plan for information technology applications and e-government; and (ii) public–private partnerships in infrastructure and public services.

The government's financial sector development strategy. The reform of state-owned banks is a critical component of Uzbekistan's financial sector development strategy. The threshold between banking and nonbank finance activities is still unclear. For example, commercial banks provide microcredit loans and leasing to customers, as do independent microcredit organizations and leasing companies. The removal of duplicative functions between banking and nonbank finance industries is one of the financial sector reform targets. The government has planned to create a new financial regulatory authority for nonbank finance industries including a securities market, leasing, microcredit organizations, and pawnshops. This is separate from banking supervision by the CBU. The reform of financial regulatory authorities will bring more transparency to the financial sector, and business activities of state-owned banks will be streamlined.

The role of SOEs for private sector-led economic growth. SOEs should facilitate private sector development. Strategically and socially important enterprises may continue as SOEs, but an exit strategy is needed to support the creation of more competitive private sector markets. Public–private partnership should be encouraged, with potential participation from SMEs. The shift to the banking system led by the private sector, by rationalizing loss-making state-owned banks, should be encouraged as well. The creation of specialized state-owned banks, e.g., an SME bank and an agriculture development bank, may be worth considering with appropriate exit strategies, given the socially oriented nature of their activities.

4.5. Policy Implications for Accelerating Inclusive Economic Growth

Uzbekistan is currently in the most important stage of its transformation toward a market-based economy aimed at sustainable and resilient growth. Private sector development is critical for a smooth shift from state-driven to private sector-led economic growth, where SMEs play a key role. Six policy implications are drawn from the above discussion, with a view to assisting the design of a comprehensive policy framework for SME development and financial inclusion for private sector development in Uzbekistan.

Strengthening business competitiveness of services-related and tech-based SMEs. The most numerous SMEs are service-related, but their job creating capacity has been relatively low and their GVA is below its potential. Retail trade and catering services are the predominant SMEs and major borrowers of bank credit among services-related small businesses. However, they are not expected to support the country's goal of sustainable economic growth as their business is domestically focused with limited operating areas, whereas highly productive services-related and tech-based SMEs could create more good quality jobs or skilled labor and help boost national productivity. Among several constraints, limited access to long-term finance impedes their growth. The government needs to facilitate the structural change of private businesses and support creating the enabling business environment for services-related SMEs, including those in education, health, transport, tourism, and information technology. In particular, tech-based SMEs should be a primary target for assistance. SMEs typically lack access to information about new markets, products, and opportunities to develop their business models. To ease this situation, the government's support measures should include business development services for SMEs and young entrepreneurs, and business literacy and education programs for potential workers.

Promoting internationalization of SMEs through global value chains. Uzbekistan's export structure has changed from heavy reliance on cotton and natural resources to a more diverse range of processed products and services, bringing new business opportunities for export-oriented and internationalized SMEs. The government could usefully promote the internationalization of SMEs by encouraging their active participation in global value chains. Benefits for SMEs could include increased competitiveness through vertical linkages with multinational lead firms, enhanced technology transfer to upgrade product quality, and resultant business expansion to overseas marketplaces, with associated job creation. It would be difficult for SMEs to grow by themselves, but they could do so if engaged in relationships and business partnerships with lead firms and value chain actors in their areas of operations. The government support measures should include developing agricultural value chains, given the growth potential of agribusinesses and their contribution to agriculture and manufacturing. Special economic zones for SMEs may be worth considering as well.

Establishing high-quality financial infrastructure to modernize the banking sector. Financial sector development is essential to promote private sector development, associated job creation, and sustainable economic growth. A sound financial system requires high-quality financial infrastructure to support effective financial outreach to private sector businesses, especially SMEs. Three essential infrastructure components are a credit data platform, a secured lending legal system, and credit guarantees. These need to be supplemented by a financial education system to facilitate the active use of the infrastructure. The credit market has been expanding in Uzbekistan, but SMEs have yet to benefit sufficiently from that expansion. Credit enhancement schemes supported by a credit bureau, a collateral registry, and credit guarantees should be created and strengthened to modernize the banking sector and enhance SMEs' access to finance. Developing a credit risk database modeled on Japan's also is worth considering.

Developing the nonbank finance industry and market-based instruments with a road map. The nonbank finance industry and capital market have yet to become a viable substitute for bank lending for private businesses, while the demand for diversified financing options has been increasing among SMEs. Tech-based SMEs especially need long-term financing for R&D investments. Leasing is a promising alternative financing option for SMEs. The need for access to trade finance and supply chain finance also will increase among SMEs and associated businesses, given the potential for developing global value chains. In the long run, the creation of a specialized equity market for innovative and viable SMEs may be worth considering. The government needs to prepare a road map for developing the nonbank finance industry and market-based instruments to promote their balanced development alongside the banking sector.

Making the best use of digital finance solutions to promote financial inclusion. Fintech has been rapidly changing the financial sector's architecture and landscape. SMEs are considered a key beneficiary of fintech, given their limited access to traditional lending models. Digital finance can have a significant positive impact on promoting access to finance for traditionally underserved groups including SMEs. Online supply chain finance could be a pilot test for using digital finance. The government needs to recognize digital finance solutions to promote financial inclusion. It also needs to enhance financial and digital literacy for SMEs and consider establishing a national strategy for financial inclusion. Such a strategy has been introduced in some developing Asian countries (e.g., Indonesia in 2012 and 2016, and Pakistan and the Philippines in 2015).

Designing institutional reform plans for SME development with advancing SOE reforms. Last, given the complexity of the business environment around SMEs, the government needs to coordinate policy discussions with line ministries and the CBU to set an SME development master plan covering both financial and nonfinancial issues, with the Cabinet of Ministers playing the leading role. The government could create a specialized SME agency to effectively design a comprehensive policy framework on SME development and efficiently implement the designated action plans. A set of policy frameworks for SME development and financial inclusion should supplement Uzbekistan's national development strategy for 2017–2021. Given that SOE reforms create more space for private businesses, the government needs to consider the institutional reform plans for SME development, together with ongoing SOE reforms, which will include clarifying the role of state-owned banks. Meanwhile, creating specialized state-owned banks, such as an SME bank and an agriculture development bank, is worth considering, given the socially oriented nature of their activities. An exit strategy for such specialized banks should be discussed at the outset, to avoid competing with private sector development.

4.6. Conclusion

Uzbekistan's present growth pattern is led by labor-intensive industries in agriculture, manufacturing, and construction, but the service sector holds great potential for quality job creation. The sectoral and employment structures of the country's economic activities have not been changed in more than a decade. Labor mobility should be facilitated between low and high productive activities. Highly productive services-related SMEs include SMEs in education, health, transport, tourism, and information technology. Such SMEs, especially tech-based ones, will be able to boost national productivity through their innovation and skilled labor, benefiting from foreign direct investment and technological breakthroughs.

Export-oriented and internationalized SMEs could also boost national productivity through their active participation in global value chains. They could grow further by strengthening firm relationships and partnerships with lead firms and value chain actors in their industries. Agriculture-related SMEs could create more jobs by restructuring their business models to highly productive businesses using technology obtained through participating in agricultural value chains.

Several factors constrain SME development: e.g., insufficient product quality control and standards, skilled labor, market access, logistics, business literacy, networking, corporate governance, and access to finance. Among others, funding constraints weaken SMEs' innovation capabilities. Enhanced financial sector development is needed for the private sector to develop further. Growth-oriented SMEs are seeking diversified financing options that go beyond traditional bank credit to support their growth potential. SME access to finance should be high on the government's policy agenda for private sector development. In particular, the balanced development of banking and the nonbank finance industry, using new digital technologies, is crucial to broadening the financing models available for viable SMEs, including start-ups and young entrepreneurs.

The government's institutional reforms should be well coordinated, together with SOE reforms, to advance private sector and financial sector development agendas.

References

Asian Development Bank (ADB). 2017. *Accelerating Financial Inclusion in Southeast Asia with Digital Finance*. Manila.

_____. 2018. State-Owned Enterprise Engagement and Reform. Supplementary Appendix 3: Case Assessment (Uzbekistan). Manila.

Central Bank of Uzbekistan. Indicators of Banking System and Non-Banking Credit Organizations. https://www.cbu.uz/ (accessed 15 October 2018).

Government of Uzbekistan. 2017. Presidential Decree No.4947: About the Strategy of Actions for Further Development of the Republic of Uzbekistan. Tashkent.

_____. 2018. Presidential Decree No. UP-5544: About Approval of Strategy for Innovative Development of the Country for 2019–2021. Tashkent.

International Finance Corporation (IFC). 2017. *MSME Finance Gap*. Washington, DC.

International Monetary Fund (IMF). 2018. *Republic of Uzbekistan Staff Report for 2018 Article IV Consultation*. Washington, DC. April.

Japan External Trade Organization (JETRO). 2018. *Securities Market in Uzbekistan*. Tashkent.

Mckinsey Global Institute. 2016. *Digital Finance for All: Powering Inclusive Growth in Emerging Economies*. https://www.mckinsey.com/~/media/mckinsey/featured%20insights/Employment%20and%20Growth/How%20digital%20finance%20could%20boost%20growth%20in%20emerging%20economies/MGI-Digital-Finance-For-All-Executive-summary-September-2016.ashx

McMillan, M. and D. Rodrik. 2011. Globalization, Structural Change and Productivity Growth. *National Bureau of Economic Research Working Paper*. No. 17143. http://www.nber.org/papers/w17143

Michielse, G., R. Krelove, N. Nersesyan, and JF. Wen. 2018. *Uzbekistan Review of the Tax System*. International Monetary Fund (IMF).

Organisation for Economic Co-operation and Development (OECD). 2017. *Boosting SME Internationalisation in Uzbekistan through Better Export Promotion Policies*. Peer Review Note. Paris. http://www.oecd.org/eurasia/competitiveness-programme/central-asia/Uzbekistan_Peer_review_note_dec2017_final.pdf

Republican Stock Exchange Tashkent. http://www.uzse.uz/ (accessed 20 September 2018).

Schwab, K. 2017. The Fourth Industrial Revolution. Geneva: World Economic Forum.

Shinozaki, S. 2015. Financing SMEs in Global Value Chains. *Integrating SMEs into Global Value Chains—Challenges and Policy Actions in Asia*. pp.66-100. Manila: ADB.

State Committee of the Republic of Uzbekistan on Statistics (Uzbekistan Statistics). 2017a. Demography of Enterprises and Organizations. 24 July. https://www.stat.uz/en/435-analiticheskie-materialy-en1/2074-demography-of-enterprises-and-organizations (accessed 20 September 2018).

_____. 2017b. Innovation Activity of Enterprises and Organizations. 14 July. https://stat.uz/en/435-analiticheskie-materialy-en1/2080-innovation-activity-of-enterprises-and-organizations (accessed 20 September 2018).

UZDaily. 2018. Uzbekistan Adopts Strategy of Innovative Development for 2019–2021. 21/09/2018.

Uzbekistan Lessors Association. 2018. *Overview of the Uzbekistan Leasing Services Sector on the Results of the First Half of 2018*. Tashkent.

World Bank. 2013. Enterprise Surveys. Uzbekistan (2013) http://www.enterprisesurveys.org/data/exploreeconomies/2013/uzbekistan (accessed 20 September 2018).

_____. 2015. *Principles for Public Credit Guarantee Schemes for SMEs*. http://documents.worldbank.org/curated/en/576961468197998372/pdf/101769-REVISED-ENGLISH-Principles-CGS-for-SMEs.pdf (accessed 20 September 2018).

_____. 2017. The Global Findex Database 2017. http://www.globalfindex.worldbank.org/ (accessed 20 September 2018).

_____. 2018. *Growth Diagnostics for Uzbekistan*. Tashkent.

_____. Doing Business Reports (various years). http://www.doingbusiness.org/ (accessed 20 December 2019).

_____. World Development Indicators. http://www.databank.worldbank.org/ (accessed 20 September 2018).

CHAPTER 5

Trade and Foreign Direct Investment in Uzbekistan

Jozef Konings and Aigerim Yergabulova

Uzbekistan's external trade is currently dominated by the export of primary commodities and other low-value-added goods. The development of regional trade and cooperation in the past was hampered by state intervention, which included import substitution strategies and foreign exchange restrictions. In addition, the continued slowdown in economic growth of the country's major trading partners—the People's Republic of China (PRC) and the Russian Federation—and falling world commodity prices have adversely affected trade tax contributions to the government's budget in recent years. Moreover, Uzbekistan attracts the least foreign direct investment (FDI) inflows among Central Asian economies.[1] This challenging external position suggests the need to transform toward a more open, diversified, and market-based economy.

To this end, a set of reforms advocating a new development strategy has been initiated to accelerate the country's modernization and development of key industries. An important priority is liberalizing trade via tariff reductions and initiating structural reforms in the state sector to boost both domestic and foreign competition. In line with that agenda, government authorities have already implemented a series of policy actions. In particular, to strengthen monetary policy, the national currency has floated freely since September 2017. That has reduced the negative impact of external competitiveness on domestic enterprises. Other actions include resuming negotiations to accede to the World Trade Organization (WTO), improving relations with regional trading partners, and introducing legislative changes to attract foreign investors. Membership in trade agreements and FDI liberalization would further promote domestic competition and contribute to the efficiency of the country's economy.

---

[1] Data from the World Bank. World Development Indicators. https://databank.worldbank.org/source/world-development-indicators (accessed December 2019)

Trade liberalization can boost economic growth, especially in an emerging economy such as Uzbekistan's. Trade facilitates productivity improvements and more efficient allocation of resources, and hence boosts economic output. For example, Pavcnik (2002) found evidence that aggregate productivity in Chile increased due to its trade liberalization, and Amiti and Konings (2007) show that accession to the WTO and a subsequent reduction of input tariffs significantly contributed to productivity gains in Indonesian manufacturing during the late 1990s.

However, liberalized trade may not necessarily foster aggregate growth if there exist cumbersome business and labor regulations or excessive government support for enterprises (Rodrik 1988, Bolaky and Freund 2004). For example, reductions in trade protectionism in India led to higher productivity growth in private firms but productivity in public sector firms remained unchanged (Topalova 2004). While state-owned firms enjoy soft budget constraints, they tend to retain excessive labor, which depresses their productivity and prevents efficient reallocation of resources (De Loecker and Konings 2003). Furthermore, Donaldson (2018) concluded that improved railroads decreased trade costs and increased trade and real incomes in India. That is, other trade facilitation mechanisms also are important, including transport and logistics infrastructure (Nordas et al. 2006, Hong et al. 2011); indirect transport costs (Hausman et al. 2013); and nontariff measures (Kee et al. 2009).

The role of FDI to facilitate growth through human resource development and technology transfer also has been discussed extensively in the literature. One reason to attract FDI is to create new jobs in the economy. FDI not only opens up opportunities, but also tends to result in higher wages in developing countries as foreign employers offer more on-the-job training than do domestic employers (Javorcik 2012). Hence, FDI boosts aggregate productivity in the host country. However, the amount and type of FDI received depend on a number of factors, such as absorptive capacities within the recipient country, institutional and political regulations, trade openness, and scale factors (de Mello 1999).

This chapter analyzes the scope for economic activities to enhance the role of trade and FDI in Uzbekistan. The chapter starts by discussing Uzbekistan's institutional background in economic and trade cooperation. Section 5.2 draws out stylized facts from export, import, and FDI data. Section 5.3 discusses why Uzbekistan needs to further liberalize its trade and FDI, and section 5.4 reviews how international trade and FDI can promote economic growth. The chapter then takes a "granular" approach to analyzing firm size distribution in Uzbekistan (section 5.5). Section 5.6 estimates a gravity model to explain Uzbekistan's trade pattern, using a sample of major trading partners. Section 5.7 summarizes and provides policy recommendations to improve the country's trade and investment climate.

5.1. Uzbekistan's Trade and International Economic Cooperation: An Overview

A fundamental principle in international economics is that reducing trade barriers to free up flows of goods and services between countries raises social welfare. It provides welfare gains to consumers through increased product variety, lower prices and improved quality of goods, as well as opportunities for producers to specialize more and so reap greater economies of scale. In this context, the WTO plays a key role in promoting free trade by setting the rules of international trade, providing a platform for negotiating bilateral, regional, plurilateral, and especially multilateral trade agreements to reduce tariffs and other trade barriers. As of 2019, 164 countries were members of the WTO.

Regional and bilateral cooperation can stimulate national transit systems, harmonize transport regulations, and facilitate customs transit, which can significantly reduce transport costs (ADB 2006). Lower transport costs and shorter transit times in turn increase the gains from trade by attracting FDI, diversifying source and destination countries through global supply chains, and differentiating exports in terms of product composition.

Economic integration in Central Asia reflects institutional trade policies and the geography and geopolitics of the region (Table 5.1). As of 2019, only three Central Asian economies are WTO members—the Kyrgyz Republic (from 1998), Tajikistan (from 2013), and Kazakhstan (from 2015). Uzbekistan is currently an observer economy. Its accession to the WTO would help it access export markets and achieve higher returns on investment.

In terms of regional cooperation, Uzbekistan is a member of the Commonwealth of Independent States (CIS), the organization formed by the former Soviet Union countries at the end of 1991. The initial aims of creating the organization were to sustain free trade and movement of people, protect human rights, and prevent armed conflicts in the territory of the CIS. However, the integration started to fail due to large differences between the economy and territorial potential of the Russian Federation versus other member states (Kononczuk 2007).

The Economic Cooperation Organization involves all Central Asian economies, including Uzbekistan, however its preferential trade agreements do not apply to all members. For example, the organization's trade cooperation agreement has been ratified only by Kazakhstan, the Kyrgyz Republic, and Tajikistan.

The Eurasian Economic Union, founded in 2015, was formed to establish a single market, involving a lower number of participant countries than the CIS. However, the treaty has recently received substantial criticism due to its inability to stimulate integration and economic modernization (Ferrari 2016).

Table 5.1: Trade and Economic Organization Memberships, Uzbekistan

Organization/Agreement	Membership	Notes
World Trade Organization	No	Observer country.
Commonwealth of Independent States	Yes	Joined in 1992, ratified in 1994.
Eurasian Economic Union	No	Founded in 2015. Current members are Armenia, Belarus, Kazakhstan, the Kyrgyz Republic, and the Russian Federation.
Economic Cooperation Organization	Yes	Preferential trade agreements do not involve Uzbekistan.
Partnership and Cooperation Agreement	Yes	Bilateral trade agreements with the European Union.

Source: Batsaikhan and Dabrowski (2017).

Recently the role of trade and investment between Uzbekistan and the European Union (EU) has been increasing, as shown in the next section. This has been triggered by the signing of the bilateral Partnership and Cooperation Agreement in 1996, which offered the Generalized System of Preferences to Uzbekistan. Other Central Asian economies, including the Kyrgyz Republic and Tajikistan also benefit from bilateral agreements with the EU. Uzbekistan benefits less than others under the free trade agreements with the EU because it is not a WTO member and has not completed its market reforms. The incomplete reforms include restructuring state-owned enterprises and privatization; increasing banking competition and interest rate liberalization; eliminating barriers to entry and exit; and reducing subsidies for food, energy, and water.

One form of integration for Uzbekistan is through the gas pipelines from Turkmenistan to the PRC and the Russian Federation via Uzbekistan and Kazakhstan. The World Energy Council ranks Uzbekistan among the top natural gas producers in the world—at 14th largest in 2014. The construction of a major gas pipeline from Turkmenistan has been completed and a second pipeline through Uzbekistan is scheduled (Farchy 2016).

In the last decade, the PRC has been actively reviving the old Silk Road trading route through its Belt and Road Initiative (BRI) that came into force in 2015. The BRI aspires to create a new Eurasian land bridge through transport and infrastructure development, financial integration, and trade liberalization (NDRC 2015). The BRI contains land- and marine-based routes, of which the former runs through the PRC–Central Asia–West Asia economic corridor.

Asia and Europe account for more than a quarter of world trade, hence lowering trade costs could have a significant global impact (Konings 2018). Individual countries' potential trade gains from the BRI have been estimated using gravity models of international trade. Specifically, a 50% reduction in trade costs[2] could increase world trade from 4% to 12%, depending on the locality. For Uzbekistan, the estimated increase in trade was approximately 28%, one of the largest increases due to the BRI projects.

Improved logistics and infrastructure are also believed to increase FDI in the region. However, until recently, one of the biggest issues concerning FDI into Uzbekistan was the ability to repatriate profits to the home country in the face of restrictions on capital outflows. In this regard, recently the Central Bank of Uzbekistan proposed amending the law on currency regulation and currency control, to remove restrictions on profit repatriation of FDI. Moreover, the Central Bank proposes to allow residents to open and use accounts in foreign banks. This, in combination with BRI projects, should improve Uzbekistan's investment climate, facilitate its trade, and attract more foreign investors.

5.2. The Evolution of Trade and Foreign Direct Investment in Uzbekistan: Stylized Facts

5.2.1. Exports and imports

Figure 5.1 shows Uzbekistan's total nominal exports and imports for 1995–2018. Imports and exports increased simultaneously until the global economic crisis of 2008. Total exports and imports had increased from about

---

[2]   A 50% fall in trade costs was adopted because the BRI projects combine both transport costs reduction and trade facilitation measures. The WTO (2015) calculated that trade facilitation among the BRI countries could reduce the trade costs by 12%–23%.

$2 billion in 1995 to $6 billion in 2007. Note that the crisis had a larger negative impact on exports than imports, increasing the trade deficit between 2008 and 2014. A key driver behind this trend was the downturn in international petroleum and gas prices. While accounting for about 40% of total exports in 2016, the share of exports fluctuated between 15% and 85% during 2008 to 2017 due to the global movement in commodity prices. This suggests that Uzbekistan, like other economies with abundant natural resources that lack diversification of their exports, has been vulnerable to external trade shocks.

Figure 5.1: Total Imports and Exports, Uzbekistan, 1995–2018

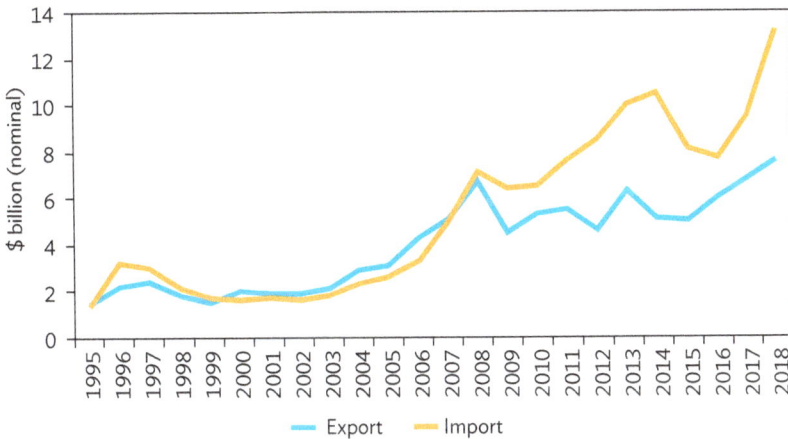

Source: UN Comtrade. https://comtrade.un.org/db/default.aspx (accessed 12 December 2019).

Since Soviet times, Uzbekistan's major trading partner, both in terms of export destinations and import origins, has been the Russian Federation. Following independence after 1991, the destination markets have been diversified away from the Russian Federation and more toward the PRC for imports, and PRC and Switzerland for exports (Figures 5.2 and 5.3). Evidence of a declining share of Russian exports and imports has also been documented for other Central Asian countries, in particular for Kazakhstan (ADB 2018). Nevertheless, the Russian Federation remains a key trade partner of Uzbekistan, accounting for 15% of exports and 22% of imports in 2017. The steady increase in imports from the PRC matched the steady decline in imports from the Russian Federation, eventually exceeding the latter's share beginning 2016. The first year the share of exports to the PRC exceeded the exports to the Russian Federation was in 2013. Also, in 2012 exports (mostly gold) to Switzerland began to increase and in 2017, the country become the top export destination for Uzbek goods.

Figure 5.2: Major Export Destinations, Uzbekistan, 1996–2017

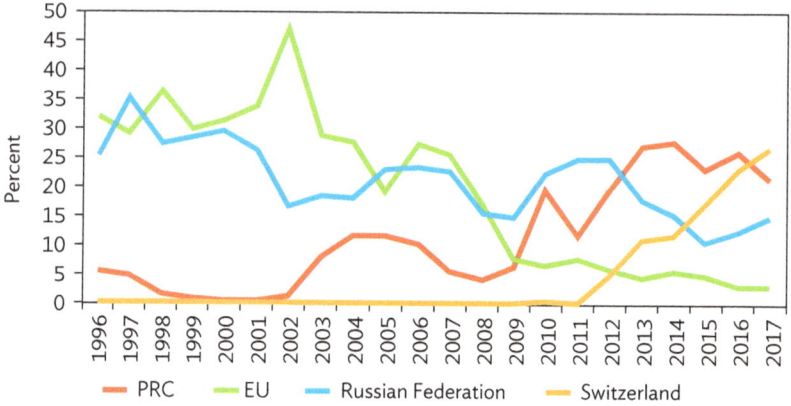

EU = European Union, PRC = People's Republic of China.
Source: Observatory of Economic Complexity. 2018. Export and Imports of Uzbekistan. Retrieved from https://atlas.media.mit.edu/en/profile/country/uzb/ (accessed 12 December 2019).

Figure 5.3: Origins of Major Imports to Uzbekistan, 1996–2017

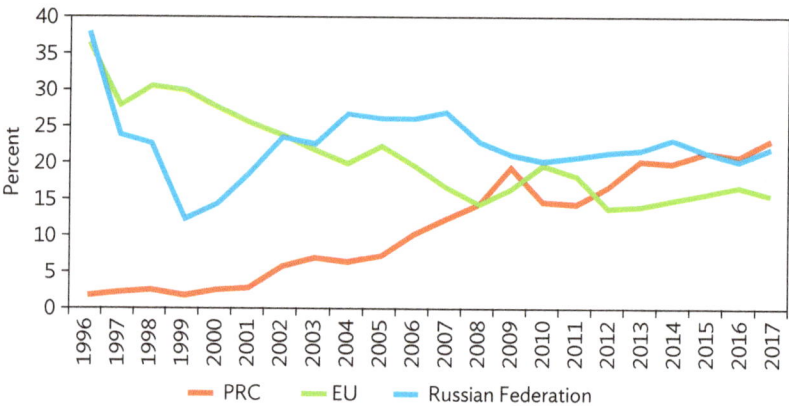

EU = European Union, PRC = People's Republic of China.
Source: Observatory of Economic Complexity. 2018. Export and Imports of Uzbekistan. Retrieved from https://atlas.media.mit.edu/en/profile/country/uzb/ (accessed 12 December 2019).

The composition of Uzbekistan's exports remains substantially concentrated in primary commodities, including precious metals and mineral products (Figure 5.4). Gold accounted for 23% of Uzbekistan's exports in 2018, up from 14% in 1995. On the other hand, textiles, including cotton fiber declined in total exports, from 77% in 1995 to only 8% in 2018. ADB (2006) estimated that the rapid growth of exports in Uzbekistan during 2000 and 2004 was due to the increased prices of primary commodities. In particular, 18 percentage points of the 46% increase in Uzbekistan's exports was due to the rise in world prices for gold and cotton fiber.

Uzbekistan's major import products in 2018 comprised of machines, transport equipment, and metal products (Figure 5.5). Such a diversified structure of imports suggests that many branches of the economy depend on imports.

Figure 5.4: Major Export Products, Uzbekistan, 2018
(%)

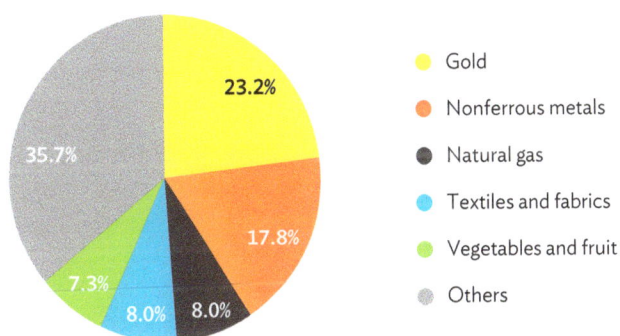

- Gold — 23.2%
- Nonferrous metals — 17.8%
- Natural gas — 8.0%
- Textiles and fabrics — 8.0%
- Vegetables and fruit — 7.3%
- Others — 35.7%

Source: UN Comtrade. https://comtrade.un.org/db/default.aspx (accessed 12 December 2019).

Figure 5.5: Major Import Products, Uzbekistan, 2018
(%)

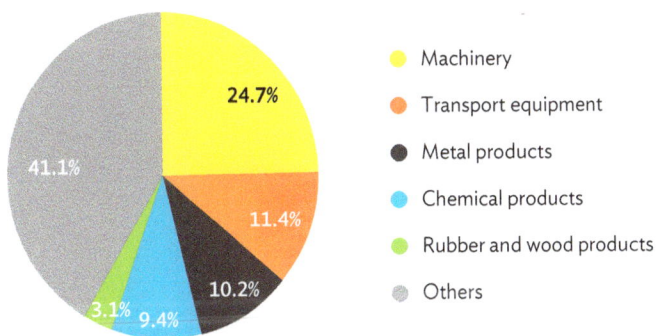

- Machinery — 24.7%
- Transport equipment — 11.4%
- Metal products — 10.2%
- Chemical products — 9.4%
- Rubber and wood products — 3.1%
- Others — 41.1%

Source: UN Comtrade. https://comtrade.un.org/db/default.aspx (accessed 12 December 2019).

5.2.2. Foreign direct investment inflows

Although the Government of Uzbekistan stresses the importance of attracting FDI, it follows a selective approach by encouraging export-oriented industries and discouraging investments in import-consuming sectors (Bendini 2013). Consequently, the FDI inflows are heavily concentrated in the extractive industries and play a negligible role in the Uzbekistan economy. Figure 5.6 depicts the evolution of FDI inflows to Uzbekistan during 1996 and 2018. The FDI had increased from $170 million in 2006 to $1.64 billion in 2010, reaching 4% of gross domestic product (GDP). Since 2011, FDI has been declining gradually to the 2006 level, indicating that the volatility of FDI inflows is closely linked to a decline in world commodity prices. Figure 5.7 confirms that the oil and gas industry accounted for the largest part of FDI inflows in 2012. In 2017, the share of extractive resources, although aggregated, represented 57% of total FDI received. Thus, diversifying the economy away from the reliance on natural resources extraction could reduce the volatility of FDI inflows.

Figure 5.6: FDI Inflows and Share of GDP, Uzbekistan, 1996–2018

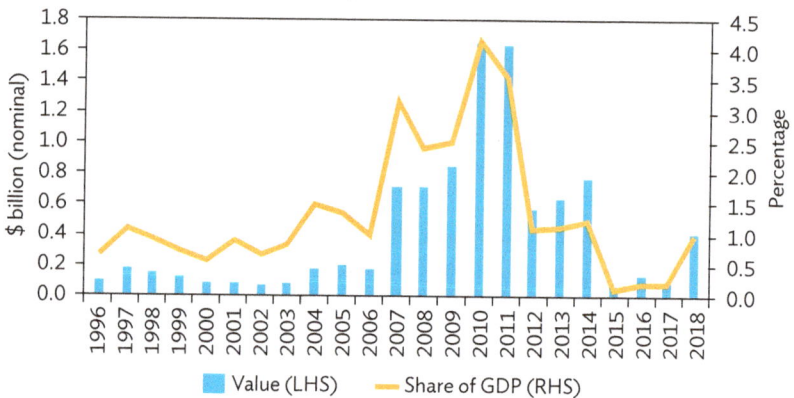

FDI = foreign direct investment, GDP = gross domestic product, LHS = left-hand scale, RHS = right-hand scale.
Source: UNCTADSTAT. https://unctadstat.unctad.org/ (accessed 12 December 2019).

Figure 5.7: FDI Inflows in Share of GDP (%), Uzbekistan, 2012 and 2017

2012

2017

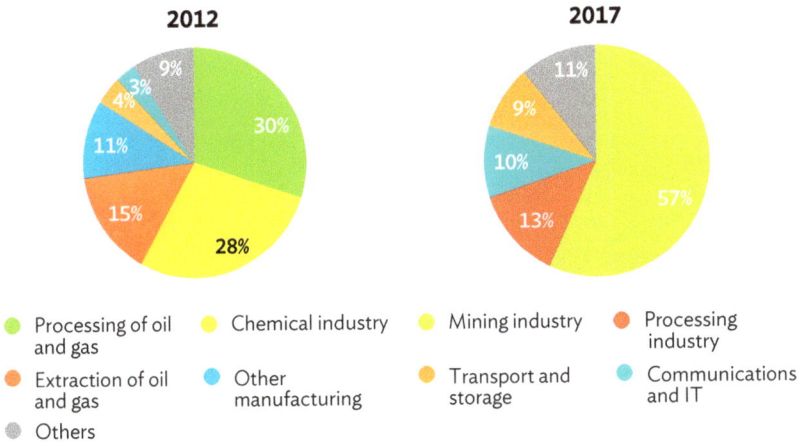

- Processing of oil and gas
- Chemical industry
- Mining industry
- Processing industry
- Extraction of oil and gas
- Other manufacturing
- Transport and storage
- Communications and IT
- Others

FDI = foreign direct investment, GDP = gross domestic product, IT = information and technology.
Sources: ADBI (2014) and Uzbekistan Statistics (2018).

5.3. Why Does Uzbekistan Need to Liberalize Its Trade and Foreign Direct Investment?

Uzbekistan's current trade policy challenge is to expand its investment and trade opportunities. To do so, the country needs to open up to foreign trade and liberalize its FDI. The government's past strategies limited foreign trade to a certain group of commodity exports, and protected domestic firms from external competition. The total trade (the sum of exports and imports of goods and services) as a share of GDP in Uzbekistan has been declining since 2008 and this has also happened in other Central Asian economies (Figure 5.8). The fall was triggered by a sharp decline in global commodity prices, plus government restrictions on interregional trade activities (World Bank 2018). Moreover, the ratio of trade to GDP has been smaller in Uzbekistan throughout the entire period since 1995 than in comparator countries. During 2013–2017, the average has been 40% of GDP for Uzbekistan, 61% of GDP in Kazakhstan, 115% in the Kyrgyz Republic, and 58% in Tajikistan. This suggests that Uzbekistan's state-driven approach of import substitution, together with its relatively high trade costs because it is double-landlocked, has led its economy to be less reliant on foreign trade than the comparators' economies.

Figure 5.8: Total Trade as a Share of GDP in Central Asian Countries, 1995–2018[a]

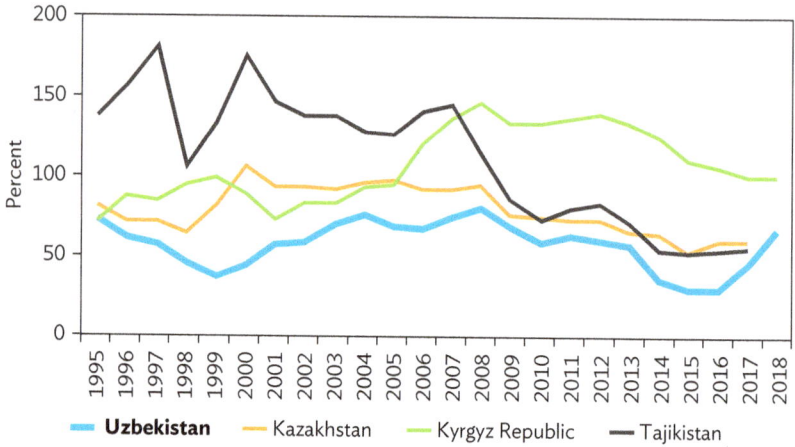

[a] The year 2018 is not reported for Kazakhstan and Tajikistan.
GDP = gross domestic product.
Source: World Bank. World Development Indicators. https://databank.worldbank.org/source/world-development-indicators (accessed 12 December 2019).

5.3.1.   Tariff and Nontariff trade barriers

Even though the government shelters domestic firms from foreign competition, many branches of the economy rely on imports (World Bank 2018). In terms of import duty levels, Uzbekistan's trade policies remain the most restrictive in the Central Asian region. Figure 5.9 shows the weighted average import tariff rate for Uzbekistan during 2006–2014. Although the rate is declining over time, it was still high at 16.2% in 2014 compared with the average rates that year of 4.6% for the Kyrgyz Republic, 8.3% for Tajikistan, and 8.6% for Kazakhstan. The Central Asian economies' underlying lower tariffs can be explained by their involvement in regional agreements such as the Eurasian Economic Union, and in the WTO.

Table 5.2 shows the decomposition of import tariffs in Uzbekistan by major product categories in 2014. The highest import tariffs are observed in apparel and textile industries, such as footwear, leather, and furs manufacturing. This is no coincidence, because textiles accounted for 15% of Uzbekistan's exports in 2016.

Figure 5.9: Weighted Average Import Tariffs, Selected Central Asian Countries, 2006–2014

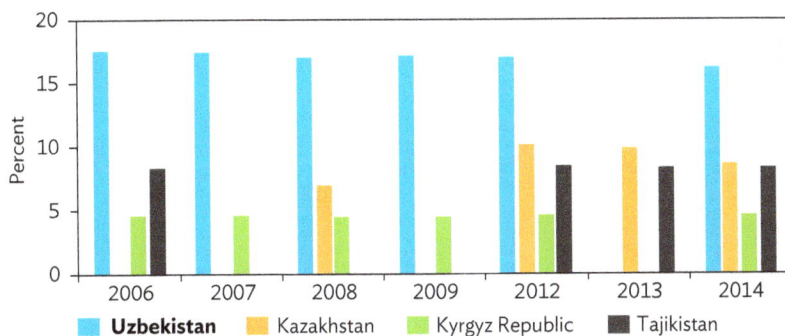

Sources: Authors' calculations based on World Bank. UNCTAD Trade Analysis Information System (TRAINS).https://databank.worldbank.org/reports.aspx?source=UNCTAD-~-Trade-Analysis-Information-System-%28TRAINS%29 (accessed 16 November 2018); and World Bank. World Development Indicators. https://databank.worldbank.org/source/worlddevelopment-indicators (accessed 16 November 2018).

Table 5.2: Average Import Tariffs, by Product, Uzbekistan, 2014
(%)

Product Code (HS)	Product Category	Weighted Average Tariff (%)
01–05	Animal and animal products	13.4
06–15	Vegetable products	14.4
16–24	Foodstuffs	14.4
25–27	Mineral products	12.4
28–38	Chemical and allied industries	13.7
39–40	Plastics and rubbers	11.5
41–43	Rawhides, skins, leather, and fur	20.5
44–49	Wood and wood products	13.2
50–63	Textiles	24.0
64–67	Footwear and headgear	27.0
68–71	Stone and glass	23.0
72–83	Metals	11.9
84–85	Footwear and headgear	9.1
86–89	Transport	8.8
90–97	Miscellaneous	17.5

HS = harmonized system.
Source: Authors' calculations based on World Bank. UNCTAD Trade Analysis Information System (TRAINS). https://databank.worldbank.org/reports.aspx?source=UNCTAD-~-Trade-Analysis-Information-System-%28TRAINS%29 (accessed 16 November 2018); and World Bank. World Development Indicators. https://databank.worldbank.org/source/worlddevelopment-indicators (accessed 16 November 2018).

As a result of negotiations under the WTO, the average level of applied tariffs has fallen by one-third during 1998–2014 (Table 5.3). Uzbekistan misses the opportunity to trade freely with other economies. In addition to tariff cuts, WTO members (developed and developing), have implemented duty-free and quota-free market access to goods from least-developed economies.

Table 5.3: Decline in Global Applied Most-Favored Nation Tariffs, 1998–2014

(%)

Category	Applied Most-Favored Nation Tariffs	
	Average: 2012–2014	Decrease from 1998*
Agricultural	14.9	2.9
Nonagricultural	8.1	4.1
All	9.0	3.9

Source: WTO (2016).

In addition to high import tariffs, Uzbekistan imposes import-exclusive excise taxes and nontariff barriers such as foreign exchange controls, convertibility delays, and conformity assessments, all of which interfere considerably with trade. While tariffs clearly inhibit cross-border trade, nontariff measures often also function as serious impediments to trade. For example, Kee et al. (2009) found that in 34 of 78 studied countries, the contribution of nontariff measures to the overall level of barriers was higher than that of tariffs.

Entrepreneurs' perception of nontariff measures in Uzbekistan is not reported in the literature. However, the World Bank (2018) undertook a firm-level survey of state support measures demanded by manufacturers. Some of the measures include introducing free convertibility for import of inputs, abolishing restrictions for firms selling their output to anyone in domestic and foreign markets, reducing time and simplifying procedures for issuing licenses and permits, and reducing the time needed for getting foreign exchange convertibility.

5.3.2. Investment and business climate

Per the World Investment Report (UNCTAD 2018), Uzbekistan attracts the least FDI inflows among Central Asian economies (Figure 5.10). The foreign exchange, banking, and profit repatriation restrictions, together with the overall tough business environment, have caused a number of foreigners to cut back their investment activities in Uzbekistan (World Bank 2013). Thus, creating a favorable investment climate and competitive environment in the domestic market, and expanding the industrial and export potential of local producers would be critical to attracting greater FDI and creating new jobs in the economy. Evidence from literature suggests that trade and FDI liberalization is associated with increases in productivity and output, but perhaps more importantly to politicians, is the association with new job opportunities in the economy. For example, the employment attributable to both direct and indirect FDI (productivity spillovers) in the United States accounted for 12 million jobs or 8.5% of the labor force in 2013 (Richards and Schaefer 2016).

Figure 5.10: Foreign Direct Investment Flows into Selected Economies, 2005–2017
($ billion)

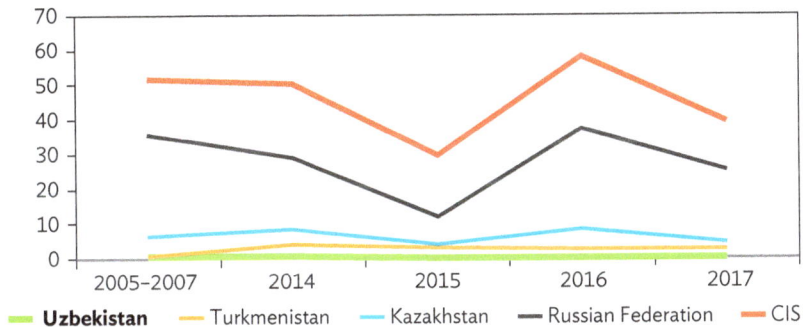

CIS = Commonwealth of Independent States.
Source: UNCTAD. 2018. World Investment Report 2018: Investment and New Industrial Policies. New York: United Nations.

To provide a sense of the level of business dynamics and entrepreneurship in Uzbekistan—the World Bank Doing Business report ranked Uzbekistan 69th among 190 countries in 2020. The ranking is based on assessing 11 indicators, such as regulation for starting a new business, registering properties, trading across borders, and labor market adjustments. Figure 5.11 shows these indicators based on 2020 estimates. Although Uzbekistan ranks relatively well in starting a new business (8th out of 190 countries), the country faces large constraints in trading across borders (152nd), dealing with construction permits (132nd), and resolving insolvency (100th).

Figure 5.11: Ranking on Doing Business Indicators, Uzbekistan, 2020

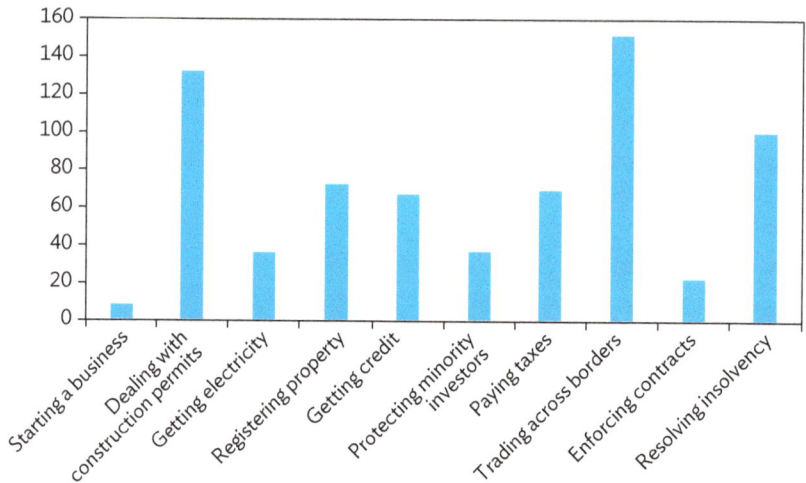

Note: Rank 1 is the highest, 190 is the lowest.
Source: World Bank. 2020. *Doing Business 2020: Comparing Business Regulation in 190 Economies.* Washington, DC.

5.3.3. Logistics and infrastructure

Table 5.4 provides indexes measuring the performance of logistics[3] and infrastructure, as computed by the World Bank. Uzbekistan scores the second lowest in both indexes, after the Kyrgyz Republic. Thus, Uzbekistan can still improve a lot to achieve the full potential of its logistics and infrastructure. For transit to benefit the domestic Uzbekistan economy, a cross-border investment push is required to improve transport infrastructure. In this context, the PRC's Belt and Road Initiative could play a substantial role in facilitating logistics infrastructure. When accompanied with the necessary institutional harmonization, policy cooperation on cross-border investment can lead to a more transparent market for goods and services (EBRD 2003). Furthermore, a recent analysis from Kazakhstan shows that improving the efficiency of transport and logistics could significantly help to increase firm-level productivity (ADB 2018).

---

[3]   The logistics performance index is a weighted average of the efficiency of the clearance process, quality of trade infrastructure, ease of arranging competitively priced shipping, quality of logistics services, ability to track and trace assignments, and timeliness in shipments reaching destinations.

Table 5.4: Logistics Performance Index and Infrastructure Index Scores, Uzbekistan and Comparators

Country	Logistics Performance Index	Infrastructure Index
PRC	3.7	3.8
Kyrgyz Republic	2.2	2.0
India	3.4	3.3
Kazakhstan	2.8	2.8
Russian Federation	2.6	2.4
Uzbekistan	**2.4**	**2.4**

Note: 1 = low, 5 = high.
PRC = People's Republic of China.
Source: World Bank. World Development Indicators. http://www.databank.worldbank.org/ (accessed 12 December 2019).

5.4. Potential Gains from Trade and Foreign Direct Investment

International trade and FDI are essential catalysts for economic growth in developing economies. Trade facilitates innovation and more efficient production of goods and services in which countries have a comparative advantage. Trade liberalization or openness to trade reflects the removal of barriers to trade between countries. These barriers include tariff obstacles, such as import and export duties and nontariff measures, including licensing rules (e.g., quotas) and antidumping measures. Conventional wisdom is that the more open economies grow faster than the less open ones. A study by Wacziarg and Welch (2008) indicated that the average annual growth rates of countries that lowered trade barriers were about 1.5 percentage points higher than those not undertaking trade liberalization.

Furthermore, trade fosters economic growth by encouraging innovation, reducing poverty and reallocating resources from less efficient to more efficient uses. After trade liberalization, economies experience better market access and a tougher competitive environment. Improved access to external markets in turn increases profits, leading to more innovation. A seminal work by Aghion et al. (2001) suggests that the more competitive markets may induce firms to innovate more to escape from competition. Coelli et al. (2016) investigated whether the global tariff reductions during the 1990s had any effect on innovation (patenting) in more than 60 countries. Between 1990 and 2000, as a result of regional trade agreements and unilateral trade liberalization, developed economies experienced an average reduction in tariffs of 8%–5%, and developing economies' average reduction was 25%–15%. Their results suggest that freer trade accounted for a 7% increase in innovation (patenting), thus emphasizing an important role of trade liberalization on innovation and thereby economic growth.

Openness to international trade is also believed to affect growth through poverty reduction. If trade fosters economic growth, then absolute poverty will be alleviated more quickly with faster economic growth (Cockburn and Giordano 2008). However, poverty is linked to other factors, such as access to capital, health and education services, logistics, and infrastructure. Thus, trade liberalization itself may not guarantee faster growth because it requires that other structural changes and policies are addressed simultaneously. For example, Africa is the poorest continent, yet African economies have made substantial progress in trade liberalization (Le Goff, Rocher, and Singh 2014). But it has weak institutions, limited access to finance, poor education, and geographical isolation. This suggests that poor policies and strategies not only negatively affect total welfare, but also hamper developing economies from benefiting from the gains from trade. The situation is also relevant for Uzbekistan, because over 11% of its population lived below the poverty line in 2018 (ADB 2019). Thus, trade liberalization policies should not be seen in isolation: reforms to other policies are needed to maximize the potential of liberalizing effects, including the alleviation of poverty and wage inequality.

From the micro-level perspective, trade openness promotes the reallocation of resources where the least productive firms exit the market and the most productive ones expand and enter the export market, thus increasing average industry productivity (Bernard and Jensen 1999, Pavcnik 2002, Melitz 2003, Bernard et al. 2012). Another channel through which trade affects the production decision and price adjustments is the extent to which firms face foreign competition. Mayer, Melitz, and Ottaviano (2014) show that exporting to more competitive markets increases the relative market share of the best performing products within firms. Trade openness also induces lower average prices and markups due to increased product varieties and tougher competition in a trading country (Melitz and Ottaviano 2008).

The literature on the impacts of trade liberalization on the economic growth of Central Asian economies, including Uzbekistan, is limited. Nannicini and Billmeier (2011) attempted to answer whether open transition economies (Armenia, Azerbaijan, Georgia, and Tajikistan) grow faster than a closed one (Uzbekistan). The paper found that trade liberalization had a positive effect on economic growth in the transition economies. It concluded that, for Uzbekistan, missing the opportunity for trade liberalization could come at a substantial cost in the medium-to-long run. Mogilevskii (2012) provided an overview of the trade initiatives and recent trade trends and patterns in Central Asian economies, including Uzbekistan. The study found that openness to trade has increased, and ranged from 20% (share of trade in GDP) for Uzbekistan to 50% for Turkmenistan in 2010.

FDI also enhances economic growth by upgrading skills (including managerial skills) and infrastructure and due to technological spillovers from developed economies to developing ones (Dunning 1994). FDI liberalization includes reforming a wide range of policies favoring FDI, including tax incentives, flexible foreign exchange policies, investment guarantees, and removal of administrative barriers. From the theoretical perspectives, FDI is linked to growth through capital accumulation and to introduction of new inputs and technologies in the production process of the host country. However, empirical studies that test the relationship between FDI and economic growth have shown varying results. A few studies, such as De Mello (1999) for 32 developed and developing economies and Chakraborty and Basu (2002) for India, found weak or no evidence for FDI contributing to growth. But many other studies show positive effects of FDI, including Haskel et al. (2007), Damijan and Decramer (2014) on productivity improvements, Head and Ries (2002) on skill upgrading, and Javorcik (2012) on job creation. An important conclusion is that countries that grow faster also attract more FDI inflows (Choi 2006, Fidrmuc and Kostagianni 2015). Moreover, where an emphasis has been given to trade openness, there are also well-developed financial markets and strong institutions to facilitate FDI growth. Chile provides a further example of how FDI and trade liberalization accompanied with reforms to regulatory policies have played a positive role in economic growth (Box 5.1).

Box 5.1: Role of Trade and Foreign Direct Investment Liberalization in the Chilean Economy

Chile's economy experienced phenomenal growth when its annual rate of gross domestic product was 7% between the late 1980s and the 2000s. The determinants of the economic success were the radical market reforms involving foreign trade practices; elimination of government controls on economic activity; infrastructure developments; social programs to reduce poverty; and improved private pension, health, and education systems. Other features that contributed to Chile's success include its advantageous geographic location and abundant natural resources.

In terms of foreign trade policies, in the mid-1970s import tariffs were brought down to a common level of 11%, with a further reduction to 6% by the mid-2000s (Box Figure). Financial markets were opened to foreign competition and trade agreements were enacted with Canada, Latin America, and Mexico. Moreover, in 1976 Chile withdrew from the Andean Pact (involving Bolivia, Colombia, Ecuador, Peru, and Venezuela), which at the time was described as a model of economic integration marked by protectionism and an adverse view of foreign

Continued on next page

Box 5.1 continued

direct investment. Further, as a result of ratifying free trade agreements with the European Union, Japan, and the United States, the share of trade covered by trade agreements increased from 25% to 85% between 2002 and 2007. The goal of joining such treaties was to improve the welfare by attracting foreign investment and becoming a regional export hub.

To this end, trade openness, as measured by the sum of exports and imports as a share of gross domestic product, rose rapidly in Chile, from 56% in 1992 to 81% in 2008. The increase was triggered partly by the steep rise in copper prices (Chile's most abundant natural resource) and partly by the increase in exports and imports of other products.

Evolution of Average Tariffs and Trade as a Share of GDP in Chile, 1992–2008
(%)

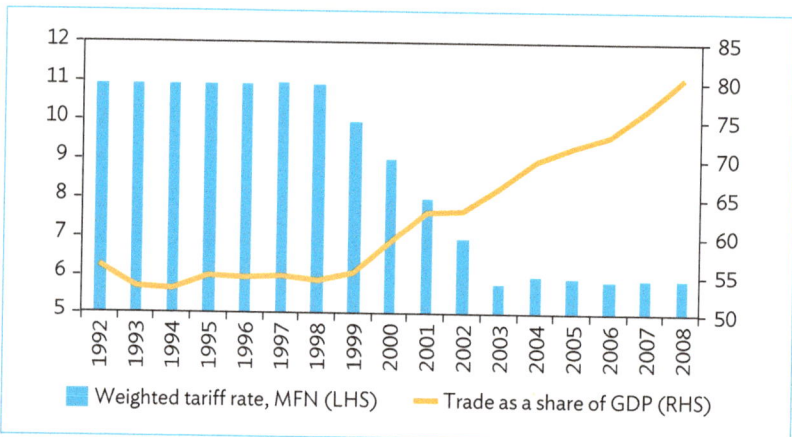

Weighted tariff rate, MFN (LHS)   Trade as a share of GDP (RHS)

GDP = gross domestic product, LHS = left-hand scale, MFN = most favored nation, RHS = right-hand scale.
Sources: World Integrated Trade Solution (2018), World Bank. World Development Indicators. https://databank.worldbank.org/source/world-development-indicators (accessed 12 December 2019).

Today, Chile is ranked as a high-income economy by international institutions and remains the best-performing nation in South America, with relatively high investment rates, low inflation, and stable financial markets. Moreover, it is among the most attractive business destinations in the world. To sum up, Chile's experience demonstrates that with coherent institutions and policies, opening up to trade and foreign direct investment can be very beneficial to economic growth, linking long-term economic and social prospects.

Source: Brid and Hernandez (2004).

5.5. Firm Size Distribution Analysis

This section takes a firm-level perspective to examine the structural channels of competiveness and growth in Uzbekistan. During 2009–2018, a growing body of research has focused on the variation in firm-level growth to carefully assess a range of economic policies that affect both product and factor markets. The underlying interest is driven by the enormous variation in firm growth within narrowly defined industries (e.g., Syverson 2011, Haltiwanger et al. 2013). Hence, many countries have started to explicitly take into account firm heterogeneity as well as the interconnectivity between firms via supply chains when implementing new industrial policies (Aghion et al. 2015).

More importantly, understanding firm-specific or idiosyncratic shocks helps us identify micro-origins of an economy's macroeconomic fluctuations. For example, idiosyncratic shocks to a specific industry can have important aggregate effects if the sector is strongly interlinked with other industries in the economy through supply chains. Recent insights confirm the existence of such interlinkages and find that firm-specific shocks can have a significant impact on cyclical fluctuations in GDP growth (Gabaix 2011; Acemoglu et al. 2012); unemployment (Moscarini and Postel-Vinay 2012); and aggregate prices (Amiti et al. 2014). A study by Di Giovanni et al. (2016) uses firm-level data to show how trade linkages at the firm level are associated with aggregate comovement. They find that 8% of firms in France directly connected to a trading country accounts for 56% of total value added generated by the French economy.

A hitherto unexploited data set of firms in Uzbekistan, collected through Bureau van Dijk's Orbis database is used here. The data reported in Orbis are limited; however, they provide useful insights about the firm size distribution to document a number of key microeconomic structural features of the Uzbekistan economy, which can guide economic policy. The focus is on the year 2012 because the data set for this year reports the most observations, with total employment in private firms amounting to 98,976. Although this is only a small fraction of total registered employment, it provides a good first approximation for understanding firm-level heterogeneity. The data set contains 8,668 firms and allows the documentation of stylized facts characterizing Uzbekistan: in particular, the firm size distribution.

Figure 5.12 shows the firm size distribution in Uzbekistan. As in most countries, Uzbekistan has many micro and small firms employing less than 20 workers, but also has a "fat tail" of very large firms. That the firm size distribution is "fat-tailed" indicates that idiosyncratic shocks matter, which may affect the entire economy.[4] This implies that a shock to, for example, GM Uzbekistan, the country's largest automobile manufacturer, can ripple through the entire supply chain and affect overall macroeconomic performance. In transition economies, including Uzbekistan, large state-owned firms were part of many countries' basic make-up. Dismantling these state-owned enterprises has caused substantial output declines, at least in the short run, in most transition economies of Central and Eastern Europe and in the Russian Federation (Blanchard 1997).

Figure 5.13 plots a Lorenz curve using firm employment levels, which indicates quite some heterogeneity between firms in terms of employment. About 20% of the firms account for 60% of all employment. If all firms were of equal size, the Lorenz curve would be at the diagonal. The further away from the diagonal, the more skewed is the size distribution. The curve indicates that the size distribution in Uzbekistan is less skewed than is typical in advanced countries. For example, Duparcq and Konings (2016) found that for Italy, 20% of the firms account for 80% of all employment. This suggests that relative to firms in advanced countries, Uzbekistan may have constraints to firm growth, preventing them from fully exploiting scale economies. Examples of such constraints include access to finance, access to global markets, and lack of good managerial practices. Moreover, a less skewed size distribution might reflect a lower level of entrepreneurship, resulting in fewer micro firms. This would imply a less intensive process of "creative destruction," an essential process to achieve innovation and growth.

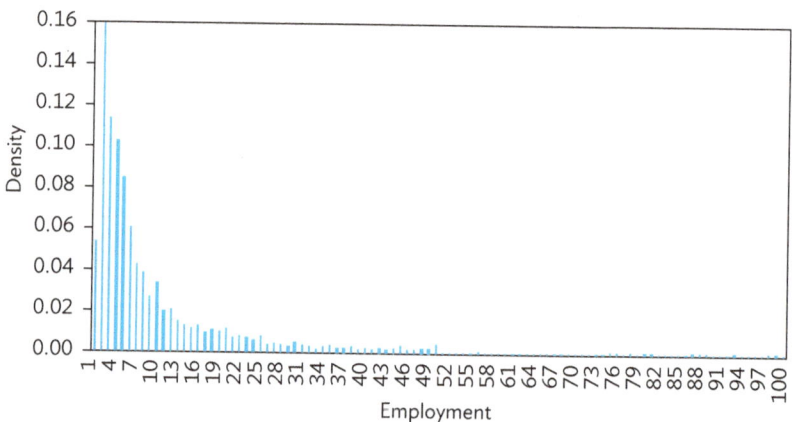

Figure 5.12: Firm Size Distribution in Uzbekistan, 2012

Source: Authors' calculations.

---

4   Examples include General Motors during the financial crisis of 2008 and the recent Volkswagen "diesel gate."

Figure 5.13: Skewed Firm Size Distribution in Uzbekistan, 2012

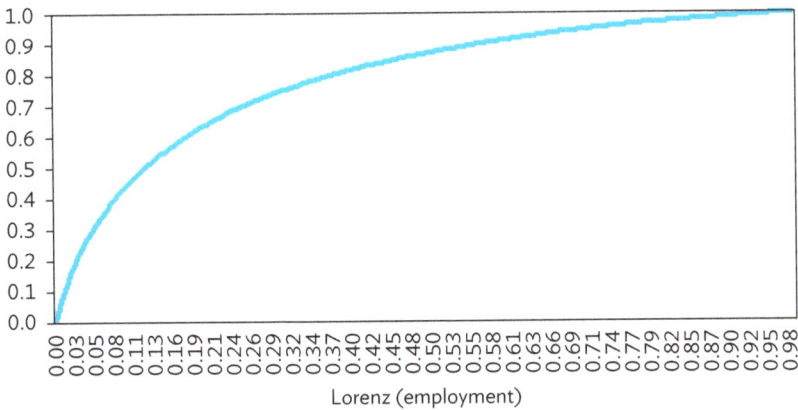

Lorenz (employment)

Source: Authors' calculations.

5.6. Gravity Model of Exports

This section estimates a gravity model of international trade to better understand the determinants of export flows of Uzbekistan. The gravity model explains the volume of trade as a function of distance and size of the countries of origin and destination. The model has become a workhorse of international trade for 50 years after being implemented by Tinbergen (1962).

One of the important features of the gravity equation is that exports rise with the economic size of the destination country (Head and Mayer 2013). Using GDP as a proxy for economy size, this feature is illustrated by taking the trade flows between Uzbekistan and its major export destinations. Data on export values for 47 of Uzbekistan's trading partners (listed in the Appendix) between 2000 and 2016 are used from the International Monetary Fund's Direction of Trade Statistics database. Together the 47 countries accounted for about 75% of Uzbekistan's total exports in 2016. GDP in current dollars, converted at the current exchange rate were extracted from CEPII.[5] Figure 5.14 shows the log of Uzbekistan's bilateral exports on the vertical axis and the log of destination countries' GDP on the horizontal axis. The red line shows predicted values from a simple regression of the log of export flow on the log of GDP. The GDP elasticity is 0.24 and is statistically significant, indicating a positive relation between the export volume and GDP of the destination country.

---

[5]   Centre d'Etudes Prospectives et d'Informations Internationales.

Figure 5.14: Uzbekistan's Exports and the Size of Destination Countries

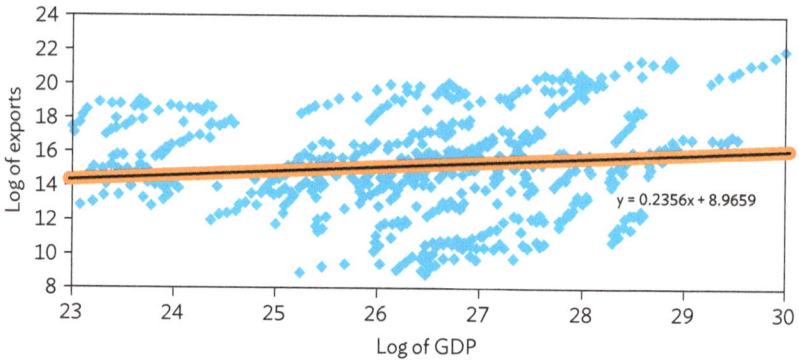

$$y = 0.2356x + 8.9659$$

GDP = gross domestic product.
Source: Authors' calculations based on data from International Monetary Fund. Direction of Trade Statistics. https://data.imf.org/?sk=9D6028D4-F14A-464C-A2F2-59B2CD424B85 (accessed 16 November 2018).

Next is the second key empirical relationship of the gravity equation—the strong negative relationship between physical distance and exports. Figure 5.15 shows that the flow of exports diminishes with as the distance to the trading partner increases. Distance is often interpreted as a trade impediment because it creates "barriers to trade" in terms of transport costs. Similar to the previous graph (Figure 5.14), the red line depicts predicted values of a regression of the log of the export flow on the log of distance. The elasticity of distance is –1.4

Figure 5.15: Uzbekistan's Exports and the Distance to Destination

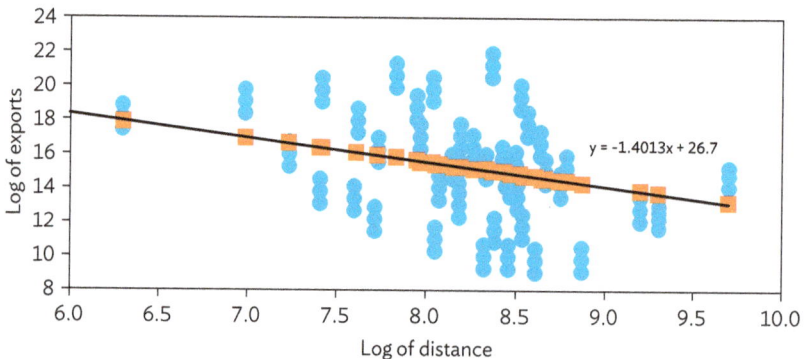

$$y = -1.4013x + 26.7$$

Source: Authors' calculations based on data from International Monetary Fund. Direction of Trade Statistics. https://data.imf.org/?sk=9D6028D4-F14A-464C-A2F2-59B2CD424B85 (accessed 16 November 2018).

and is statistically significant, which confirms the results of a series of other empirical studies (Head and Mayer 2013, Kang and Dagli 2018).

Finally, the GDP and distance are combined with other measures to estimate the export determinants of Uzbekistan. We use the extended gravity model[6] similar to Kang and Dagli (2018), which takes the following log-linear form:

$$lnX_{it} = \beta_0 + \beta_1 lndist_i + \beta_2 lnGDP_t + \beta_3 lnPOP_{it} + \beta_4 C_i + \beta_5 lnRER_{it} + \phi_i + \gamma_t + \varepsilon_{it},$$

where ln denotes log, X_{it} is the value of deflated exports of Uzbekistan to its trading partner i at year t, $dist_i$ is the population-weighted distance between Uzbekistan and its importers, and GDP_t is the value of deflated GDP of Uzbekistan. POP_{it} is the population of partner destinations that vary over time. C_i are the common control variables that include dummies[7] for geographical contiguity, membership in the EU, and WTO membership. RER_{it} is the bilateral real exchange rate, calculated by the consumer price index weighted nominal exchange rate (Kang and Dagli 2018). ϕ_i and γ_t are importer and year fixed effects, respectively. Together they control for endogeneity arising from omitted variables, such as tariff and nontariff barriers. With the inclusion of importer fixed effects, the initial GDP variables of importing countries drop out. Finally, ε_{it} is the error term. The dataset on control variables as well as the population and distance were extracted from CEPII. The nominal exchange rates were retrieved from the Thomson Reuters DataStream platform, and consumer price indexes were retrieved from the World Bank's World Development Indicators. The data cover 47 importers and 17 years (2000–2016), generating 799 observations.

In practice, the estimated parameters of a gravity equation are interpreted in terms of elasticities. For example, the distance parameter (in logarithms) is the elasticity of trade to distance, reflecting the percentage variation in trade following a 1% increase in distance. The distance parameter typically serves as a proxy for trade costs. Intuitively, the longer the bilateral distance, the higher the associated trade costs. A geographical contiguity variable in the analysis is used to capture information costs. In our dataset the countries include dummies for Kazakhstan, the Kyrgyz Republic, and Tajikistan, which share common cultural and language features. Such features help to decrease information costs because firms share similar business environments. The dummies for membership in the EU and the WTO reflect the importer's

---

[6] The naive form of the gravity equation includes the GDP of country of origin and country of destination, and their physical distance.

[7] Dummies are variables that take a value of 0 or 1. For example, a dummy takes the value 1 if an importing country is a member of the WTO, and 0 otherwise.

trading status. In this context, Uzbekistan is not the WTO member; however, it benefits from the preferential trade agreements with the EU. Finally, the real exchange rates explain how the depreciation or appreciation of Uzbekistan's currency affect its trade. The hypothesis is that a depreciation increases the export flows because firms in Uzbekistan experience increased demand for goods sold abroad as they appear cheaper for foreigners. Evidence from the gravity model literature suggests that all of the above described factors can have significant implications for trade flows by increasing or decreasing the costs of moving goods globally. In this exercise, the objective is to obtain estimates of all parameters and relate them to Uzbekistan's export flows.

Table 5.5 presents the regression results and points to important and expected directions of the gravity factors (such as distance, population, GDP, and real exchange rates) on exports of Uzbekistan. In particular, a 10% increase in distance between Uzbekistan and its trading partner is associated with a 19% decrease in exports. This underlines the important roles of transit, logistics, and infrastructure, which may help reduce transport costs. Uzbekistan's GDP is also crucial—a 10% GDP increase leads to a 5% increase in exports. The

Table 5.5: Estimates of Gravity Model for Uzbekistan

Variable	(1)	(2)	(3)
Log(distance)	−1.928[b]	−1.877[b]	−1.851[b]
	(0.918)	(0.879)	(0.857)
Log(GDP$_{exporter}$)	0.525[a]	0.483[b]	0.404[a]
	(0.160)	(0.191)	(0.210)
Log(population$_{importer}$)	0.772[a]	0.748[a]	0.748[a]
	(0.246)	(0.250)	(0.251)
Contiguity dummy	0.280	0.265	0.263
	(2.407)	(2.329)	(2.282)
EU member dummy	0.101	0.0487	0.00988
	(0.0829)	(0.0767)	(0.0708)
WTO member dummy	0.0525	0.0259	0.0188
	(0.0770)	(0.0901)	(0.0991)
Log(RER)	0.347[a]		
	(0.0338)		
Log(RER(-1))		0.302[a]	
		(0.0432)	
Log(RER(-2))			0.275[a]
			(0.0453)
Observations	799	752	705

Robust standard errors in parentheses.
[a] p<0.01, [b] p<0.05, [c] p<0.1
EU = European Union, GDP = gross domestic product, RER = real exchange rate.
Source: Authors' calculations.

effects of control variables such as geographical contiguity and membership in the EU and WTO are positive, but not statistically significant. Uzbekistan is not a WTO member and thus it faces more trade restrictions than between the EU and other WTO member countries (as discussed in section 5.1). This suggests that preferential tariffs are less applicable to Uzbekistan and, hence, membership factors may not play a significant role on exports. Not surprisingly, the impact of real exchange rates on export flows is positive and significant, suggesting that the weaker the Uzbekistan currency, the larger the export values vis-à-vis trading partners. Specifically, a 10% depreciation of Uzbekistan's currency on average is associated with a 3% increase in its exports. When a lagged real exchange rate is considered, its magnitude decreases over time. This indicates that the impact of currency depreciation is strongest in the year it occurs and its pace declines over time.

5.7. Policy Recommendations for Trade and Foreign Direct Investment Liberalization in Uzbekistan

As noted in previous sections, Uzbekistan is lagging behind its neighbors in exploiting benefits from global trade, as reflected in its lower share of trade in GDP, higher import tariffs, and lower FDI inflows compared with other Central Asian economies. The results suggest both government and market constraints on export and import growth; investment; and, subsequently, job creation. This section discusses some policy recommendations to address these constraints.

Improving market access to open up to global trade. As discussed in section 5.3, which reviewed the necessity to liberalize trade and FDI, Uzbekistan's trade policies remain the most restrictive in the Central Asian region. The weighted average import tariff rate is still high compared with the average rates for Kazakhstan, the Kyrgyz Republic, and Tajikistan. In terms of product classification, the highest import tariffs are on apparel and textile manufacturing industries, such as footwear, leather, and fur manufacturing, which were among the main exports in 2016. Because the average level of applied tariffs has fallen globally by one-third over the last 2 decades, Uzbekistan is missing the opportunity to trade more freely with other economies. Reducing the high levels of import tariffs, excise taxes on imported goods, and nontariff barriers would allow Uzbekistan to access better and cheaper imports, which is likely to boost productivity of domestic firms. Higher productivity in turn triggers many firms to start exporting. Thus, trade liberalization would boost firm growth and trade, which in turn would create new job opportunities in the economy.

Greater involvement in regional integration to facilitate trade, FDI, and job creation. An important step toward trade facilitation is participation in regional and international agreements, including the Eurasian Economic Union and the WTO. To this end, the negotiation process to accede to the WTO needs to be accelerated. Second, greater involvement in regional integration is needed to harmonize and coordinate general liberalization policies. The lack of regional cooperation on trade facilitation measures constrains international integration with important trade blocks such as the EU, where a lot of growth could be generated. While multilateral trade agreements typically take a long time, progress could be made by starting with bilateral trade agreements with a number of countries. Further trade integration through and increased trade flows emerging from such agreements would boost FDI and jobs.

Improving the business climate to attract more FDI and create new jobs. To ensure that regional integration is successful, open trade policies need to be implemented in combination with strengthening the institutional framework supporting a dynamic business environment. The analyses in section 5.3 and Chapter 4 suggest that the business climate needs improving, including by simplifying procedures for issuing licenses and permits and reducing the time required to convert foreign exchange. Firm size analysis (section 5.5) indicates a less-skewed firm distribution in Uzbekistan than in advanced countries. This suggests the presence of constraints to firm growth, such as access to finance, access to global markets, and lack of good managerial practices, which prevent firms from fully exploiting scale economies. It would be helpful to document such obstacles by surveying enterprises. This would highlight the key problems related to business regulations and nontariff barriers. Deregulation would be the way forward to generate a dynamic business environment to allow firms to grow and create jobs.

Establishing a single investment and export promotion agency to disseminate business opportunities. That Uzbekistan attracts less FDI inflows than any other Central Asian economy suggests the government needs to survey existing and potential investors to understand their negative perceptions about Uzbekistan. Better coordination between government agencies, foreign investors, and domestic enterprises is needed to promote investment opportunities and to help enterprises with their export plans, as also suggested by the World Bank (2018). Creating a single public–private or private agency could help promote export opportunities for domestic enterprises and attract investors by providing research on new markets, measuring export capacities, and assisting with all regulatory aspects of establishing a new project in Uzbekistan.

Improving transport and logistics infrastructure to increase trade flows.
The gravity equation analysis (section 5.6) underlines the important role of
transport costs and hence of the extent and quality of Uzbekistan's transit,
logistics, and infrastructure, which are among the lowest in Central Asia. This
suggests that for transit services to become more important in Uzbekistan's
economy, a push for cross-border investment is required to improve transport
infrastructure. In this context, the BRI could play a substantial role in improving
the country's transport and logistics infrastructure. Modern infrastructure
would help leverage Uzbekistan's central location in the region and reduce
transit costs, expand market access, and integrate domestic markets with
those abroad.

**Greater investment in human capital development, innovation, and
research.** Greater investment in human capital and research and development
(R&D) is needed for several reasons. First, exports in Uzbekistan are
concentrated in low-value-added products and resource extractive industries,
which suggests a lack of entrepreneurial and innovative activities. Second, a
significant part of the working age population is low-skilled or does not have
the skills most demanded in the market (World Bank 2018). Third, Uzbekistan
invests very little in R&D, amounting in 2017 to just 0.19% of GDP, which is one
of the lowest rates in the world.[8] Most importantly, opening up to both trade
and FDI would ensure that domestic firms compete with foreign firms, which
are larger, have higher labor productivity, and have more capital per worker. A
stronger focus on R&D, innovation, and skill upgrading would lead industries
to enhance their technologies and employ better-trained workers. That in turn
would increase domestic competitiveness and create new and better jobs for
meeting market trends globally.

---

[8]   World Bank. World Development Indicators. https://databank.worldbank.org/source/world-development-
indicators (accessed December 2019)

Appendix 5.1: Uzbekistan's Trading Partners

Armenia

Azerbaijan

Bangladesh

Belgium

Bulgaria

Canada

Chile

China, People's Republic of

Czech Republic

Egypt

France

Georgia

Germany

Hong Kong, China

India

Indonesia

Iran

Iraq

Israel

Italy

Kazakhstan

Korea, Republic of

Kyrgyz Republic

Latvia

Lithuania

Malaysia

Moldova

Netherlands

Nigeria

Pakistan

Poland

Portugal

Romania

Russian Federation

Singapore

Spain

Sri Lanka

Sweden

Switzerland

Tajikistan

Thailand

Tunisia

Turkey

Ukraine

United Kingdom

United States

Viet Nam

References

Acemoglu, D., V. Carvalho, A. Ozdaglar, and A. Tahbaz-Salehi. 2012. The Network Origins of Aggregate Fluctuations. *Econometrica*. 80(5): pp. 1977–2016.

Aghion, P., J. Cai, M. Dewatripont, L. Du, A. Harrison, and P. Legros. 2015. Industrial Policy and Competition. *American Economic Journal: Macroeconomics*. 7(4): pp. 1–32.

Aghion, P., C. Harris, P. Howitt, and J. Vickers. 2001. Competition, Imitation and Growth with Step-by-Step Innovation. *The Review of Economic Studies*. 68(3): pp. 467–92.

Amiti, M., O. Itskhoki, and J. Konings. 2014. Importers, Exporters, and Exchange Rate Disconnect. *American Economic Review*. 104(7): pp. 1942–78.

Amiti, M. and J. Konings. 2007. Trade Liberalization, Intermediate Inputs, and Productivity: Evidence from Indonesia. *American Economic Review*. 97(5): pp. 1611–38.

Asian Development Bank (ADB). 2006. *Central Asia: Increasing Gains from Trade through Regional Cooperation in Trade Policy, Transport, and Customs Transit*. Manila.

_____. 2018. *Kazakhstan: Accelerating Economic Diversification*. Manila.

_____. 2019. *Basic Statistics*. Manila.

Asian Development Bank Institute (ADBI). 2014. *Connecting Central Asia With Economic Centers*. Washington, DC: Brookings Institution Press.

Batsaikhan, U. and M. Dabrowski. 2017. Central Asia—Twenty-Five Years after the Breakup of the USSR. *Russian Journal of Economics*. 3(3): pp. 296–320.

Bendini, R. 2013. Uzbekistan: Selected Trade and Economic Issues. *European Parliament Policy Department, Directorate-General for External Policies*. Brussels: European Union.

Bernard, A. and J. Jensen. 1999. *Exporting and Productivity* (No. w7135). Cambridge, MA: National Bureau of Economic Research.

Bernard, A., J. Jensen, S. Redding, and P. Schott. 2012. The Empirics of Firm Heterogeniety and International Trade. *Annual Review of Economics*. 4(1): pp. 283–313.

Blanchard, O. 1997. *The Economics of Post-Communist Transition*. Oxford: Clarendon Press.

Bolaky, B. and C. Freund. 2004. *Trade, Regulations, and Growth*. Wshington, DC: World Bank.

Brid, J. and R. Hernández. Chile: The Lonely Success Story. *Harvard Review of Latin America*. 3(3): pp. 18–21.

Chakraborty, C. and P. Basu. 2002. Foreign Direct Investment and Growth in India: A Cointegration Approach. *Applied Economics*. 34(9): pp. 1061–73.

Choi, C. 2006. Does Foreign Direct Investment Affect Domestic Income Inequality? *Applied Economics Letters*. 13(12): pp. 811–14.

Cockburn, J. and P. Giordano. 2008. *Trade and Poverty in the Developing World*. Washington DC: Inter-American Development Bank.

Coelli, F., A. Moxnes, and K. Ulltveit-Moe. 2016. *Better, Faster, Stronger: Global Innovation and Trade Liberalization* (No. w22647). Cambridge, MA: National Bureau of Economic Research.

Damijan, J. and S. Decramer. 2014. Productivity Gains after Outward FDI: Evidence from Slovenia. KU Leuven Discussion Papers 2014. 46. Leuven: Katoleike Universidad Leuven.

De Loecker, J. and J. Konings. 2003. Creative Destruction and Productivity Growth in an Emerging Economy: Evidence from Slovenian Manufacturing. IZA Discussion Paper No. 971. Bonn: IZA Institute of Labor Economics.

de Mello, L. 1999. Foreign Direct Investment-Led Growth: Evidence from Time Series and Panel Data. *Oxford Economic Papers*. 51(1): pp. 133–51.

Di Giovanni, J., A. Levchenko, and I. Mejean. 2016. *The Micro Origins of International Business Cycle Comovement* (No. w21885). Cambridge, MA: National Bureau of Economic Research.

Donaldson, D. 2018. Railroads of the Raj: Estimating the Impact of Transportation Infrastructure. *American Economic Review*. 108(4–5): pp. 899–934.

Dunning, J. 1994. Reevaluating the Benefits of Foreign Direct Investment. *Discussion Paper No. 188*. Reading: Department of Economics, University of Reading.

Duparcq, P. and J. Konings. 2016. An Enterprise Map for Kazakhstan: A Guide for Industrial Policy. Economic Policy Paper 1, Economics Department. Astana: Nazarbayev University.

European Bank for Reconstruction and Development (EBRD). 2003. *Transition Report 2003: Integration and Regional Cooperation*. London.

Farchy, J. 2016. New Silk Road Will Transport Laptops and Frozen Chicken. *Financial Times*. Special Report, 9 May. https://www.ft.com/content/e9d35df0-0bd8-11e6-9456-444ab5211a2f

Ferrari, A. (ed.). 2016. *Putin's Russia: Really Back?* (Vol. 1). Milan: Ledizioni.

Fidrmuc, J. And S. Kostagianni. 2015. Impact of IMF Assistance on Economic Growth Revisited. *Economics and Sociology*, 8(3): pp. 32–40.

Gabaix, X. 2011. The Granular Origins of Aggregate Fluctuations. *Econometrica*. 79(3): pp. 733–72.

Haltiwanger, J., R. Jarmin, and J. Miranda. 2013. Who Creates Jobs? Small Versus Large Versus Young. *Review of Economics and Statistics*. 95(2): pp. 347–61.

Haskel, J., S. Pereira, and M. Slaughter. 2007. Does Inward Foreign Direct Investment Boost the Productivity of Domestic Firms? *Review of Economics and Statistics*. 89(3): pp. 482–96.

Hausman, W., H. Lee, and U. Subramanian. 2013. The Impact of Logistics Performance on Trade. *Production and Operations Management*. 22(2): pp. 236–52.

Head, K. and T. Mayer. 2013. Gravity Equations: Workhorse, Toolkit, and Cookbook. In E. Helpman, G. Gopinath, and K. Rogoff, eds. *Handbook of International Economics*. 4, Elsevier.

Head, K. and J. Ries. 2002. Offshore Production and Skill Upgrading by Japanese Manufacturing Firms. *Journal of International Economics*. 58(1): pp. 81–105.

Hong, J., Z. Chu, and Q. Wang. 2011. Transport Infrastructure and Regional Economic Growth: Evidence from China. *Transportation*. 38(5): pp. 737–52.

International Monetary Fund. Direction of Trade Statistics. https://data.imf.org/?sk=9D6028D4-F14A-464C-A2F2-59B2CD424B85 (accessed 16 November 2018).

Javorcik, B. 2012. *Does FDI Bring Good Jobs to Host Countries?* Washington, DC: World Bank.

Kang, J. and S. Dagli. 2018. International Trade and Exchange Rates. *Journal of Applied Economics*. 21(1): pp. 84–105.

Kee, L., A. Nicita, and M. Olarreaga. 2009. Estimating Trade Restrictiveness Indices. *Economic Journal*. 119(534): pp. 172–99.

Konings, J. 2018. *Trade Impacts of the Belt and Road Initiative*. ING Bank NV. https://think.ing.com/uploads/reports/Tradebelt_final1.pdf

Kononczuk, W. 2007. The Failure of Integration. The CIS and Other International Organizations in the Post-Soviet Ara, 1991–2006. OSW Study 26/2007. Warsaw: Center for Eastern Studies (OSW).

Le Goff, E., E. Rocher, and R. Singh. 2014. *Does Migration Foster Exports? Evidence from Africa*. Policy Research Working Paper No. 6739. Washington, DC: World Bank.

Mayer, T., M. Melitz, and G. Ottaviano. 2014. Market Size, Competition, and the Product Mix of Exporters. *American Economic Review*. 104(2): pp. 495–536.

Melitz, M. 2003. The Impact of Trade on Intra-Industry Reallocations and Aggregate Industry Productivity. *Econometrica*. 71(6): pp. 1695–725.

Melitz, M. and G. Ottaviano. 2008. Market Size, Trade, and Productivity. *Review of Economic Studies*. 75(1): pp. 295–316.

Mogilevskii, R. 2012. Trends and Patterns in Foreign Trade of Central Asian Countries. Institute Of Public Policy And Administration, Working Paper No. 1. Bishkek: University of Central Asia.

Moscarini, G. and F. Postel-Vinay. 2012. The Contribution of Large and Small Employers to Job Creation in Times of High and Low Unemployment. *American Economic Review*. 102(6): pp. 2509–39.

Nannicini, T. and A. Billmeier. 2011. Economies in Transition: How Important is Trade Openness for Growth? *Oxford Bulletin of Economics and Statistics*. 73(3): pp. 287–314.

National Development and Reform Commission (NDRC) of the People's Republic of China. 2015. *Vision and Actions on Jointly Building Silk Road Economic Belt and 21st-Century Maritime Silk Road*. http://en.ndrc.gov.cn/newsrelease/201503/t20150330_669367.html

Nordas, H., E. Pinali, and M. Grosso. 2006. Logistics and Time as a Trade Barrier. OECD Trade Policy Working Papers No 35. Paris: OECD Publishing.

Observatory of Economic Complexity. 2018. *Export and Imports of Uzbekistan*. Retrieved from https://atlas.media.mit.edu/en/profile/country/uzb/ (accessed 12 December 2019).

Pavcnik, N. 2002. Trade Liberalization, Exit, and Productivity Improvements: Evidence from Chilean Plants. *Review of Economic Studies*. 69(1): pp. 245–76.

Richards, J. and E. Schaefer. 2016. Jobs Attributable to Foreign Direct Investment in the United States. *International Trade Administration*. *http://www.trade.gov/mas/ian/build/groups/public/@tg_ian/documents/webcontent/tg_in_005496.pdf*

Rodrik, D. 1988. Closing the Technology Gap: Does Trade Liberalization Really Help? NBER Working Paper No. 2654. Cambridge, MA: National Bureau of Economic Research.

State Committee of the Republic of Uzbekistan on Statistics (Uzbekistan Statistics). 2018. *Investments in Fixed Capital*. https://stat.uz/uploads/docs/investitsiya-yan-dek-2017en2.pdf

Syverson, C. 2011. What Determines Productivity? *Journal of Economic Literature*. 49(2): pp. 326–65.

Tinbergen, J. 1962. An Analysis of World Trade Flows. *Shaping the World Economy*. 3: 1–117.

Topalova, P. 2004. Trade Liberalization, Poverty and Inequality: Evidence from Indian Districts. In *Globalization and Poverty* (pp. 291-336). Chicago: University of Chicago Press.

UN Comtrade. https://comtrade.un.org/db/default.aspx (accessed 12 December 2019).

United Nations Conference on Trade and Development (UNCTAD). 2018. *World Investment Report 2018: Investment and New Industrial Policies.* New York: United Nations. https://doi.org/10.18356/ebb78749-en

UNCTADSTAT. https://unctadstat.unctad.org/ (accessed 12 December 2019).

Wacziarg, R. and K. Welch. 2008. Trade Liberalization and Growth: New Evidence. *World Bank Economic Review.* 22(2): pp. 187–231.

World Bank. 2013. *Uzbekistan-Economic Development and Reforms: Achievements and Challenges (English).* Washington, DC.

_____. 2018. *Growth Diagnostics for Uzbekistan.* Washington, DC.

_____.2020. *Doing Business 2020: Comparing Business Regulation in 190 Economies.* Washington, DC.

_____. UNCTAD Trade Analysis Information System (TRAINS). https://databank.worldbank.org/reports.aspx?source=UNCTAD-~-Trade-Analysis-Information-System-%28TRAINS%29 (accessed 16 November 2018)

_____. World Development Indicators (WDI). Washington, DC. https://databank.worldbank.org/source/world-development-indicators (accessed 16 November 2018 and 12 December 2019)

World Energy Council. https://www.worldenergy.org/data/resources/country/uzbekistan/gas/

World Integrated Trade Solution. 2018. *Tariffs.* Washington DC: World Bank. https://wits.worldbank.org/

World Trade Organization (WTO). 2015. *World Trade Report 2015: Speeding up Trade: Benefits and Challenges of Implementing the WTO Trade Facilitation Agreement.* Geneva.

_____. 2016. *World Trade Report 2016: Levelling the Trading Field for SMEs.* Geneva.